W0046324

FiNALEonline.de ist die digitale Ergänzung zu deinem Arbeitsbuch. Hier findest du eine Vielzahl an Angeboten, die dich zusätzlich bei deiner Prüfungsvorbereitung in Englisch unterstützen!

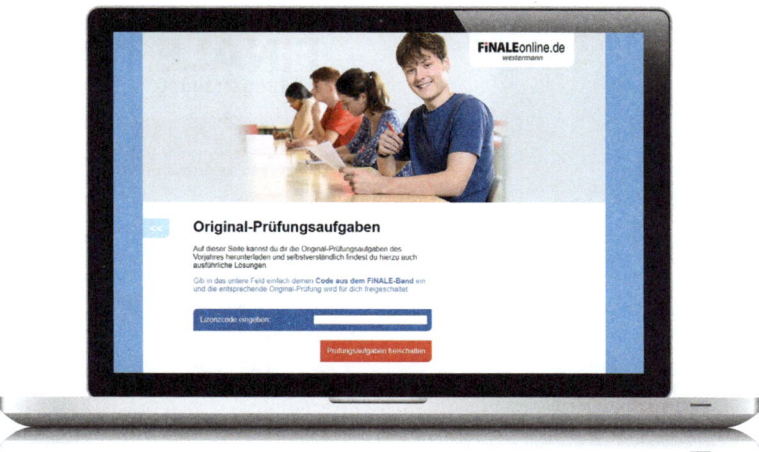

Das Plus für deine Prüfungsvorbereitung:

→ Original-Prüfungsaufgaben mit Lösungen (bitte Code von S. 4 eingeben)

→ Tipps zur Prüfungsvorbereitung, die das Lernen erleichtern

→ Audiodateien zu den Hörverstehens- übungen (bitte Code von S. 4 eingeben)

Online-Grundlagentraining

Du hast noch Lücken aus den vorherigen Schuljahren? Kein Problem! Das Online-Grundlagentraining auf FiNALEonline.de hilft dir dabei, wichtigen Lernstoff nachzuarbeiten und zu wiederholen. Und so funktioniert es:

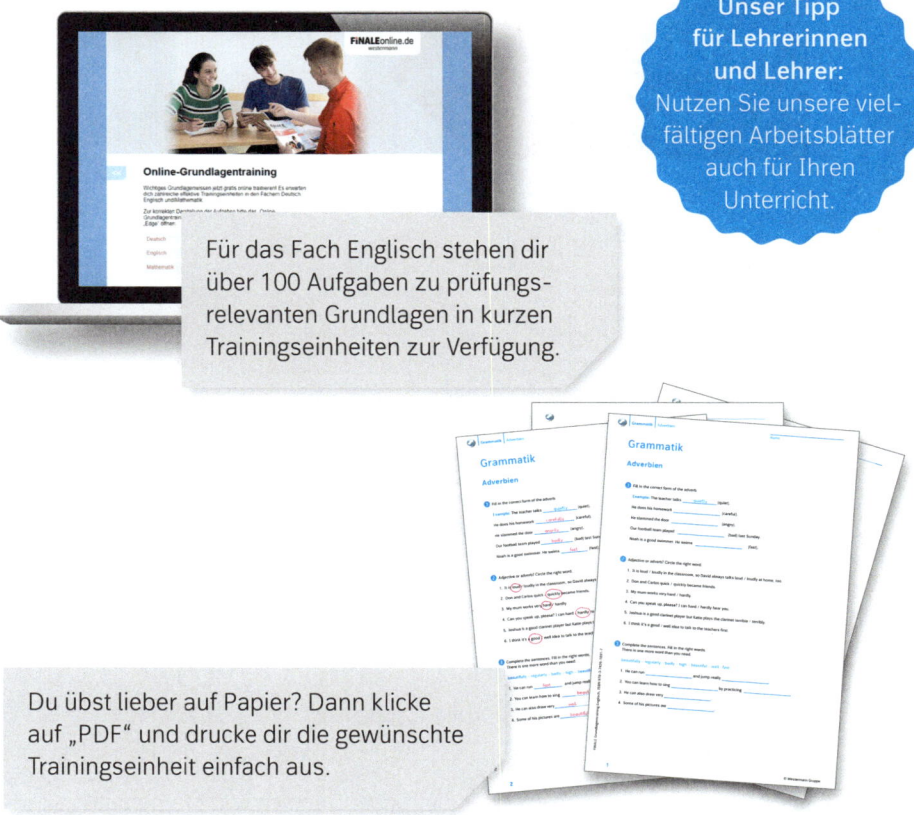

Unser Tipp für Lehrerinnen und Lehrer: Nutzen Sie unsere viel- fältigen Arbeitsblätter auch für Ihren Unterricht.

Für das Fach Englisch stehen dir über 100 Aufgaben zu prüfungs- relevanten Grundlagen in kurzen Trainingseinheiten zur Verfügung.

Für Lehrerinnen und Lehrer: Die Lehrerhandreichung für den optimalen Einsatz der Arbeitsbücher im Unterricht zum kosten- losen Download!

Du übst lieber auf Papier? Dann klicke auf „PDF" und drucke dir die gewünschte Trainingseinheit einfach aus.

FiNALE Grundlagentraining Englisch

Das FiNALE Grundlagentraining ist die ideale Ergänzung zu diesem Arbeitsbuch. Es bietet eine große Auswahl an Materialien, mit deren Hilfe du prüfungsrelevantes Grundlagenwissen auffrischen und aktiv trainieren kannst.

Folgende Inhalte werden in diesem Band behandelt:

→ umfangreiche Übungen zur Grammatik
→ Hörverstehen (mit Audiodateien)
→ Leseverstehen
→ Schreiben
→ Sprachmittlung (Mediation)
→ Sprechen
→ die wichtigsten Operatoren im Fach Englisch

Zu jeder Trainingseinheit gibt es anschauliche Lösungen.

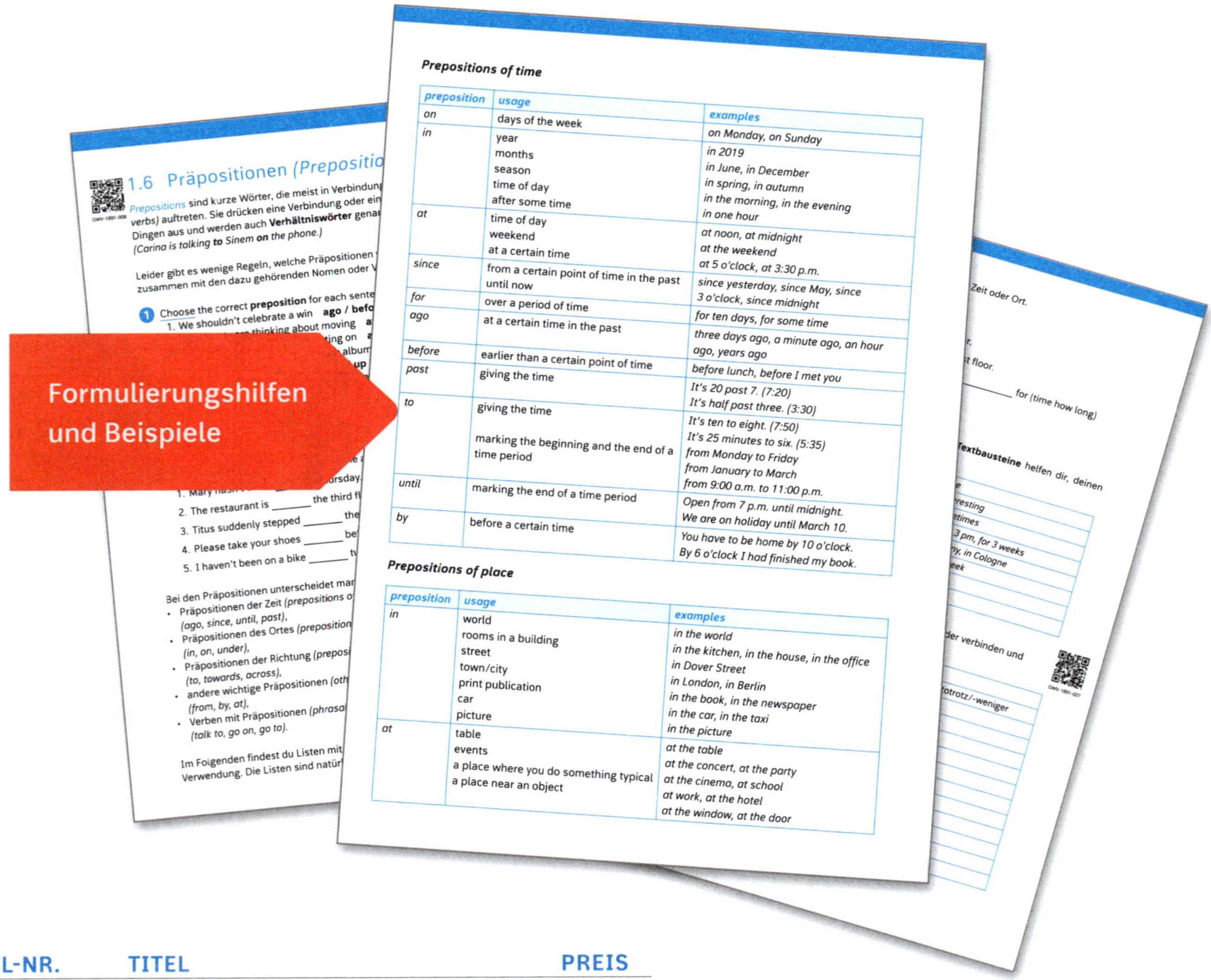

Formulierungshilfen und Beispiele

BESTELL-NR.	TITEL	PREIS
978-3-7426-1891-7	FiNALE Grundlagentraining Englisch	13,95 €

FiNALE Grundlagentraining gibt es auch für die Fächer Deutsch und Mathematik.

westermann

FiNALE
Prüfungstraining

Niedersachsen

**Abschluss
10. Klasse Realschule
Englisch**

2024

Katja Werthen-Giles

Liebe Schülerin, lieber Schüler,

sobald die Original-Prüfungsaufgaben zur Veröffentlichung freigegeben sind, können sie unter **www.finaleonline.de**
zusammen mit ausführlichen Lösungen kostenlos heruntergeladen werden. Gib dazu einfach diesen Code ein:

EN7p1Lp

Einfach mal reinschauen: www.finaleonline.de

© 2023 Westermann Lernwelten GmbH, Georg-Westermann-Allee 66, 38104 Braunschweig
www.westermann.de

Bildnachweis:
|Courtesy of Pest Control Office - Banksy, London: 11.1, 120.1. |Feldhaus, Hans-Jürgen, Münster: 5.2, 18.1, 19.2,
19.3, 19.4, 20.1, 27.1, 27.2, 27.3, 27.4, 28.1, 28.2, 28.3, 28.4, 28.5, 28.6, 28.7, 28.8, 28.9, 28.10, 28.11, 28.12, 29.1,
30.1, 30.2, 61.1, 64.1, 66.1, 91.1, 91.2, 91.3, 91.4, 92.1, 92.2, 92.3, 92.4, 92.5, 92.6, 92.7, 92.8, 92.9, 92.10, 92.11,
92.12, 93.1, 93.2, 93.3, 93.4, 94.1, 95.1, 110.1, 113.1, 114.1, 115.1. |fotolia.com, New York: dmitimaruta 21.4;
Kneschke, Robert 21.2; moodboard 21.1. |iStockphoto.com, Calgary: Arsty 9.1, 118.1; edenwithin 16.4; Fertnig 17.1;
Feverpitched 13.1, 13.2, 122.1, 122.2; Hlystov, Pavel 15.2, 124.1; sturti 15.1. |Kumpe, Bettina, Braunschweig: 1.1, 1.2,
1.3, 1.4, 1.5, 1.6, 2.1, 2.2, 2.3, 2.4, 2.5, 2.6, 2.7, 2.8, 2.9, 2.10, 2.11, 2.12, 3.1, 3.2, 3.3, 3.4, 3.5, 3.6, 7.2, 8.1, 46.1,
101.1, 101.2, 101.3, 110.2, 110.3, 110.4, 110.5, 110.6, 110.7, 111.1, 111.2, 111.3, 111.4, 111.5, 111.6, 111.7, 111.8,
111.9, 111.10, 111.11, 111.12, 112.1, 112.2, 112.3, 112.4, 112.5, 112.6, 116.2, 117.1. |Peter Wirtz Fotografie,
Dormagen: Titel. |Picture-Alliance GmbH, Frankfurt a.M.: Robert Harding World Imagery 16.2. |stock.adobe.com,
Dublin: @ Delphine Poggianti 19.1, 127.1; fizkes 6.1, 115.2; joyt 5.1, 114.2; Kneschke, Robert 16.1, 125.1; pixelliebe
7.1, 8.3, 116.1, 117.3; Stalvalki 8.2, 117.2; SUDIO 1ONE 16.3; Wellnhofer Designs 21.3.

Druck A[1] / Jahr 2023
Alle Drucke der Serie A sind im Unterricht parallel verwendbar.

Redaktion: Claudia Lüdtke / der springende punkt, Berlin
Kontakt: finale@westermanngruppe.de
Layout: LIO Design GmbH, Braunschweig
Umschlaggestaltung: Gingco.Net, Braunschweig
Umschlagfoto: Peter Wirtz, Dormagen
Druck und Bindung: Westermann Druck GmbH, Georg-Westermann-Allee 66, 38104 Braunschweig

ISBN 978-3-07-**172427**-3

Was erwartet dich in diesem Buch?

Du bist in der 10. Klasse und vor dir liegt die Zentrale Abschlussprüfung, das große „Finale".
Darauf will dich dieses Buch vorbereiten. Es gibt dir die Möglichkeit,
1. dich mit den Prüfungsaufgaben und ihren Anforderungen vertraut zu machen,
2. deine sprachlichen Möglichkeiten in den für die Zentrale Abschlussprüfung geforderten Bereichen zu erweitern und zu trainieren.

Teil A informiert dich über die Voraussetzungen der Abschlussprüfung, die einzelnen Teile und die Bewertung deiner Leistung.

In **Teil B** findest du Informationen und drei Übungstests zur mündlichen Prüfung. Du erfährst, wie die Prüfung abläuft und wie du dich gut darauf vorbereiten kannst.

Im **Teil C** erhältst du Hinweise, wie du dich gezielt und sinnvoll auf die schriftliche Prüfung vorbereiten kannst. Dieser Teil führt dich in kleinen Schritten an die Aufgabentypen und -formate heran und macht dir deutlich, was in den Aufgaben von dir erwartet wird. Außerdem bekommst du Tipps zur Erweiterung deines Wortschatzes (z. B. Wörterbucharbeit) und genaue Textbeispiele und Redemittel für das Schreiben von unterschiedlichen Textsorten.

In **Teil D** und **E** findest du Prüfungsbeispiele, die aufgebaut sind wie die Originalprüfung. Am Anfang wirst du dabei durch Lösungshilfen sehr intensiv unterstützt, später gehst du zunehmend selbstständig vor. Die Prüfungsbeispiele orientieren sich nicht nur in der Art der Aufgabenstellung, sondern auch thematisch an den Vorgaben für die Zentrale Abschlussprüfung.

In **Teil F** wird dir die Originalprüfung aus dem Jahr 2022 präsentiert.

Die Originalprüfung für 2023 bekommst du im Internet, sobald sie geschrieben und zur Veröffentlichung freigegeben ist. Sie ist dann zu finden unter www.finaleonline.de und kann mit diesem Codewort heruntergeladen werden: EN7p1Lp
Hast du noch Lücken aus den vorherigen Schuljahren? Dann empfehlen wir dir das FiNALE Grundlagentraining Englisch (ISBN 978-3-7426-1891-7). Es bietet prüfungsrelevantes Grundlagenwissen zum Nachschlagen und Üben. Ergänzend dazu findest du unter www.finaleonline.de/grundlagentraining ein kostenloses Online-Training mit interaktiven Übungsaufgaben und Arbeitsblättern zum Ausdrucken.
Und natürlich gibt es ein Lösungsheft, in dem du die Richtigkeit jedes Arbeitsschritts überprüfen kannst. Außerdem findest du auch zur Original-Prüfungsaufgabe eine mögliche Musterlösung, sodass du einschätzen kannst, was von dir in der Abschlussprüfung erwartet wird.
In diesem Arbeitsbuch findest du Schreiblinien, um deine Lösungen direkt ins Buch zu schreiben.
Manchmal musst du deine Texte auf einem Extrablatt anfertigen.
Damit du ein Gefühl für die zur Verfügung stehende Arbeitszeit bekommst, solltest du beim Bearbeiten der Prüfungsaufgaben eine Uhr bereitstellen.
Alle Übungen, zu denen es Audio-Dateien gibt, erkennst du an diesem Symbol: 🎧. Um die Audio-Dateien anzuhören, gib auf der Internetseite www.finaleonline.de diesen Code ein: EN7p1Lp

Wir sind sicher, dass du dich nach der Bearbeitung dieses Buches sicher für das „Finale" fühlst, und wünschen dir für die Prüfung viel Erfolg.

Die Autorin

Teil A Vorbereitung auf die Abschlussprüfung

Die zentrale Abschlussprüfung für Realschulen in Niedersachsen unterscheidet sich kaum von einer normalen Klassenarbeit im Fach Englisch. Mit diesem Format kennst du dich gut aus, denn du hast in jedem Schuljahr mindestens sechs Klassenarbeiten geschrieben. Der Unterschied besteht darin, dass die Aufgaben nicht von deinem Englischlehrer oder deiner Englischlehrerin entworfen wurden, sondern von Menschen, die dich, deine Klasse, deine Schule und den Unterricht bei euch gar nicht kennen. Dein Lehrer oder deine Lehrerin weiß genau, auf welchem Leistungsstand deine Klasse ist und wird die Übungen entsprechend schwer oder leicht gestalten. Die Planungsgruppe, die die Aufgaben der Abschlussarbeit entwickelt, geht von den Lernzielen im Kerncurriculum aus, die am Ende der zehnten Realschulklasse erreicht werden sollen. Anhand der Abschlussarbeit soll herausgefunden werden, wie der Lernstand an den einzelnen Schulen beziehungsweise in den einzelnen Klassen ist. Die Themen, Inhalte und Aufgaben werden nicht in jedem Jahr neu festgelegt, vielmehr gibt das Kerncurriculum den Rahmen für die Abschlussprüfung vor.

A 1 Das Kerncurriculum

Im Kerncurriculum (oder Lehrplan) ist genau festgelegt, was ein Schüler oder eine Schülerin am Ende der zehnten Realschulklasse in den einzelnen Bereichen können soll.
Diese Bereiche nennt man auch **Kompetenzen** und sie beziehen sich auf

1. Hörverstehen,
2. Leseverstehen,
3. Mediation,
4. Schreiben und
5. Sprechen.

> **INFO** Kerncurriculum
>
> Das Kerncurriculum ist der Lehrplan, der festlegt, was du im Fach Englisch lernen sollst. Die Unterrichtsziele für die einzelnen Klassenstufen (6, 8, 10) sind schriftlich formuliert.

Es geht also weniger um konkretes Wissen (Wie viele Staaten hat die USA? Wie heißt die Hauptstadt von Schottland?), sondern um deine Fähigkeiten beim Hören, Lesen, Schreiben von Texten und beim Verstehen von Inhalten und dem Übertragen in die eigene Sprache.
Zum **Hörverstehen** steht im Kerncurriculum, dass du in der Lage sein sollst, aus einem gehörten Text mit bekanntem Thema die Hauptaussage und auch Einzelinformationen zu entnehmen. Die Angaben zum **Leseverstehen** beziehen sich auf das globale Verstehen (Hauptgedanken erfassen), das selektive Verstehen (eine bestimmte Information erhören) und das Detailverständnis (den Hörtext genau und mit allen Einzelheiten verstehen) von Texten. Im **Bereich** Schreiben sollst du einen zusammenhängenden Text zu dir bekannten Themen verfassen können. Die **Sprachmittlung *(Mediation)*** bezieht sich auf deine Fähigkeit, Texte und Äußerungen zu vertrauten Themen ins Deutsche zu übertragen.
All diese Forderungen kannst du mit ein wenig Übung erfüllen. Sie werden anhand von ausgewählten Aufgabenformaten in der Abschlussarbeit überprüft. Das **Sprechen** teilt sich in zwei Bereiche ein („an Gesprächen teilnehmen" und „zusammenhängendes Sprechen"). Beide werden in der mündlichen Prüfung abgeprüft. Du musst zum einen ohne Vorbereitung an einem Gespräch über ein dir vertrautes Thema teilnehmen können. Dies beinhaltet die Darstellung deiner Meinung zu einem bestimmten Thema und das Austauschen von Informationen.

A 2 Die Vorgaben

Die Themen, Inhalte und Aufgaben werden in Niedersachsen nicht in jedem Jahr neu festgelegt. Vielmehr legen die Ausführungen im Kerncurriculum den Rahmen für die Abschlussprüfung fest. Darauf verweist das Kultusministerium (die oberste Schulbehörde in Niedersachsen) in jedem Jahr und betont, dass man die Vorjahresprüfung zur Vorbereitung nutzen soll.

Häufig werden die Themen, die im Jahrgang 9 und 10 im Englischunterricht behandelt wurden, auch für die Prüfung genutzt. Wenn du dein Lehrbuch für Englisch durchblätterst, werden dir Inhalte wie Berufswahl beziehungsweise Bewerbung, Arbeitswelt, Freizeitgestaltung und Freunde, aber auch Medien, Reisen, Alkohol und Drogen begegnen. Ebenfalls werden unterschiedliche englischsprachige Länder thematisiert wie z. B. Australien, Neuseeland, England und die USA. All diese aufgezählten Themen sind dir aus deinem Unterricht bekannt, da die Lehrbücher dem Kerncurriculum entsprechend konzipiert werden. Außerdem geht es wie gesagt nicht darum, Wissen über ein bestimmtes Land oder Ähnliches abzufragen. Du sollst vielmehr beweisen, dass du Englisch verstehen, lesen, schreiben und an Gesprächen in der Fremdsprache teilnehmen kannst. Nachdem du die Beispieltests in diesem Arbeitsbuch durchgearbeitet hast, bist du gut auf die Prüfung vorbereitet.

A 3 Die mündliche Prüfung im Fach Englisch

Seit dem Schuljahr 2013/2014 müssen alle Schüler des 10. Schuljahrgangs an Realschulen an einer mündlichen Prüfung im Fach Englisch teilnehmen. Der zeitliche Umfang für die mündliche Teilprüfung beträgt 12–15 Minuten. Die mündliche Prüfung findet zu einem anderen Zeitpunkt als die schriftliche Abschlussprüfung statt, im Jahr 2024 findet die verbindliche mündliche Prüfung in Englisch im Zeitraum von Montag, dem 11. März bis Freitag, dem 15. März sowie von Montag, dem 3. April bis Freitag, dem 26. April statt. In der Regel wird sie als Tandemprüfung (zwei Schüler pro Prüfung – bei ungerader Schülerzahl in einer Klasse auch eine Dreiergruppe) durchgeführt. Es gibt keine Vorbereitungszeit. Die Prüfung besteht aus drei Teilen, in denen deine mündliche Sprechfähigkeit auf unterschiedliche Weise geprüft wird. Für die Prüfung sind keine Hilfsmittel zugelassen. Die Prüfungsgruppen werden entweder ausgelost oder festgelegt und von deinem Lehrer oder deiner Lehrerin bekannt gegeben.
Deine Fachlehrerin oder dein Fachlehrer ist häufig der Prüfer oder die Prüferin, erläutert jeweils kurz die entsprechenden Aufgaben und greift nur ein, wenn ihr nichts mehr sagt oder Fragen äußert. Ansonsten ist seine oder ihre Rolle zurückhaltend passiv. Der Protokollant oder die Protokollantin bewertet mithilfe eines vorgegebenen Bewertungsrasters die Prüfungsleistung.

Leistungsfeststellung
Du musst in dieser Prüfung beweisen, dass du Fragen zu verschiedenen Themen in der Fremdsprache sprachlich richtig und fließend beantworten, Bilder beschreiben und interpretieren und mit einem Partner über ein bestimmtes Thema diskutieren und deine eigene Meinung darlegen kannst. Du darfst jedoch nicht „rumlabern", sondern musst dich auf die gestellten Aufgaben konzentrieren. All diese Bereiche werden vom Protokollanten oder der Protokollantin und vom Prüfer oder der Prüferin bewertet.
Die einzelnen Teile der Prüfung werden nicht gesondert beurteilt, obwohl unterschiedliche Ansprüche gestellt werden. Du bekommst eine Note für deine Gesamtleistung. Die Prüfer und Protokollanten verwenden dafür vorgegebene Beurteilungsbögen. Beide geben direkt nach der Prüfung ihre Beurteilung ab, ermitteln die Gesamtnote und teilen sie euch zeitnah mit.

Insgesamt können 40 Punkte verteilt werden. Der Prüfer oder die Prüferin, der oder die die Prüfung durchführt und vielleicht dein Fachlehrer oder deine Fachlehrerin in Englisch ist, vergibt 20 Punkte. Der Protokollant oder die Protokollantin, der oder die nur zuhört, vergibt ebenfalls 20 Punkte. Beide Personen haben einen Bewertungsbogen.
Der Prüfer oder die Prüferin beurteilt den Gesamteindruck deiner sprachlichen Äußerungen. Ziel ist eine flüssige Beantwortung der Fragen oder Aufgaben, eine problemlose Kommunikation, aufgabenbezogene Beiträge und die Aufrechterhaltung der Kommunikation mit dem Prüfer oder der Prüferin und deinem Partner beziehungsweise deiner Partnerin.

Der Protokollant oder die Protokollantin beurteilt das kommunikative Handeln, Verständlichkeit und sprachliche Flexibilität, Wortschatz, Aussprache, Betonung und Satzmelodie.

Kommunikatives Handeln	Verständlichkeit und sprachliche Flexibilität	Wortschatz	Aussprache Betonung Satzmelodie
– Sprichst du fließend? – Lieferst du relevante Beiträge zum Bild oder zur Partneraktivität? – Benötigst du Hilfen? – Wendest du Strategien zur Aufrechterhaltung der Kommunikation an?	– Verwendest du abwechslungsreiche Satzstrukturen? – Verwendest du richtige Strukturen? – Formulierst du inhaltlich sinnvolle und zusammenhängende Beiträge?	– Hast du einen umfangreichen Wortschatz? – Wendest du diesen Wortschatz angemessen an?	– Kann man dich problemlos verstehen? – Verwendest du die richtige Aussprache und Satzmelodie? – Nutzt du die Satzmelodie, um deine Sprechabsicht zu verdeutlichen?

Die Note für die Abschlussprüfung in Englisch Klasse 10 besteht aus einer mündlichen und einer schriftlichen Teilprüfung. Die Note für die mündliche Teilprüfung fließt zu einem Drittel in die Gesamtnote der Abschlussprüfung ein. Hier ist eine Übersicht für die Punkte der mündlichen Prüfung:

40–35 = 1
34–27 = 2
26–19 = 3
18–12 = 4
11– 4 = 5
 3– 0 = 6

Die Landesschulbehörde Niedersachsens hat einen Leitfaden zur mündlichen Prüfung im Fach Englisch herausgebracht. Unter folgendem Link kannst du diesen einsehen oder auch herunterladen:
https://www.nibis.de/uploads/redriedl/EN/Materialien_mdl_Pruefung_SI.pdf

Ablauf der mündlichen Prüfung für den Mittleren Bildungsabschluss an Realschulen (12–15 Minuten)
1. *speaking about yourself: questions and answers* (1–2 Minuten pro Kandidat)
2. *speaking promts:* überwiegend monologische Aufgabe mithilfe von *pictures, audio materials oder reali*a (2–3 Minuten pro Kandidat)
3. *paired/group discussion:* Diskussion von visual material o. Ä. (2–4 Minuten pro Kandidat)

A 4 Zum Aufbau der schriftlichen Abschlussprüfung

Die Abschlussprüfung am Ende der zehnten Realschulklasse dauert **120 Minuten** und findet am 8. Mai 2024 statt (Nachschreibtermin: 22. Mai 2024). Du darfst ein zweisprachiges Wörterbuch benutzen.
Die Prüfung setzt sich aus vier Teilen zusammen:
Der erste Teil testet das **Hörverstehen** und dauert etwa 25 Minuten. Für die übrigen drei Prüfungsteile stehen dir ungefähr 90 Minuten zur Verfügung. Behalte die Zeit immer im Blick (nimm am besten eine Uhr mit) und teile sie dir gut ein! Bekanntlich dauert das Schreiben von Texten immer am längsten. Das Bearbeiten der Aufgaben in diesem Buch wird dir beim Zeitmanagement helfen, da du anschließend besser einschätzen kannst, wie lange du für die einzelnen Prüfungsteile brauchst. Notiere in der **Checkliste** am Ende der einzelnen Kapitel immer die Anzahl der Minuten, die du für die einzelnen Teile benötigst. So behältst du den Überblick und kannst dir eine Strategie für den Ernstfall zurechtlegen.

INFO Prüfungsteile	
Listening	23 (oder 24) Punkte
Reading	24 (oder 23) Punkte
Mediating	8 Punkte
Writing	25 Punkte
Gesamt:	**80 Punkte**

In manchen Jahren konnte man im Hörverstehen 23 Punkte und im Leseverstehen 24 Punkte erreichen. In anderen Jahren waren die Punktezahlen umgekehrt (Listening 24 Punkte und Reading 23 Punkte).

Im ersten Teil, dem **Hörverstehen,** gibt es **vier Aufgabentypen,** die im Schwierigkeitsgrad ansteigend sind. Du hörst unterschiedliche Textsorten (z. B. Interview, Bericht, Ansagen, Dialog, Telefongespräch) und erhältst dazu verschiedene Aufgabenformate, bei denen du ein Bild auswählen, ein Formular ausfüllen, aus mehreren Anworten die richtige aussuchen oder richtig beziehungsweise falsch ankreuzen sollst.

Auch der Teil zum **Leseverstehen** beinhaltet **vier Teilaufgaben,** die ähnliche Aufgabentypen präsentieren wie der Hörteil *(true or false, matching,* Multiple Choice, Lückentext). Mögliche Lesetexte umfassen Briefe, Formulare, Artikel, E-Mails, Berichte usw. Denke daran, dass du nicht jedes einzelne Wort im Text verstehen musst. Viele Wörter kannst du aus dem Kontext erschließen. Schlage nur die wichtigen Vokabeln nach, da Nachschlagen viel Zeit in Anspruch nimmt.

Die Aufgaben zu **Mediation** (Sprachmittlung) bestehen aus **zwei Teilbereichen.** Häufig müssen Informationen aus der englischen in die deutsche Sprache und anschließend vom Deutschen ins Englische übertragen werden. Dabei kann es sich zum z. B. um Hinweisschilder, Anzeigen, Speisekarten oder Fahrpläne handeln.

Du bekommst für das *Writing* zwei Aufgabenvarianten und hast 15 Minuten Zeit, um dich für die eine oder andere zu entscheiden. Du solltest dir die Aufgabentypen genau ansehen und die Aufgabenstellung durchlesen, um inhaltlich zu entscheiden, ob dir die Themen liegen. Entscheide nicht nach Länge oder Art des Textes, sondern nach Inhalt und Thema. Nimm dir Zeit und überlege genau, welche Variante du besser bearbeiten kannst. Für diese Aufgaben gibt es insgesamt 25 Punkte. Deine Entscheidung ist also wichtig.

INFO Bewertungsschlüssel für die schriftliche Abschlussarbeit	
Prozentualer Anteil der Gesamtpunktzahl	**Endnote**
100 – 93% (80 – 73 points)	sehr gut (1)
92 – 83% (72 – 65 points)	gut (2)
82 – 72% (64 – 57 points)	befriedigend (3)
71 – 60% (56 – 48 points)	ausreichend (4)
59 – 30% (47 – 24 points)	mangelhaft (5)
29 – 0% (23 – 0 points)	ungenügend (6)

Die Punkte beider Prüfungen werden zusammengerechnet, um dann eine Note zu erhalten:

INFO Gesamtbewertung	
120 – 108 Punkte	sehr gut (1)
107 – 92 Punkte	gut (2)
91 – 76 Punkte	befriedigend (3)
75 – 59 Punkte	ausreichend (4)
58 – 27 Punkte	mangelhaft (5)
26 – 0 Punkte	ungenügend (6)

A 5 Zum Aufbau des Buches – und zum Umgang damit

Dieses Arbeitsbuch wird dir alle nötigen Informationen wie Inhalte, Themen und Aufgabenstellungen zu den Prüfungen vermitteln und dich optimal auf beide vorbereiten.

In **Teil B** geht es um die mündliche Prüfung. Du erfährst genau, wie die Prüfung abläuft, welche Themen vorkommen und auch, wie du dich am besten vorbereiten kannst. Du findest Übungsaufgaben, die genau erklärt werden. Im Anschluss kannst du drei Übungstests „durchspielen".

In **Teil C** wirst du dich intensiv mit den verschiedenen Bereichen der Prüfung (Hörverstehen, Leseverstehen, Mediation, Schreiben und Sprechen) beschäftigen. Du wirst Übungen mit Tipps und Tricks finden, die dir beim Verbessern deiner Fähigkeiten in allen Kompetenzen helfen. Es ist wichtig, dass du die Aufgaben nacheinander durcharbeitest und dir genug Zeit nimmst, denn nur so kannst du davon auch wirklich profitieren. Zu Beginn solltest du nicht zu viele Übungen bearbeiten. Setze dir einen Schwerpunkt (z. B. Hörverstehen), nimm dir die Zeit und bearbeite den Teil dazu. Beantworte die Aufgaben in der vorgegebenen Zeit und sieh dir die Lösungen an. Hake die richtigen Antworten ab, aber mache dir bei den Fehlern bewusst, warum du welche gemacht hast. Gab es Probleme mit dem Akzent des Sprechers? Hast du ein wichtiges Wort nicht verstanden? Waren die Sprecher zu schnell? Hat dich eine Aufgabenstellung verwirrt? Hast du dir nicht genug Zeit genommen? Du musst aus deinen Fehlern lernen, damit sie sich nicht wiederholen. Nutze die Checkliste am Ende jedes Tests und werte die Ergebnisse richtig aus. Anhand deiner Notizen zur Fehlerquelle fällt es dir leichter, die Ursachen zu erkennen und so Fehler in Zukunft zu vermeiden.

In **Teil D** wird dir ein angeleiteter Test präsentiert. Hier kannst du das Format der Prüfung mit Hilfen und Hinweisen richtig kennen lernen und nach und nach durcharbeiten. Du kannst feststellen, welche Aufgaben dir leicht fallen und wo du dich noch verbessern musst. Die Lösungshilfen und Hinweise unterstützten dich und machen dich am Beispiel der Übungen auf Probleme und mögliche Schwierigkeiten aufmerksam, auf die du achten solltest.

Der **Teil E** bietet dir einen Test an, den du nun fast selbstständig bearbeiten kannst. Den Test solltest du unter Prüfungsbedingungen bearbeiten. Du hast 120 Minuten Zeit (möglichst ohne Unterbrechungen oder Pausen), um alle Aufgaben zu lösen. Ziehe dich an einen Ort zurück, an dem du so lange ungestört arbeiten kannst. Folgendes Material benötigst du: zweisprachiges Wörterbuch, Getränke und Snacks, Papier, Stifte (bunt), Computer oder Tablet (zum Anhören der Audio-Dateien), eine Uhr und dieses Arbeitsbuch.

Teil F ist die schriftliche Abschlussprüfung aus dem Jahr 2022. Diesen Test solltest du als Generalprobe betrachten und ihn entsprechend ernst nehmen. Bevor du ihn bearbeitest, hast du in den vorangegangenen Teilen deine Stärken festgestellt, Schwächen verbessert und Lücken gefüllt. Erst dann ist es sinnvoll, diese Aufgaben zu bearbeiten. Bevor du das tust, lies dir die Checklisten zu den einzelnen Teilen noch einmal durch und erinnere dich an deine Strategien, die du erfolgreich eingesetzt hast. Denke an mögliche Fehlerquellen, die du vermeiden kannst. Dann bist du fit für die Prüfungen im Fach Englisch.

INFO Aufbau des Buches

Teil A   Einführung
Teil B   Sprechen
Teil C   Die Kompetenzen (Hör-, Leseverstehen, Mediation, Schreiben)
Teil D   Angeleiteter Test
Teil E   Test mit wenig Hilfen
Teil F   Test ohne Hilfen – Abschlussprüfung 2022

Teil B Die mündliche Prüfung

B 1 Ablauf der mündlichen Prüfung

Wie schon in Kapitel A 1.3 „Die mündliche Prüfung im Fach Englisch" (S. 9) erwähnt, besteht die mündliche Prüfung aus drei Teilen.

Ablauf der mündlichen Prüfung für den Mittleren Bildungsabschluss an Realschulen (12–15 Minuten)
1. *speaking about yourself: questions and answers* (1–2 Minuten pro Kandidat)
2. *speaking promts:* überwiegend monologische Aufgabe mithilfe von *pictures, audio materials* oder realia (2–3 Minuten pro Kandidat)
3. *paired/group discussion:* Diskussion von *visual material* o. Ä. (2–4 Minuten pro Kandidat)

Die Prüfungsteile
In der folgenden Tabelle kannst du sehen, was in den drei Prüfungsteilen gefragt wird, welche Themen vorkommen und was du zur Vorbereitung auf die Prüfung üben kannst. Genauere Hinweise dazu findest du im Verlauf dieses Kapitels. Das Material für die mündliche Abschlussprüfung wird im Gegensatz zur schriftlichen Abschlussprüfung nicht von der Landesschulbehörde zusammengestellt, sondern von der Fachkonferenz Englisch oder den Englischlehrerinnen und -lehrern an deiner Schule.

Prüfungsteil	mögliche Themen und Inhalte	Übungshinweise
1. *Warm-up*-Fragen	– Fragen beantworten zur eigenen Person (persönliche Angaben), Familie, Schule, Freizeitgestaltung, Haustiere, Vorlieben, Hobbys, Berufswunsch, Zukunftspläne etc.	– Wortschatz zu den Themen z. B. anhand von Mindmaps üben – Frage- und Antwortspiele mit Partner oder Partnerin üben – buchstabieren üben
2. Bildbeschreibung	– Bilder, die sich zum Beschreiben anbieten z. B. Straßenszene, Großstadt – Dorf, öffentliche Plätze wie Marktszene, Bahnhof, Café, Restaurant – Bilder von Menschen, die Sport treiben, einen Konflikt austragen, arbeiten, essen, einem Hobby nachgehen	– typische Phrasen zur Bildbeschreibung einüben – *simple present/ present progressive* – mit Partner oder Partnerin üben
3. Partneraktivität	– Planung einer Party, einer Sprachreise, Auslandsjahr etc. – Auswahl eines Ferienjobs, Geschenk, Urlaubsziel, Freizeitaktivität etc.	– typische Phrasen für eine Diskussion einüben (eigene Meinung äußern, Argumente vorbringen usw.) – mit Partner oder Partnerin üben

B 2 Aufgabenformate für das Sprechen

Trainingsmöglichkeiten

Auf den folgenden Seiten findest du Tipps, Übungen und Methoden, um dich auf die einzelnen Prüfungsaufgaben intensiv vorzubereiten. Entsprechende Satzanfänge und Redemittel *(phrases)* unterstützen dich in deiner Vorbereitung. Da die Prüfung eine Tandemprüfung ist, ist das gemeinsame Üben mit einem Partner sinnvoll.

INFO

Internetadressen für Material bzw. Aufgaben:
– https://www.cambridgeenglish.org
– https://www.cambridgeenglish.org/test-your-english/
– www.splendidspeaking.com
– www.teachingenglish.org.uk

So könnt ihr möglichst realistisch die Prüfungssituation simulieren. An manchen Schulen werden die Paare frühzeitig bekannt gegeben, sodass du dich eventuell mit deinem Prüfungspartner vorbereiten kannst. Ihr könnt euch gegenseitig Tipps geben und auf Fehler hinweisen. Solltest du noch zusätzliches Material benötigen, kannst du die Internetadressen in der Infobox nutzen.

B 2.1 Aufgabenformate für Prüfungsteil 1

In diesem Prüfungsteil werden dir und deinem Partner nacheinander oder abwechselnd Fragen gestellt. Gemeinsam mit einem Partner oder einer Partnerin kannst du Fragen und Antworten trainieren und das Buchstabieren wiederholen.

Übungsaufgabe zu Prüfungsteil 1
– *What's your name?*
– *What's your last/family name?*
– *Can you spell your first/last/family name?*
– *How old are you?*
– *What's your favourite colour/food/animal/pet/music/subject/hobby?*
– *Where do you live?*
– *Do you have any brothers or sisters?*
– *How do you get to school?*
– *How long does it take?*

Sucht euch ein Thema aus *(family, school, pets, hobbies, plans for the future)* und denkt euch viele passende Fragen aus. Stellt euch diese Fragen gegenseitig und wechselt euch mit dem Fragen und Antworten ab.

Mindmaps und *word webs*

Anhand von Mindmaps und *word webs* kannst du dir den Wortschatz zu den Themen ins Gedächtnis rufen und so einüben. Bei *word webs* schreibst du ein Wort in die Mitte und schreibst in Felder um diesen Begriff alles, was dir dazu einfällt.
Bei einer Mindmap kannst du stärker sortieren. Du kannst zu den einzelnen Begriffen Unterpunkte hinzufügen. Auf Seite 61 (und im Lösungheft auf Seite 16) findest du als Beispiel eine Mindmap zum Thema *school*.

B 2.2 Aufgabenformate für Prüfungsteil 2

Im zweiten Prüfungsteil sollst du ein Bild oder Foto möglichst detailliert beschreiben. Schau dir das Bild auf der folgenden Seite an und beschreibe es anschließend. Denk daran, dass man ein Bild im *simple present* beschreibt, aber die Tätigkeiten der Personen im *present progressive* benennt, da sie in diesem Moment ablaufen. (Beispiel: *The woman on the left is cleaning the bathroom.*) Stelle Vermutungen über die Gefühle und Gedanken der Personen an und/oder nenne das Thema beziehungsweise die Hauptaussage des Bildes.

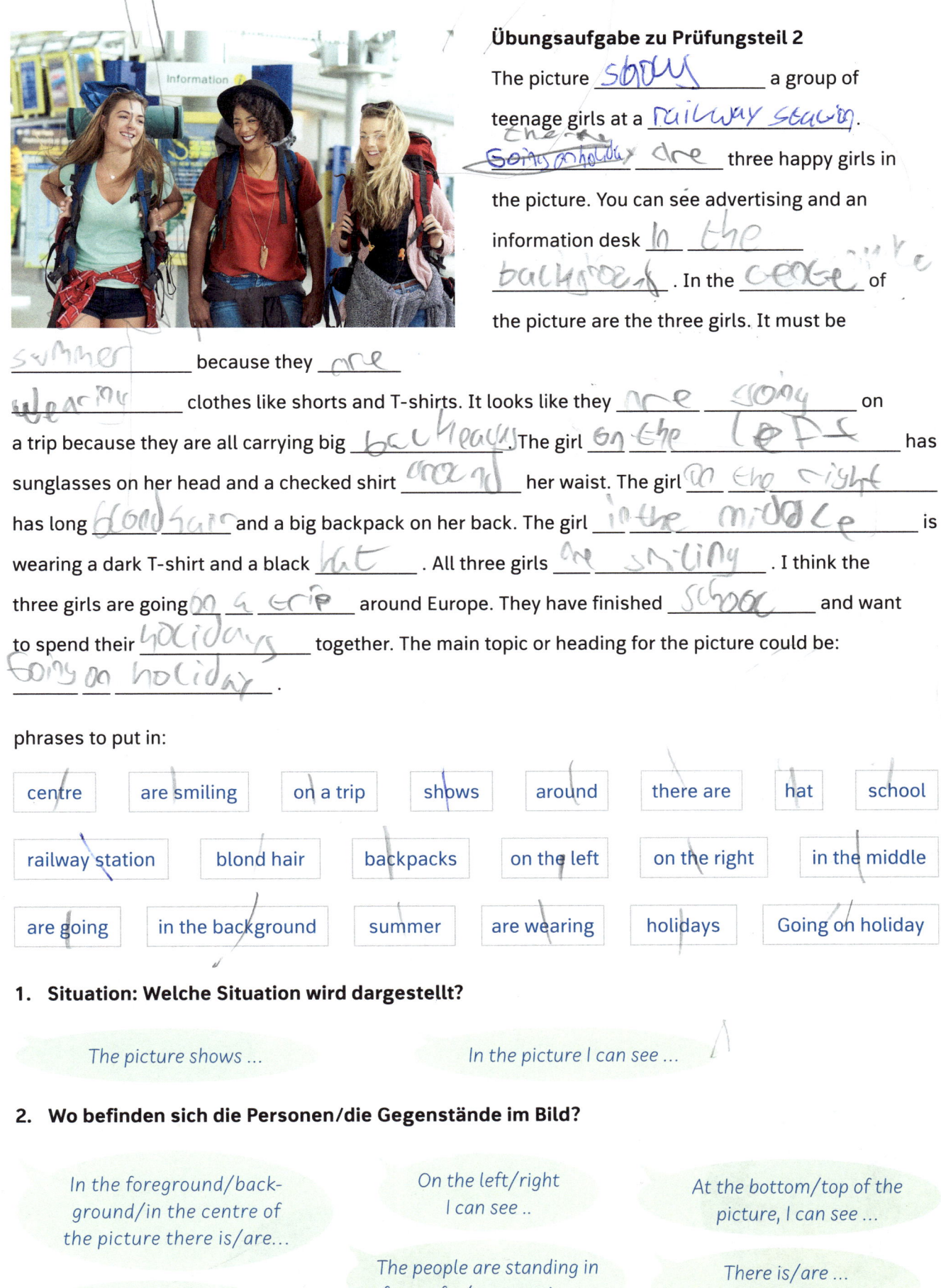

Übungsaufgabe zu Prüfungsteil 2

The picture _shows_ a group of teenage girls at a _railway station_. _there are_ ~~there going on holiday~~ three happy girls in the picture. You can see advertising and an information desk _in the background_. In the _centre_ of the picture are the three girls. It must be _summer_ because they _are wearing_ clothes like shorts and T-shirts. It looks like they _are going_ on a trip because they are all carrying big _backpacks_. The girl _on the left_ has sunglasses on her head and a checked shirt _around_ her waist. The girl _on the right_ has long _blond hair_ and a big backpack on her back. The girl _in the middle_ is wearing a dark T-shirt and a black _hat_. All three girls _are smiling_. I think the three girls are going _on a trip_ around Europe. They have finished _school_ and want to spend their _holidays_ together. The main topic or heading for the picture could be: _Going on holiday_.

phrases to put in:

centre	are smiling	on a trip	shows	around	there are	hat	school
railway station	blond hair	backpacks	on the left	on the right	in the middle		
are going	in the background	summer	are wearing	holidays	Going on holiday		

1. **Situation: Welche Situation wird dargestellt?**

   The picture shows …   *In the picture I can see …*

2. **Wo befinden sich die Personen/die Gegenstände im Bild?**

   In the foreground/back-ground/in the centre of the picture there is/are…

   On the left/right I can see ..

   At the bottom/top of the picture, I can see …

   The people are standing in front of…/are meeting …

   There is/are … behind/under …

   In the top right-hand corner there is/are…

15

3. Was tun die Menschen? Was sagen sie zueinander? Was denken und fühlen sie?

> *The old woman is reading/ talking to a friend/eating …*

> *The children are probably talking about …*

> *The man looks happy/sad/ worried, because …*

> *Maybe he is thinking that …*

B 2.3 Aufgabenformate für Prüfungsteil 3

Im letzten Teil sollst du mit deinem Partner oder deiner Partnerin ein Gespräch zu einem vorgegebenen Thema führen und je nach Aufgabenstellung zu einer Einigung beziehungsweise zu einer gemeinsamen Planung gelangen. Dabei ist es wichtig, dass du deine Meinung darstellst und gute Argumente nennst, um diese zu unterstützen. Du musst auf Argumente deines Partners oder deiner Partnerin reagieren und das Gespräch aufrechthalten, indem du nach seiner oder ihrer Meinung zu deinen Ideen fragst. Folgende Satzanfänge können dir dabei helfen:

1. Expressing an opinion
I think …
In my opinion …
I believe that …
I would suggest that …

2. Giving reasons and examples
For example, …
That's why …
Let me explain …
because …
And finally, …
What do you think about …

3. Agreeing with someone
I agree (with you) …
That's a good point.
You're right.
That sounds great.

4. Disagreeing with someone
I don't think you can say …
I see what you mean, but …
Sorry, I don't agree with you …
Yes, but …

5. Keeping a conversation going
What do you think about …?
How do you feel about …?
Maybe we should try …
We could …

Übungsaufgabe zu Prüfungsteil 3
Imagine you want to go on holiday. Look at the pictures and talk about the possibilities. You must decide where you want to spend your vacation. Give reasons for your choice.

B 3 Speaking Tests

Die folgenden drei *Speaking Tests* solltest du entweder mit einem Partner oder einer Partnerin oder mit mehreren Personen bearbeiten. Ihr könnt dabei die Rollen verteilen: Einer von euch könnte z. B. der Prüfer oder die Prüferin sein, einer der Protokollant oder die Protokollantin und einer der zweite Prüfling. Nimm das Gespräch auf und höre es dir anschließend an. So kannst du feststellen, ob du fließend sprichst und ob deine Aussprache verständlich ist. Vergleiche deine Aufnahme anschließend mit dem Lösungstext und überprüfe, ob du eventuell entscheidende Aspekte der Themen vergessen hast. Achte auf die Zeit. Die mündliche Prüfung ist sehr kurz.

B 3.1 Speaking Test 1

Introduction: Good morning. Please come in and have a seat. How are you today? This is Mrs/Mr X. She/he will listen to us and take notes. In the first part of the test I will ask you some questions.

Part 1 – Questions

AUFGABENSTELLUNG

	Partner A/Partner B	possible answers
Answer the following questions. (Partner A and B are asked identical questions.)	What's your first/last name? Can you spell your last name, please?	
	Please tell me where you live!	
	How long have you been living there?	
	Do you live in a house or a flat?	
	Please describe your room!	
	Do you have any hobbies?	
	Tell us more about your favourite hobby.	

Part 2

AUFGABENSTELLUNG

Examiner:
I'd like each of you to talk on your own about something. I'm going to give each of you a picture.
Here is your picture. Please show it to your partner and tell him/her what you can see in the picture and what the people are doing/talking about/thinking/feeling.

Questions picture 1/partner A:
What can you see? What is the boy doing? What jobs do you think children should do at home?

Questions picture 2/partner B:
What can you see? What is the problem? What is the boy thinking? What jobs do you have to do at home?

Part 3

Examiner: I am going to describe a situation to you. Imagine that students in your class want to have a party. Talk to each other about possible places, times and things to do and organize, and agree on a plan of action. Here is a mind map with some ideas to help you.

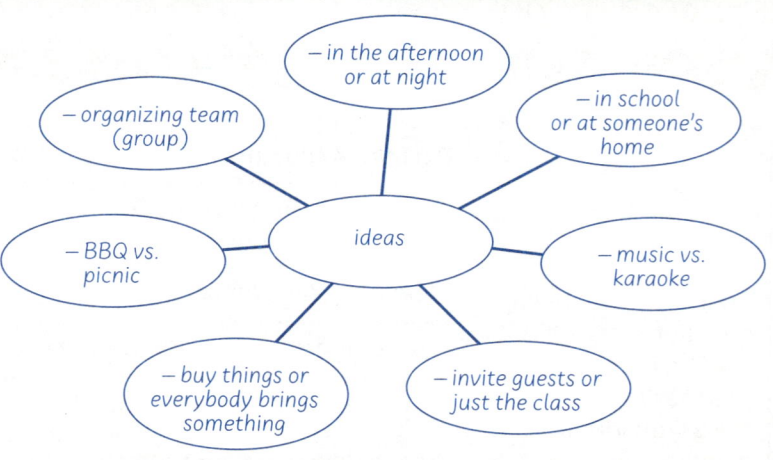

B 3.2 Speaking Test 2
Part 1 – Questions

Answer the following questions. (Partner A and B are asked identical questions.)	Partner A/Partner B	possible answers
	Hello, how are you today? What's your name? Can you spell your first name, please?	
	Tell me something about your hometown. What can you do there in your free time?	
	Can you talk about your family? Do you have sisters or brothers?	
	Tell me about your friends.	
	Do you have a pet?	

Part 2

Here is a picture. Talk about the picture and answer the questions.

Questions: What can you see? What are they talking about? What kind of rules do you have to follow at home?

In der Prüfung bekommt – wie in Speaking Test 1 gezeigt – jeder von euch ein Bild zu einem gemeinsamen Thema. Ihr zeigt es eurem Partner oder eurer Partnerin und sprecht dann über das Bild, das ihr bekommen habt. In Part 3 redet ihr dann gemeinsam zu einer Situation, die euch vorgegeben wird.

Part 3

In this part of the test you are going to talk to each other. Imagine your school wants to introduce school uniform. Talk to each other about the advantages and disadvantages of school uniform and come to a decision in the end.

Talk about the clothes you would choose and the colours/styles etc. for boys and girls.

B 3.3 Speaking Test 3
Part 1 – Questions

	Partner A/Partner B	possible answers
Answer the following questions. (Partner A and B are asked identical questions.)	What's your first name? Can you spell your first name, please?	
	Where do you go to school?	
	What is/are your favourite subject(s)?	
	What other activities do you do in school?	
	What is the atmosphere like in your class?	
	Do you have a lot of friends in school?	

Part 2

Talk about the picture and answer the questions.

Questions
What can you see? Describe the situation.
What would you do if you were the person without a cigarette?

Part 3

You want to take driving lessons to get your driver's licence as soon as possible. To earn some money you and your friend want to get a summer job. Look at the following pictures and discuss the different possibilities with your partner. Make a decision about which job you would like to do.

summer jobs

Lösungshilfen

Die Fragen im ersten Teil solltest du ohne Probleme beantworten können. Wenn dir keine Antworten einfallen, kannst du auch Aktivitäten oder Ähnliches erfinden. Deine Antworten müssen sprachlich richtig sein, aber nicht der Wahrheit oder deiner Meinung entsprechen.

Das Thema des zweiten Teils betrifft dich direkt, denn es geht um *peer pressure* – Jugendliche üben Druck auf Mitglieder ihrer Gruppe aus, sich anzupassen, z. B. in diesem Fall Zigaretten zu rauchen. Stell dir die Situation vor und versetze dich in die Person ohne Zigarette. Es ist wichtig, dass du flüssig und ohne viele Pausen antwortest.

Ihr bekommt einige Bilder, die euch Ideen vorgeben. So kommt ihr schnell ins Gespräch. Ihr könnt natürlich auch andere Vorschläge diskutieren.

Nun hast du erfahren, wie die mündliche Prüfung abläuft und hast drei Übungstests durchgearbeitet. Versuche nun, nach der Bearbeitung der Aufgaben in diesem Kapitel die Checkliste auszufüllen.

CHECKLISTE nach der Bearbeitung der Aufgaben Teil B

Aufgabe	Zeit	Was hat mir geholfen?	Fehlerquellen
Speaking Test 1 Sprechübung Part 1 Questions			
Sprechübung Part 2 Helping at home			
Sprechübung Part 3 Organizing a party			
Speaking Test 2 Sprechübung Part 1 Questions			
Sprechübung Part 2 Rules at home			
Sprechübung Part 3 School uniforms			
Speaking Test 1 Sprechübung Part 1 Questions			
Sprechübung Part 2 Smoking			
Sprechübung Part 3 Summer jobs			

Im nächsten Teil lernst du die wichtigsten Arbeitstechniken, Strategien und Aufgabenformate für die schriftliche Prüfung kennen.

Teil C Arbeitstechniken für die schriftliche Prüfung

Im Kerncurriculum des Landes Niedersachsen wird im Fach Englisch zwischen produktiven und rezeptiven Kompetenzen unterschieden. Mit den rezeptiven sind das **Hör-** und das **Lesverstehen** gemeint, da man hier gesprochene oder geschriebene Sprache verstehen muss.
Die produktiven Fertigkeiten sind das **Schreiben** und das **Sprechen.** Hier muss Sprache entweder schriftlich oder mündlich produziert werden. In der schriftlichen Abschlussprüfung werden die vier Kompetenzen Hörverstehen, Leseverstehen, Sprachmittlung und Schreiben abgeprüft.

C 1 Arbeitstechnik Hörverstehen

Die Überprüfung des Hörverstehens ist der **erste Teil** der zentralen Abschlussprüfung der zehnten Realschulklassen in Niedersachsen im Fach Englisch. Er dauert **etwa 25 Minuten** und besteht aus vier unterschiedlichen Aufgabenformen. Jeder Text oder Dialog wird zweimal nacheinander vorgespielt. Insgesamt kannst du in diesem Bereich 23 (oder 24) Punkte erreichen. Im Folgenden werden dir unterschiedliche Aufgabenformen mit entsprechenden Hörtexten vorgestellt, die du so oder ähnlich auch in der Abschlussprüfung lösen musst. Du hast in den vergangenen Schuljahren viele Aufgaben zum Hörverstehen in den Klassenarbeiten in den Fächern Englisch oder Französisch und Deutsch bearbeitet und bist daher schon ein halber Profi. Wahrscheinlich fällt dir das Leseverstehen leichter, weil du einen Text mehrmals lesen kannst, während das beim Hören nicht möglich ist. Die Vorbereitung auf diese Aufgaben ist daher sehr wichtig. Dieses Kapitel hilft dir dabei und macht dich mit den wichtigsten Arbeitsschritten und Tricks vertraut, sodass die Prüfung für dich kein Problem sein wird.

Es gibt verschiedene Formen des Hörverstehens. Hierbei kommt es immer darauf an, welche Informationen für den Hörer wichtig sind. Ein Beispiel: Du möchtest abends ins Kino gehen, weißt aber nicht, wann der Film anfängt. Du rufst das Kino an und hörst dir die Ansagen der einzelnen Filme an. Du wirst nicht bei allen Filmtiteln genau zuhören, denn du willst nur eine Uhrzeit zu dem Film erfahren, der dich interessiert. Die Informationen müssen von dir aussortiert oder „selektiert" werden. Dein Verhalten wäre ein anderes, wenn dein Freund dir einen Witz erzählt, bei dem jede Einzelheit wichtig ist, um ihn zu verstehen.
Daher unterscheidet man drei Formen des Hörverstehens. Beim **globalen Hörverstehen** musst du nur die Hauptgedanken erfassen, nicht alle Einzelheiten. Beim **selektiven Hörverstehen** musst du eine bestimmte Information heraushören, z. B. eine Zahl, ein Datum oder eine Uhrzeit. Beim **detaillierten Hörverstehen** solltest du den Hörtext möglichst genau und in allen Einzelheiten verstehen. Die Aufgabenformen in der Abschlussprüfung beinhalten alle drei Formen des Hörverstehens. Daher wirst du sie anhand von Beispielaufgaben intensiv üben.

INFO Hörverstehen

1. Globales Hörverstehen – Hauptgedanken erfassen.
2. Selektives Hörverstehen – eine bestimmte Information erhören.
3. Detailliertes Hörverstehen – den Hörtext genau und mit allen Einzelheiten verstehen.

C 1.1 Aufgabenformate für das Hörverstehen

Multiple Choice
Bei diesen Aufgaben musst du die richtige Antwort aus mehreren heraushören. Meistens gibt es drei oder vier Möglichkeiten (manchmal auch mit Bildern), aber nur eine ist richtig. Die Anweisungen auf Englisch lauten wahrscheinlich so:

- You will hear five conversations.
- You will hear each conversation twice.
- There is one question for each conversation.
- For questions **1 – 5** put a tick in the box under the right answer.

What would the boy like for his birthday?

A a new TV ☐

B a new bike ☐

C a new mobile phone ☐

True – false – **not in the text**

Bei diesen Aufgaben musst du entscheiden, ob die Aussage zu dem gehörten Text richtig *(true)* oder falsch *(false)* ist. Manchmal wird die Übung noch um eine dritte Spalte ergänzt: *not in the text*. Die Aussage kann also richtig oder falsch sein oder gar nicht erwähnt werden.

Beispiel:

- You will hear a radio programme about visiting Scotland.
- Listen and answer questions 16–23 (oder 24).
- For questions 16–23 decide whether each sentence is true or false.
- Put a tick in the correct box 'true' or 'false'.
- You will hear the programme twice.

	true	false
Edinburgh is the capital of Scotland.	☐	☐

Matching

Bei dieser Aufgabe geht es darum, passende Zuordnungen zu bilden. Welche Überschrift passt zu welchem Text? Welcher Sprecher im Dialog sagt was? Häufig müssen die Antworten in eine Tabelle eingetragen werden.

Beispiel:

- You will hear five teachers talking about the subjects they teach.
- Listen and complete the chart by filling in the correct subject.
- You will hear all the texts twice.

Teacher	Subjects
Teacher 1	History
Teacher 2	Maths

Fill in-**Aufgaben**

Bei diesem Aufgabenformat handelt es sich um eine Einsetzaufgabe. Häufig musst du fehlende Informationen in einen Satz, eine Tabelle oder ein Formular eintragen.

Beispiel:

- You will hear an American student talking about her new job.
- Listen and complete questions 14–19.
- You will hear the text twice.

Susan started her job in March _____ .

C 1.2 Was passiert beim Hörverstehen?

Beim Hörverstehen laufen drei verschiedene Phasen nacheinander ab. Diese nennt man 1. *pre-listening* (vor dem Hören), 2. *while-listening* (während des Hörens) und 3. *post-listening* (nach dem Hören). In jeder Phase gibt es bestimmte Tipps und Tricks, die dir beim Bearbeiten der Höraufgaben helfen können.

C 1.3 *Pre-Listening* (vor dem Hören)

Vorwissen aktivieren

Stelle dir vor dem Hören des Textes folgende Fragen:

1. Gibt dir die Überschrift Hinweise auf den Inhalt des Hörtextes?
2. Wenn die Aufgabe ein Bild oder eine Frage beinhaltet: Um welche Situation könnte es sich hier handeln oder welche Informationen sollen von dir herausgehört werden?
3. Wie würdest du dich in einer solchen Situation verhalten? Was würdest du tun oder sagen?

Beispiel:

Wenn du weißt, dass es sich beim Hörtext um einen Dialog zwischen einem Arzt und seinem Patienten handelt, dann verfügst du über viel Vorwissen zu dieser Situation, denn du warst bestimmt schon selbst beim Arzt. Man geht meistens dann zum Arzt, wenn man krank ist. Der Patient wird dem Arzt erklären, was ihm fehlt oder er wird seinen Zustand beschreiben. Anschließend wird der Arzt vielleicht weitere Fragen stellen oder den Patienten untersuchen und ihm Medikamente verschreiben.

Wortschatz aktivieren

Überlege vor dem Hören des Textes, welche Wörter dir zu diesem Thema einfallen und welche Redewendungen typisch für diese Situation sind.

In dem Dialog beim Arzt wirst du Vokabeln für verschiedene Körperteile, Krankheiten und Symptome erwarten: *body parts, leg, arm, hand, stomach, tummy, neck, head, back, cough, runny nose, sore throat, earache, flu, fever, pain,* etc.

Allgemeinwissen nutzen

Viele Dinge, die für dich selbstverständlich sind und die du jeden Tag tust oder benutzt, können bei diesen Aufgaben dein Vorteil sein. Du weißt, wie die Welt funktioniert und das kann dir bei der Abschlussarbeit helfen.

Beispiele:

1. Wie werden Temperaturen im Wetterbericht in europäischen Ländern angegeben?
   (Richtig: mit Zahlen und Grad Celsius)
2. Was muss man kaufen, bevor man mit öffentlichen Verkehrsmitteln (Bus, Bahn, Straßenbahn etc.) fährt?
   (Richtig: eine Fahrkarte)
3. Welche Währungseinheit gilt in vielen europäischen Ländern? (Richtig: Euro)

Mithilfe dieses Wissens kannst du Situationen gut einschätzen und weißt, worauf du beim Hören achten musst. Wenn es um Wetter und Temperaturen geht, dann musst du auf Zahlen achten. Wenn es um Reisen und Verkehrsmittel geht, dann wird vielleicht eine Fahrkarte gekauft.

Arbeitsanweisungen lesen

Lies dir die Aufgaben mehrmals durch. Stelle sicher, dass du die Aufgabe verstehst und genau weißt, was du tun sollst. Wenn du dir nicht sicher bist, dann frage deinen Lehrer oder deine Lehrerin.

– Was genau sollst du heraushören?

– Kannst du aus der Aufgabenstellung schon erkennen, worauf du achten musst?

– Erkennst du Wörter in den Aufgaben oder vielleicht die Situation wieder?

– Höre immer bis zum Ende des Texts oder des Dialogs zu.

Vorbereitung auf die Prüfungssituation

Bringe genug Verpflegung für diese Prüfung mit, sodass du zwischendurch etwas essen und trinken kannst. Stelle sicher, dass du gut funktionierende Stifte mitbringst (mindestens zwei) und eventuell auch dein zweisprachiges Wörterbuch. Konzentriere dich auf diese Situation, lass dich nicht ablenken oder durch Geräusche stören. Du bist gut vorbereitet und wirst die Prüfung mit Erfolg bewältigen.

> **TIPP** one – two – three
>
> 1. Lies die Aufgabenstellung und Erläuterungen genau durch. Um welches Thema oder welche Situation geht es?
> 2. Welche Informationen werden im Text erfragt (Zahlen, Uhrzeit, Geldbetrag)?
> 3. Überlege, welche Wörter und Vokabeln dir bei dieser Aufgabe/Frage oder diesem Bild einfallen.

C 1.4 *While-Listening* (während des Hörens)

Konzentration

In dieser Situation musst du dich gut konzentrieren. Vielleicht schließt du die Augen, wenn dir das hilft. Häufig kann man dann Gehörtes besser aufnehmen. Du kennst die Aufgabenstellung und weißt, was du tun musst. Achte gezielt auf die gesuchte Information.

> **TIPP** Vorbereitung
>
> 1. Such dir einen ruhigen Arbeitsplatz, an dem du ungestört arbeiten kannst.
> 2. Du benötigst mindestens 25 Minuten für die vier Höraufgaben. Es ist sinnvoll, alle vier Aufgaben nacheinander zu bearbeiten, da dies die Prüfungssituation simuliert.
> 3. Starte die Audio-Dateien und folge den Anweisungen in den Tracks oder im Text.

Keine Panik!

Wenn du die gesuchte Information beim ersten Durchgang nicht hörst oder im Text nicht jedes Wort verstehst, ist das kein Grund zur Panik. Bleib ruhig und konzentriere dich. Du wirst genug verstehen und kannst die Aufgaben erfolgreich lösen.

Unverhofft kommt oft!

Manchmal gibt es ein überraschendes Thema in der Abschlussprüfung, das dir noch nicht so vertraut ist oder einen Hörtext, der lang ist und von einem Sprecher gesprochen wird, der einen merkwürdigen Akzent hat. Lass dich dadurch nicht aus der Ruhe bringen. Bleib ruhig und arbeite konzentriert weiter.

> **TIPP** beim Hören
>
> – Lass dich durch das Thema des Hörtexts, die Geschwindigkeit, die Vokabeln oder die Aussprache nicht aus der Ruhe bringen.
> – Bleib ruhig und konzentriert bei der Sache.

Notizen machen

Du kannst dir während des Hörens kurze Notizen machen, die dir anschließend beim Beantworten der Aufgaben helfen. Wenn du die richtige Antwort sicher weißt, kannst die sie auch schon beim ersten Hören ankreuzen. Beim zweiten Durchgang kannst du dich ganz auf die noch fehlenden Informationen konzentrieren.

Achte auf nonverbale Informationen im Text

Aus dem Hörtext kann man nicht nur das Thema, die Situation und das Gesagte heraushören, sondern auch Informationen, die nicht ausgesprochen werden (nonverbale Informationen). Die Satzmelodie verrät dir, ob es sich um eine Frage oder einen Aussagesatz handelt. Häufig kannst du auch hören, ob ein Sprecher z. B. glücklich oder wütend ist. Diese Zusatzinformationen können beim Bearbeiten der Aufgaben hilfreich sein.

Merkmale gesprochener Sprache

Gesprochene Sprache und geschriebene Sprache unterscheiden sich deutlich voneinander. Beim Lesen kann man jedes einzelne Wort erkennen, beim Sprechen dagegen werden häufig Silben verschluckt oder Wörter zusammen gesprochen. Diese Kurzformen kennst du schon aus dem Unterricht (*I'm, I've, I'd, he's, you've* etc.). Beginnt ein Wort mit einem Vokal, verbinden Sprecher die Wörter miteinander *(an apple, an operation, an orange* usw.).

C 1.5 *Post-Listening* (nach dem Hören)

Antworten kontrollieren und vervollständigen

Wenn du Aufgaben schon nach dem ersten Hören gelöst hast, nutze den zweiten Durchgang, um diese Aufgaben zu kontrollieren und die anderen Aufgaben zu lösen.

Wenn die Höraufgabe zu Ende ist, vervollständige deine Antworten mithilfe deiner Notizen. Wenn du eine Aufgabe gar nicht bearbeiten kannst, kreuze immer eine Antwort an, denn es gibt keinen Punktabzug für falsche Antworten. So hast du eine Chance, die richtige Antwort zu erraten. Vielleicht bist du auch in der Lage, eine von drei oder vier Wahlmöglichkeiten auszuschließen, sodass sich deine Chance, die richtige Lösung zu wählen, erhöht. Wenn du nichts ankreuzt, ist deine Antwort auf jeden Fall falsch.

C 1.6 Beispielaufgaben

Learning by doing

Bisher hast du viele Informationen zur Abschlussprüfung erhalten. Jetzt gilt es für dich, diese in die Praxis umzusetzen und die Beispielaufgaben zu bearbeiten. Dafür musst du dir Audio-Dateien auf der Internetseite www.finaleonline.de anhören. Gib dort den auf Seite 4 genannten Code ein.

Am besten arbeitest du die Übungsaufgaben der Reihe nach durch. Wie in der Abschlussarbeit werden dir vier Aufgabenteile mit unterschiedlichen Aufgabenformen (siehe Infokasten auf Seite 24) präsentiert. Denk daran, dass du den Text nur zweimal hören darfst. Dann solltest du die Aufgaben gelöst haben.

Part 1 – Questions 1–5  **Track 1**

AUFGABENSTELLUNG

- You will hear five short conversations.
- There is one question for each conversation.
- For questions **1–5,** put a tick in the box under the right answer.

1. What time does the movie start?

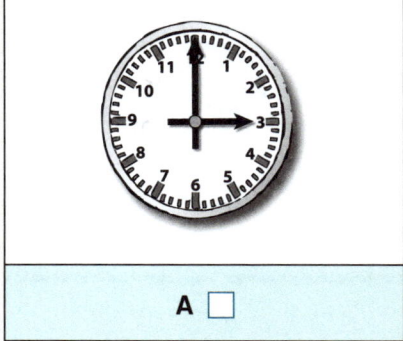

A ☐

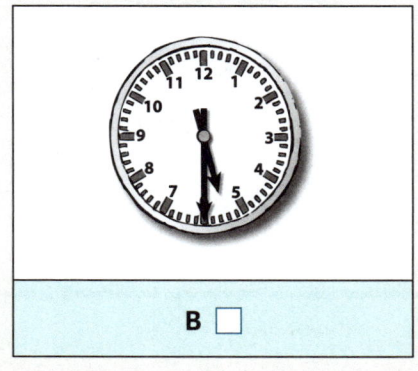

B ☐

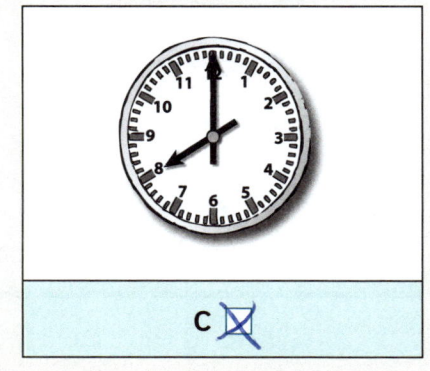

C ☒

2. **What will the weather be like today?**

A ☐   B ☒   C ☐

3. **What is the man going to eat in the restaurant?**

A ☐   B ☐   C ☒

4. **Where is she going?**

  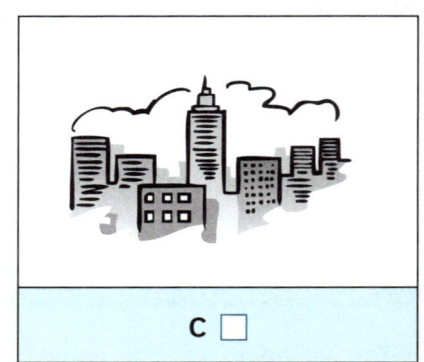

A ☒   B ☐   C ☐

5. **What can you buy in the new store?**

  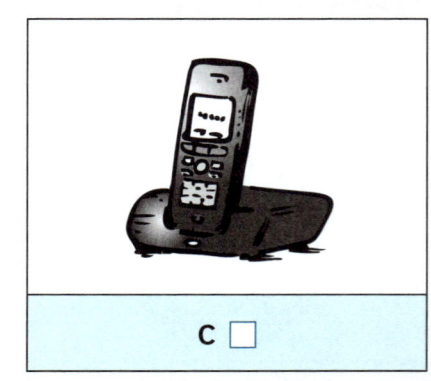

A ☒   B ☐   C ☐

Part 2 – Questions 6 – 11

 **Track 2**

AUFGABENSTELLUNG

- Listen to Tim telling his teacher about his summer job in a camp in the USA.
- For questions **6 – 11** tick **A**, **B** or **C**.

6. Tim's job started	A	in June.	☒
	B	in July.	☐
	C	in August.	☐

7. He usually worked	A	five days a week.	☒
	B	every day.	☐
	C	five hours a day.	☐

8. He really liked	A	the food.	☐
	B	working with the kids.	☒
	C	speaking English.	☐

9. He stayed in	A	a hotel.	☐
	B	his own room.	☒
	C	a youth hostel.	☐

10. He earned	A	$10 an hour.	☐
	B	$20 a day.	☐
	C	$1,000 for two months.	☒

11. His future plans are	A	to buy a new car.	☐
	B	to go to the Bahamas.	☐
	C	to write e-mails to his friends.	☒

Part 3 – Questions 12 – 17

 **Track 3**

You will hear an American student talking about her new job.

AUFGABENSTELLUNG

Listen and complete questions **12 – 17**.

12. Susan started her job ___*as a waiter in March*___ .

13. She earns ___*6 dollar an hour*___ .

14. She starts work at ___*10 am*___ .

15. Usually she has a break from ___*1*___ to ___*1:30 PM*___ .

16. In nice weather there are ___*15 tables*___ outside.

17. She gets good tips but at night ___*her feet hurt a lot*___ .

Part 4 – Questions 18 – 23

 **Track 4**

You will hear a radio program from the US talking about differences between the US and German school systems.

AUFGABENSTELLUNG

- Listen and answer questions **18 – 23**.
- For questions **18 – 23** decide whether each sentence is true or false.
  Put a tick in the correct box "true" or "false".

	true	false
18. The two school systems are the same.	☐	✗
19. German pupils don't have lockers.	✗	☐
20. American students carry their books around all day.	☐	✗
21. US students go home earlier than German kids.	☐	✗
22. German kids do their homework at home.	✗	☐
23. US students spend their afternoon in school.	✗	☐

Trainingsmöglichkeiten

Das Einhören in den Klang einer Fremdsprache wird durch den ständigen Kontakt erleichtert. In der heutigen Medienwelt stehen dir viele Möglichkeiten zur Verfügung, die englische Sprache zu hören. Englische Radio- und Fernsehsender ermöglichen dir das Hören von authentischen Inhalten wie kurze Ansagen, Wetterberichte oder Nachrichten. Im Internet bieten alle großen Fernsehsender (CNN, BBC) ihre neuesten Meldungen gesprochen an. Im Internet gibt es auch Internetseiten, die speziell für Englischlerner Hörübungen zu verschiedenen Themen mit Aufgaben und Lösungen anbieten (www.elllo.org; www.esl-lab.com; www.learnenglishfeelgood.com).

C 2 Arbeitstechnik Leseverstehen

Die Überprüfung des Leseverstehens ist der zweite Teil der Zentralen Abschlussprüfung. Dieser Bereich besteht aus vier Teilen und auch hier kannst du 24 (oder 23) Punkte erreichen. Die Aufgabenstellungen unterscheiden sich nicht übermäßig von denen der Hörübungen, doch beziehen sie sich in diesem Fall auf einen Text, den du in aller Ruhe lesen kannst. Nach den Hörübungen kannst du dir den Rest der Zeit selbstständig einteilen.

Du sollst bei den Aufgaben zum Leseverstehen beweisen, dass du den gelesenen Text verstanden hast. Häufig wirst du aufgefordert, einen Text zu lesen, und sollst dann Fragen dazu beantworten. Beliebt sind die sogenannten W-Fragen (besonders Wer? Wo? Wann? Wie?) Du liest z.B. du einen Fahrplan und musst anschließend herausfinden, wann der Zug nach Edinburgh fährt. Das Leseverstehen begegnet dir in fast jedem Unterrichtsfach, sodass du schon viele Erfahrungen sammeln konntest. Auf den nächsten Seiten werden dir die wichtigsten Lesestrategien und Aufgabenformen erklärt. Anschließend kannst du diese an Beispielaufgaben ausprobieren.

C 2.1 Aufgabenformate für das Leseverstehen

Multiple Choice

Bei diesen Aufgaben musst du die richtige Antwort aus mehreren herausfinden. Meistens gibt es drei oder vier Möglichkeiten, aber nur eine ist richtig.

Beispiel:
- Read the text and then answer the questions.
- For each question, mark the correct answer with a tick.

In schools in the United States students …	A	have their own locker.	☑
	B	have different classes every day.	☐
	C	stay in school until 5 p.m.	☐
	D	drive their car to school.	☐

True – false (giving evidence)

Du musst entscheiden, ob die Aussage zum Text richtig oder falsch ist. Zusätzlich musst du die Zeile(n) im Text angeben, in der oder in denen (es kann sich um eine oder mehrere Zeilen handeln) sich die Antwort befindet. Ohne die Zeilenangabe erhältst du keine Punkte, auch wenn du die richtige Antwort angekreuzt hast.

Beispiel:
- Read the text. Then look at the statements.
- For each statement tick the correct answer: "true" or "false" and give the line/lines in which you find the information.
- For each correct answer you must fill in both: true or false, and the line(s).

	true	false	line(s)
1. Barack Obama was President of the United States for eight years.	☑	☐	_____

True – false – not in the text

Du musst entscheiden, ob die Aussage zu dem Text richtig oder falsch ist. Manchmal wird die Aufgabe noch um eine dritte Spalte ergänzt: *„not in the text"*. Der Satz kann also richtig oder falsch sein oder wird gar nicht erwähnt.

Beispiel:

- For each question, tick the correct answer.

	true	false	not in the text
1. In Germany all the students have lockers.	☐	☑	☐

Matching

Bei dieser Aufgabe musst du passende Teile einander zuordnen. Dies können Überschriften sein, die du Textabschnitten zuordnen musst, oder Satzteile, die zerschnitten wurden und die du wieder richtig zusammensetzen musst. Eine andere Möglichkeit wäre, dass du einem Text über Eigenschaften einer Person oder eines Tieres die richtige Abbildung oder den richtigen Text zuordnen musst. Häufig gibt es zu viele Texte, sodass am Ende ein Text übrig bleibt, der sich nicht zuordnen lässt. Hier musst du sehr genau lesen und die Details erfassen. Die Abschlussprüfung 2019 enthielt folgende Matching-Aufgabe:

Beispiel:

- Here are the summaries of five different presentations on how environmental issues influence our daily lives.
- There are seven headings.
- Decide which one would be most suitable for each text.

Texten zum Thema Umwelt müssen passende Überschriften zugeordnet werden. Dabei solltest du so vorgehen: Lies zuerst die Überschriften genau und unterstreiche Schlüsselwörter. In der folgenden Überschrift kannst du *„climate change"*, *„harder"* und *„poor"* unterstreichen.

F Why climate change is harder on the poor

Der folgende Text beginnt mit dem Satz: *„Climate change is unfair."* Dies ist schon ein Hinweis, dass die Überschrift F zu diesem Text passen könnte. Im nächsten Satz findest du das Wort *„poor"*. Es werden außerdem verschiedene Auswirkungen des Klimawandels *(„rising oceans", „dying farmland", „killer storms")* genannt, gegen die sich reiche Länder wappnen könnten, im Gegensatz zu armen Menschen.

6. Climate change is unfair. While rich countries can fight against rising oceans and dying farmland, poor, people around the world are already having their lives turned upside down. Their lives are threatened. They struggle much more with killer storms, hunger and the loss of their own lands. The author asks us to join the movement for worldwide climate justice.*

Source: adapted from https://www.ted.com/talks/anote_tong_my_country_will_be_underwater_soon_unless_we_work_together/
transcript?referrer=playlist-why_climate_change_is_a_human&language=en
Anote Tong, TED Conferences LLC, New York, 10-2015

Im vorangehenden Beispiel findest du die nötigen Informationen zu Beginn des Textes. Manchmal stehen sie aber auch am Ende, wie im folgenden Beispiel:

H Cooling down the earth

11. In this perspective-shifting talk, Danny Hillis invites us to think about creative scientific solutions for global issues like climate change. He looks at controversial solutions like building a giant solar shade to lower the global temperature.*

Source: adapted from https://www.ted.com/talks/danny_hillis_should_we_create_a_solar_shade_to_cool_the_earth
Danny Hillis, TED Conferences LLC, New York, 04-2017

Im letzten Satz steht der Hinweis „... *to lower global temperature*". Daraus kannst du schließen, dass „*Cooling down the earth*" die richtige Überschrift ist. Es ist daher wichtig, alle Texte bis zum Ende genau durchzulesen.

Put the information in the correct order.
Bei einer solchen Aufgabe musst du den Text lesen und ganz bestimmte Informationen zum Beispiel in eine Tabelle eintragen.

Beispiel:
• Read the following text and find out the differences between the German and the US school systems.

German school system	US school system
Students usually go home at 1 p.m.	Students stay in school until 3 p.m.
Students don't have a locker.	Every student has a locker.
Students have different classes every day.	Students have the same classes every day.

C 2.2 Arbeitstechniken und Lesestrategien

Ähnlich wie beim Hörverstehen teilt man den Leseprozess in drei Phasen ein: ***pre-reading, while-reading*** und ***post-reading.*** Zu allen drei Phasen erhältst du Tipps, die dir beim Bearbeiten der Texte helfen.
Es gibt unterschiedliche Möglichkeiten, einen Text zu lesen. Welche Lesetechnik man einsetzt, hängt von den Informationen ab, die man dem Text entnehmen will. Im Folgenden werden dir die drei wichtigsten Methoden erklärt. Wenn du eine andere erfolgreich benutzt, solltest du diese natürlich auch in der Abschlussarbeit anwenden. Trotzdem ist das Üben der anderen Strategien anhand der Beispieltexte wichtig, da du dadurch eine größere Auswahl an Methoden hast, die du verwenden kannst.
Das ***skimming*** bezeichnet das überfliegende Lesen, durch das man sich schnell über das Thema oder den Inhalt informieren kann (globales Textverständnis). Wenn du zum Beispiel ein Referat vorbereitest und viele Texte zu deinem Thema im Internet findest, dann liest du diese quer, um schnell herauszufinden, ob du die Texte verwenden willst oder nicht.
Scanning nennt man auch suchendes Lesen. Diese Technik setzt du ein, wenn du eine ganz bestimmte Information suchst – eine Uhrzeit, eine Zahl oder Ähnliches. Wenn du die Zeitung liest und nur das Ergebnis eines Fußballspiels suchst, dann wirst du nicht die ganze Zeitung durchlesen, sondern nur den Sportteil nach dem Ergebnis absuchen.
Das detaillierte Lesen ***(careful reading)*** wendest du an, wenn du genaue Informationen aus dem Text benötigst, um die Aufgaben zu lösen. Wenn du die Hauptaussage erfassen oder die Geschehnisse einer Handlung in eine bestimmte Reihenfolge bringen musst, dann solltest du den Text sorgfältig lesen und den Großteil verstehen. Die folgenden Hinweise können dir dabei helfen.

C 2.3 *Pre-Reading* (vor dem Lesen)

> **TIPP** Vorbereitung
>
> 1. Schau dir die Bilder an und lies die
> Überschrift oder den Titel des Texts. Worum geht es?
> 2. Aktiviere dein Vorwissen zu dem Thema des Texts.
> 3. Überlege, welche Wörter du zu diesem Inhalt kennst.

Vorwissen aktivieren

Bevor man lesen lernt, schaut man sich Bilderbücher an und weiß so, was in der Geschichte passiert. Später liest man den Titel eines Buches und überlegt, wovon es handeln könnte.

Hat der Lesetext in der Prüfung ein **Bild,** so kann es dir schon den Inhalt des Textes verraten. Schau dir auch den Titel an und stelle weitere Überlegungen zur Herkunft und Art des Textes an. Ähnlich wie bei den Hörtexten (Gespräch mit dem Arzt) hast du auch an den Lesetext bestimmte Erwartungen. Wenn auf dem Bild ein Gegenstand abgebildet ist, dann wird der Text von diesem Gegenstand (z. B. ein Handy) handeln. Es könnte eine technische Beschreibung (Gebrauchsanweisung) oder ein Bericht über Neuheiten auf dem Handymarkt sein. Du besitzt wahrscheinlich selbst ein Handy und weißt, wie man es benutzt. Automatisch fallen dir viele Wörter ein, die zu diesem Thema gehören. Überlege, welche englischen Begriffe dir einfallen. Viele technische Begriffe ähneln sich in beiden Sprachen, doch achte auf *false friends.* Das sind Wörter oder Begriffe, die ähnlich oder gleich klingen, aber etwas anderes bedeuten.

> **INFO** false friends
>
> Achte auf die „falschen Freunde". Das sind Wörter, die sich genau wie deutsche Wörter anhören und manchmal ähnlich geschrieben werden, aber etwas anderes bedeuten.
>
> **Deutsch – Englisch**
> Handy – *mobile phone, cell phone*
> nützlich – *handy*
> werden – *become*
> bekommen – *get*

Aufgabenstellung beachten

Bevor du den Text das erste Mal liest, solltest du dir die Aufgabenstellung und die Fragen genau durchlesen, damit du weißt, was von dir verlangt wird und welche Informationen du herausfinden sollst. Lies den Text und markiere Textstellen und Wörter (**Schlüsselwörter),** die für das Beantworten der Fragen wichtig sind.

C 2.4 *While-Reading* (während des Lesens)

Wörter erschließen

Wenn du einen dir unbekannten Text liest, sei es nun in deiner Muttersprache oder in einer Fremdsprache, so wirst du wahrscheinlich auf Wörter treffen, die du nicht kennst. Das ist ganz normal und muss dich nicht beunruhigen. Häufig ist es nicht so wichtig, jedes Wort in einem Text zu verstehen, denn du kannst die Aufgaben auch so lösen. Manchmal ist eine Vokabel aber doch wichtig. Dann kannst du sie im Wörterbuch nachschlagen. Dies solltest du aber nur in Ausnahmefällen tun, da es sehr zeitaufwendig ist. Vorher solltest du versuchen, die Bedeutung des Wortes (oder der Wörter) aus dem Textzusammenhang zu erschließen. Dazu musst du den Satz intensiv lesen und vielleicht noch den davor und den danach zu Hilfe nehmen.

Probiere es am folgenden Beispiel aus. Zur Übung haben wir das fehlende Wort gleich ganz weggelassen:

The man walked into a restaurant.
He was very hungry and asked the waiter for the _____ .
He read it and ordered a large steak and potatoes.

Anhand dieser drei Sätze solltest du herausbekommen, welches Wort fehlt. Vielleicht kennst du das Wort auf Deutsch und nicht auf Englisch, aber das macht nichts. Du kannst dir die Bedeutung von bekannten Wörtern aus dem Zusammenhang erschließen. Manchmal hilft dir auch die deutsche Sprache weiter, denn viele Wörter werden auf Englisch ähnlich geschrieben (z. B. *intensive, logical, intelligent, friendly, guest, restaurant, family).* Bei anderen Wörtern helfen dir die Wortverwandtschaften. Wenn du die Bedeutung des Nomens kennst, dann kannst du dir die Bedeutung des Verbs selbstständig erschließen *(invention – to invent).* Diese Techniken kannst du auch in der Prüfung anwenden. Wenn das nicht funktioniert, kannst du das Wort im Wörterbuch nachschlagen.

TIPP Aufgabenstellung verstehen

Lies dir die Fragen zum Text genau durch: Welche Informationen sollst du herausfinden?
1. Sollst du gezielt nach bestimmten Informationen suchen (z. B. Uhrzeiten, Zahlen)?
2. Sollst du das Thema des Texts grob verstehen?
3. Sollst du die Hauptaussage des Texts verstehen?

Wörterbucharbeit

Das Arbeiten mit dem Wörterbuch hast du in den vergangenen Jahren im Englischunterricht und zu Hause geübt. Vielleicht besitzt du ein zweisprachiges Wörterbuch, das du auch zur Abschlussprüfung mitnehmen kannst. Wenn du ein Wort nachschlägst, solltest du folgendermaßen vorgehen:

1. Schritt: das Wort im Wörterbuch finden

Alle Wörterbücher sind alphabetisch geordnet, wobei es nicht nur auf den ersten, sondern auch auf die folgenden Buchstaben ankommt. So wird das Wort *bathrobe* vor dem Wort *bathtub* stehen, da „r" vor „t" kommt. Auf jeder Doppelseite des Wörterbuchs findest du oben links und rechts fett gedruckte Leitwörter. Durch sie kannst du auf den ersten Blick erkennen, mit welchem Stichwort die linke Seite beginnt und mit welchem die rechte Seite endet. Solltest du nach zwei zusammenhängenden Wörtern suchen, kann es vorkommen, dass du unter dem zweiten Begriff nachschlagen musst.

2. Schritt: die passende Übersetzung finden

Die erste Übersetzung, die du im Wörterbuch findest, ist nicht immer die, die du suchst. Häufig haben englische Wörter mehrere deutsche Bedeutungen – und umgekehrt. In vielen Fällen helfen die kursiv gedruckten Informationen oder die kurzen Beispielsätze, die deutlich machen, in welchem Kontext der jeweilige Begriff verwendet wird. Lies dir alle Übersetzungsvorschläge durch und entscheide, welcher passt.

C 2.5 *Post-Reading* (nach dem Lesen)

Achte auf die Zeit!

Wenn du Aufgaben schon nach dem ersten Lesen gelöst hast, bearbeite die anderen Aufgaben und kontrolliere anschließend alle Antworten.

Wenn du eine Aufgabe gar nicht bearbeiten kannst, kreuze immer eine Antwort an. Wenn du nichts ankreuzt, ist die Antwort auf jeden Fall falsch. So hast du eine Chance, die richtige Antwort zu erraten. Vielleicht bist du auch in der Lage, eine von drei oder vier Wahlmöglichkeiten (Multiple Choice) auszuschließen, sodass sich deine Chance erhöht, die richtige Lösung zu wählen.

TIPP Arbeitsschritte Textarbeit

Step 1: Lies dir die Überschrift des Textes und anschließend die Aufgabenstellung genau durch.
Step 2: Überfliege den Text *(skimming)*.
Step 3: Jetzt lies den Text sorgfältig und gründlich durch. Markiere wichtige Textstellen.

C 2.6 Textbeispiele mit Aufgaben
Part 1 – Questions 1 – 5

AUFGABENSTELLUNG

- Read the short texts.
- Then answer the questions **1 – 5.** For each question, tick the correct answer.

Fripp Island, South Carolina
1. Playing golf on Fripp
Playing golf on the private Island of Fripp is wonderful. We have two private
golf courses (18 holes) that only members can use. The price for a round of
golf is $75. You can bring your own clubs or rent a set at the course. You need
proper shoes and clothing to play. No shoes, no shirt – no service. You can rent   5
a golf cart to drive from one hole to the next. Our club house has changing
rooms and showers and a restaurant and bar.

2. Animals on the Island
There is an abundance of wildlife on Fripp. You can see deer and a variety
of birds. Alligators roam the island freely. You might encounter them in the   10
pools next to the golf course or on the greens, where they love to lie in the
sun. Do not approach them or they might attack you. You can watch pelicans
from the ramps that go out into the water.

3. The beaches
The island is surrounded by long stretches of beautiful beach. Most houses and   15
apartments are close to the beach. You can bring your own beach chairs and
sunshades or you can rent them. Remember to wear plenty of suntan lotion so
you don't get sunburned because the sun is very hot and aggressive. Beware
of the tide. You can get a chart with the tide-change times at the information
desk when you check in.

4. Going fishing   20
If you want to go fishing on Fripp, you can do so from the piers that go into
the water. There is one at each end of the island. You can bring your own
fishing rods and bait or rent the equipment. You can catch sharks, sting rays
and other kinds of ocean fish. You can also go crabbing. You need a net and
bait (chicken necks work best).   25

	true	false
1. a) There is an alligator farm on Fripp. b) You can play golf without shoes.	☐	☒
2. a) You can catch sharks on Fripp. b) You don't need suntan lotion on the beach.	☒	☒
3. a) Both golf courses have eighteen holes. b) If you see alligators, you can touch them.	☒	☒
4. a) You can take a shower after your round of golf. b) There is a restaurant, but not a bar.	☒	☒
5. a) You have to bring your own beach chairs and sunshades. b) The tide comes in at the same time every day.	☒	☐

Part 2 – Questions 6–10

AUFGABENSTELLUNG

- Decide which dream house described in the advertisements (**A – H**) would be the most suitable for the people below (**6 – 10**).
- Write the correct letters in the box.

6. Samir, Sweden Oh, my dream house? It is on the beach. You have a great view of the ocean and the beach, and it should be really big – a big house – with maybe an elevator, and maybe at least three cars and a cinema in the house as well. That would be cool.	F
7. Cheryl, Guam If I had a dream house, I think that it would first of all be next to the ocean. I love the ocean. Secondly, it would probably have really high ceilings because I like places that are very airy and big and spacious. Thirdly, my dream house would definitely have a jacuzzi, a hot tub, something like that, and a very big, big bathroom and a big balcony.	A
8. Jonathan, Canada To describe my dream house: it would actually be very simple. It would probably be a small apartment in a large city that was very strong on points of culture – maybe in Barcelona or some city like that. It would probably be a simple apartment in an entertainment, nightlife district with lots of culture around and a very lively scene.	J
9. Emily, Djibouti My dream house? I don't want a big, big house, just as long as it's surrounded by nature. I don't want to live in a modern country or a big city like New York or Tokyo. I prefer quiet places where you can really meditate and live your life fully.	D
10. Demelza, Australia My dream house would be two stories high. It would be made of wooden floor boards and plain white walls, and I think it would have Thai-style decor. [...]	B

Quelle: www.elllo.org

Houses

A For rent by real estate agent. House in large development. Ideal for families with children. Three bedrooms and two bathrooms, large garden and deck in the back. No garage. House needs some work but a little paint will help. Call between 9 a.m. and 5 p.m. (570 448 3526) or come and see the house Saturday at 10 a.m.

B Opportunity of a lifetime. Must be sold because of new job in a foreign country. Small, two-story country home with large vegetable garden. Simple floor plan and beautiful woodwork floors, ceilings and walls. Rooms painted a simple white with Asian furniture and doors. Viewing times: daily from 10 a.m. – 6 p.m.

C Oceanfront property for sale. Vacation home built in Pacific Island style with beautiful flower gardens surrounding a central villa. Spacious one-story house with attached garage. Large windows and double doors look out onto terraces in the front and rear of the home. Three bedrooms, two baths, swimming pool and whirlpool included. All rooms are large and have very high ceilings. Master bedroom has a large balcony overlooking the blue waters of the Pacific.

D For sale or rent. Small, private bungalow in a secluded corner of Pennsylvania. Direct access to national parks and quiet mountain lakes. Clean air and almost no neighbors. Fishing, hiking, biking and skiing within easy reach. Wildlife and birds come right up to your back door and windows. Leave busy, stressful life of the cities behind and find yourself again.

E Farm for sale. This farm is a gem. It is a dream come true for somebody looking for a farm to start a new life. A large stone house sits on 200 acres of land. It comes with two barns – one haybarn for animals and a barn for equipment. You can buy the machines and start your new crop right away. Call our office (467 324 9876) and take this great chance.

F For sale. Large residence with huge plot of land. Sits on a cliff overlooking the Atlantic Ocean with direct access to the beach and boathouse. Five bedrooms, three baths, in-house swimming pool, billiard room and family entertainment room with movie theater-style seating. Five car garage, workshop and large parking area. All rooms equipped with digital TV, Internet access and intercom system. The house is three stories high and includes an elevator, which also goes to the beach below.

G Cottage for sale. This small cottage lies in the heart of Ireland. It is made of brick and has three bedrooms and a small bathroom. It lies in a romantic valley and has a wonderful view of the mountains around. A stable is in the back so you could keep a horse there. Ideal for a family or a holiday cottage. Come and see it for yourself. Call us on Dublin 3674 23 876.

H For sale by owner. Small studio apartment centrally located in Rome. One bedroom, small kitchen, living room and bath. Within walking distance of the Vatican City, Circus Maximus, Colosseum, Tivoli and other sights. Easy access to theater, markets, cinema etc. Located directly in the heart of one of Rome's hottest nightclub, cafe and restaurant scenes.

Part 3 – Questions 11 – 15

- Read the texts (**1 – 5**) below and the statements **a**), **b**) and **c**) next to them.
- Decide which of the statements is the correct one for each text.
- Put a tick in the correct box.

11. Text 1	**A visit to the Statue of Liberty – plan like a ranger with these ranger tips!** 1. Book your tickets online to avoid long lines. 2. Download the new app from the National Park Service for more information. 3. Wear comfortable shoes because you have to walk long distances. 4. Pack a light bag – you have to carry it all the time. 5. If you come early in the day, you will have more time to explore. 6. Check the weather and wear the right clothes. 7. Bring a bottle of water. The temperature in the statue is higher than outside. It will get very hot in the summer, so water is important. 8. Arrive 15 to 20 minutes before the departure time of the ferry. You need time to go through security and catch the boat. Enjoy your visit!	A	Buy the ticket on the day of your visit.	☐
		B	The temperature inside the statue is lower than outside.	☐
		C	Avoid the queue and book your tickets online.	☒

12. Text 2	**Review of an electric scooter** The scooter came in a big package in just three days. I really didn't know what to expect because I only paid 300 euros. I did not want to spend too much money on my first scooter. When I took it out of the box, it looked perfect – no scratches or marks. The model I had chosen was the H25. It is light and has a good range. The 7.5 ah battery in combination with a 250 w motor is not too powerful, but it will get you where you want to go, which is about 11 miles (17 km) with one charge. The charging time is about 4 hours, so going to work or school in the morning and coming back in the afternoon works well. I can recommend the scooter, but you get what you pay for.	A	The scooter had a lot of scratches when it came in a box.	☐
		B	The scooter is light and has a good range.	☑
		C	The user can not recommend the scooter.	☒

13. Text 3	**What to do when you meet a bear!** If the bear notices you, talk calmly in low tones. Stand your ground but slowly wave your arms. Make yourself look as large as possible. If the bear is standing in one place, move away slowly and sideways. Never run away or climb a tree. Always leave an escape route for the bear. Stay calm and pick up small children. Don't make sudden moves or scream. This may feel threatening to the bear and it may attack.	A	You should stand your ground and make slow movements with your arms.	☒
		B	You should sit on the ground, cover your head and lay dead.	☒
		C	If the bear sees you, you should scream and run away.	☐

14. Text 4	**Mexico City Airport transportation** There are many different services for tourists to travel to and from the airport in Mexico City. You should choose airport-authorized services to make sure that you and your family are safe. A one way trip costs between $40 and $200 depending on the service you use. 1. You can share a van with other people who want to go to the same destination. $60 2. You can order a private van or car for more comfort on your trip to the airport. $120 3. A local personal driver will use his own vehicle and knows the area and traffic. He can also show you the sights in the city. $180 4. You can grab a cab at the airport. The drive might take you directly to your hotel or maybe not. $100 5. You can take one of the buses into town. During rush hour, the buses are full and there is no air-conditioning. $40 6. Ride in luxury and take a limousine to your hotel. Drinks and air-conditioning are included. $240	A	Sharing a van with other people is the cheapest ride to and from the airport.	☐
		B	The buses all have air-conditioning.	☐
		C	You can use your own private van or car for $120.	☒

15. Text 5	**What is XFOOD?** When you work a lot and your life is hectic, you can eat well with XFOOD. Our food is the perfect alternative to fast food. It is healthy, tasty and balanced. We have milk and vegan drinks, powder and bars. You can prepare your food the day before and take it with you to work or on a trip. We are a small company based in Berlin. All our products are produced in Germany or Switzerland. XFOOD has four different flavours – vanilla, banana, chocolate and strawberry. Our food is a nutritious replacement for an entire meal. A drink or bar has about 500 kcal and covers about 25% of your daily food and energy requirements. It will sustain you for several hours. You feel energetic and fit the whole day. You can order our food products online and pay with your credit card. Your food will arrive in your home after two days.	A	XFOOD offers three different flavours.	☐
		B	XFOOD replaces half of your daily food requirements.	☒
		C	XFOOD comes in drinks, bars and powder.	☒

Part 4 – Questions 16 – 23

Read the text and complete the sentences.

Problems for students at university

The number of registered students at German universities has steadily gone up in the last decade. More pupils leave school with a diploma that allows them to study at a university.

Confronted with this problem, the secretary of education in Kiel said that the
5 state's government is trying to make more living space available to students but that private investors would also be needed. The plan is to build more student housing in Kiel and Flensburg in the coming years but the situation is difficult. Students are sleeping and actually living in their cars, youth hostels or in retirement homes along with old people. This seems to be a good partnership
10 because the young students help the older people to deal with the everyday challenges of life like shopping, cleaning, getting dressed and preparing food, but students should be able to concentrate on their studies and not taking care of older people on the side. The number of students is increasing. Right now there are 48,000 students at the universities in Schleswig-Holstein but it
15 is expected that this number will increase by more than 20 % in the next few years. Things might get worse before they get better.

In October, about 5,000 new students will arrive to start their semester. Only about 50 % of them have an apartment or a permanent place to stay. The rest will have to improvise and basically wait and see. This will be extremely diffi-
20 cult for foreign students who arrive at the train station in Kiel with a suitcase and little money. Last week, the representative of the student body demanded an emergency plan for students who don't have a place to stay by a certain date. He explained his idea of "bed surfing". A person who has an extra bed or room can register at a university website and offer the bed to a student for
25 a short period of time like six or eight weeks. During that time the student can stay with this person for a certain amount of money while looking for a permanent place to stay. Usually things quieten down after a month or two and more apartments become available to students. But rents are high and most of the students end up on a long waiting list for student housing.

	line in the text
16. A lot of people leave school with a diploma _____	line _____
17. The number of students in Schleswig-Holstein right now is _____	line _____
18. The government in Kiel is trying to offer more _____	line _____

19. Students are sleeping and living _____	*line* _____
20. Students help older people with _____	*line* _____
21. In October, 5,000 new students will arrive but only _____	*line* _____
22. An idea to help students is "bed surfing" which is _____	*line* _____
23. Rents are high and a lot of students are on _____	*line* _____

C 3 Arbeitstechnik Mediation (Sprachmittlung)

Der Aufgabenteil der Sprachmittlung oder *mediating* besteht aus **zwei Teilen.** Von dir wird erwartet, dass du die wichtigsten Informationen aus Sach- sowie Gebrauchstexten in die jeweils andere Sprache überträgst. Es geht nicht um eine wörtliche Übersetzung. Die Bedeutung der Hinweisschilder oder kurzen Texte soll sinngemäß und verständlich wiedergegeben werden. Du sollst also zwischen Gesprächspartnern mit unterschiedlicher Muttersprache vermitteln und dabei z. B. Hinweisschilder, Mitteilungen, Formulare, Ansagen, kurze Gebrauchstexte, Interviews und Gespräche dem Sinn nach wiedergeben.

C 3.1 Aufgabenformate für die Sprachmittlung

Bevor du mit der Bearbeitung der Aufgabe anfängst, solltest du die Arbeitsanweisungen genau lesen. Denk daran, dass du jeden einzelnen Teilaspekt der Aufgabe bearbeiten musst, denn nur so kannst du die volle Punktzahl erreichen. Stelle sicher, dass du die Anforderungen der Aufgabe verstehst.
Beim ersten Lesen solltest du den Text nur überfliegen, um herauszufinden, um welches Thema es geht und um welche Textsorte es sich handelt. Beim zweiten Durchgang solltest du den Text genauer lesen und dabei wichtige Schlüsselwörter und Informationen unterstreichen. Teile längere Texte in Abschnitte ein und überlege dir Überschriften. Anschließend kannst du die Aufgaben lösen. Lass dir genug Zeit und lies genau. Schlage dir unbekannte Wörter im Lexikon nach oder versuche, sie aus dem Kontext zu erschließen.

Part 1

AUFGABENSTELLUNG

Du bist mit deinen Eltern in New York City im Urlaub. Du siehst ein Poster für eine Stadtrundfahrt durch Manhattan. Da deine Eltern kein Englisch sprechen, erklärst du ihnen, was hier angeboten wird. Schreibe auf ein Extra-Blatt.

New York City Bus Tours
Come and see the city that never sleeps.
- Buses with air-conditioning and open deck
- Over ten stops – check out the sights. See the Empire State Building, the Metropolitan Museum of Art, Macys, Grand Central Station, Central Park, the Zoo, Ground Zero and many more.
- Enjoy the commentary of a real city guide in English, Spanish or French.
- Tours start every hour at the Bus Terminal and last 3 hours.
Adults: $35   **Children:** $20   **Book online or call:** 475-9843

Part 2

AUFGABENSTELLUNG

Lorenzo from Bulgaria is now in your class. He does not understand all the rules in your school yet. His German is not very good. You help him with his questions in English.

> **Schulordnung:**
> 1. Die Pausenhalle steht den Schülerinnen und Schülern ab 7 Uhr zur Verfügung. Alle anderen Räume werden erst um 7.30 Uhr betreten.
> 2. In der Unterrichtszeit und in den Pausen darf das Schulgelände nicht verlassen werden.
> 3. Fahrräder werden in den Fahrradständern abgestellt und gegen Diebstahl gesichert.
> 4. Schüler/innen, die mit einem motorisierten Zweirad in die Schule fahren, benötigen eine Parkerlaubnis.
> 5. In den großen Pausen gehen alle Schülerinnen und Schüler auf den Schulhof oder in die Pausenhalle.
> 6. Die 5-Minuten-Pausen dienen nur zum Wechsel der Unterrichtsräume oder dem Gang auf die Toilette.
> 7. Der Aufenthalt in Fachräumen (einschl. Sport- und Schwimmhalle) ist nur in Begleitung einer Lehrkraft erlaubt.
> 8. Nach Unterrichtsschluss säubern die Schülerinnen und Schüler ihre Plätze und stellen die Stühle hoch (im Klassen- und im Fachraum).

Lorenzo: So, what do I have to do when I come to school in the morning? I don't understand the first rule. Can I go to the classroom right away?

You: No, you can't go to your classroom.

_____

Lorenzo: During the breaks can I go into town and get something to eat?

You: No, you must _____

_____

Lorenzo: Can I stay in the classroom and talk to my friends then?

You: No, you _____

Lorenzo: Where can I leave my bike?

You: _____

Lorenzo: When classes are over, can I go home right away?

You: No, you _____

Lorenzo: Are there any other rules that I need to know about?

You: Yes, during the 5-minute break _____

_____

_____

C 4 Arbeitstechnik Schreiben

INFO häufige Arbeitsanweisungen

– *Fill in a form.*	Fülle ein Formular aus.
– *Write an e-mail/letter.*	Schreibe eine E-Mail/einen Brief.
– *Sum up ...*	Fasse zusammen ...
– *Give your opinion.*	Nimm Stellung.
– *Answer x's e-mail.*	Beantworte die E-Mail.
– *Discuss the advantages and disadvantages of ...*	Diskutiere die Vor- und Nachteile von ...
– *Imagine a dialogue.*	Stelle dir einen Dialog vor.
– *Give reasons for ...*	Begründe ...

Das Schreiben von Texten macht den vierten Teil der Abschlussprüfung im Fach Englisch aus. Du hast eine Wahlmöglichkeit, d.h., du kannst dir eine Schreibaufgabe aus zwei Varianten aussuchen. Du hast 15 Minuten Zeit, um dich für die eine oder die andere Schreibaufgabe zu entscheiden. Die Schreibaufgaben enthalten entweder zwei oder drei Teilaufgaben.

Du sollst hier **zusammenhängende Texte zu vertrauten Themen** aus deinen Interessengebieten (Familie, Essen, Trinken, Sport, Arbeitswelt, Schule, Hobbys, Einkaufen, Medien, Freizeit, Reisen) verfassen. Mögliche Textformen umfassen Briefe, E-Mails, Notizen, Postkarten, Geschichten, einfache Gebrauchsanweisungen, kurze Personenbeschreibungen, Formulare, kurze Texte zu Bildvorlagen, strukturierte Berichte und Stellungnahmen.

Die Beurteilung deines Texts bezieht sich zum einen auf die kommunikativ-inhaltliche Komponente. Das bedeutet, dass die Struktur, die Flüssigkeit des Textes und die Erfüllung aller inhaltlichen Anforderungen aus der Aufgabenstellung beurteilt werden (Hast du die Aufgaben vollständig bearbeitet?). Bei deiner sprachlichen Leistung umfasst die Benotung den verwendeten Wortschatz, die Satzstrukturen (Hauptsatz, Nebensatz, Verbindungswörter usw.) und die Beherrschung von sprachlichen Mitteln wie Zeitformen, Wortarten etc. Es ist daher wichtig, dass du dich um treffende Formulierungen bemühst und damit demonstrierst, dass du einen Text in der englischen Sprache abwechslungsreich gestalten kannst.
Im Folgenden werden dir unterschiedliche Aufgabenformen und Schreibanlässe vorgestellt, die du so oder ähnlich auch in der Abschlussprüfung bewältigen musst.

Du hast während deiner Schullaufbahn schon viele Texte in deutscher und auch in englischer Sprache verfasst. Darunter befanden sich unterschiedliche Textsorten wie Steckbrief, Lebenslauf, Zusammenfassung, Dialog, Bewerbung, Brief an einen Freund/eine Freundin, Inhaltsangabe, Einkaufsliste, Geschichte anhand von Bildern schreiben, Tagesablauf, Freizeit und Hobbys beschreiben, einen freien Text über eine Stadt beziehungsweise einen Staat (z.B. USA) schreiben, eine Geschichte erfinden. Du hast also schon viele Erfahrungen mit Texten gesammelt und kennst vielleicht auch deine Stärken und Schwächen. Auf den folgenden Seiten werden dir unterschiedliche Schreibanlässe und Textsorten vorgestellt. Zusätzlich erhältst du Hinweise und Hilfen, die dich beim Bearbeiten der Schreibaufgaben unterstützen. Lies sie in aller Ruhe durch und bearbeite anschließend die vorgegebenen Aufgaben.

C 4.1 Aufgabenformate für das Schreiben

Writing a letter

Bei einem Brief unterscheidet man den persönlichen *(informal letter)* vom geschäftlichen *(formal letter)*. Den persönlichen Brief schreibt man beispielsweise an die Großmutter oder eine Freundin und schlägt einen vertraulichen Ton an. Der Geschäftsbrief sieht etwas anders aus, die Unterschiede werden in der folgenden Tabelle aufgelistet.

INFO letter	
Formal letter	**Informal letter**
Textmerkmale – Datum und Anrede – Stelle dich in einem Einleitungssatz vor! – Formuliere dein Anliegen. – Höfliche Schlussformel und Unterschrift – Beachte Sinnabschnitte. – Die Zeitform hängt vom Inhalt des Briefes ab. – Verwende nur Langformen *(it is* statt *it's)*.	– Datum und Anrede – Warum schreibst du den Brief? – Beachte Sinnabschnitte. – Schlussformel und Unterschrift – Die Zeitform hängt vom Inhalt des Briefes ab.
Words and phrases	
– *Dear Madam or Sir* (wenn der Name nicht bekannt ist) – *Dear Mr Z/Mrs Z/Ms Z,* – *I am writing because …* – *I would be very grateful for a …* – *I look forward to hearing from you.* – *Yours sincerely, …*	– *Dear/Hi/Hello …,* – *Thank you very much for your letter.* – *That's all for today.* – *Give my love / my regards to …* – *I hope to hear from you soon.* – *Love/Yours/Best wishes/Take care/ All the best from …*

AUFGABENSTELLUNG

An Au Pair Job

> - family of 4 (kids are 2 and 5)
> - looking for an au pair from December 2023 to the end of July 2024
> - offer: private bedroom with bath, pocket money, language course
> - wanted: non-smoker, honest, experience with kids (babysitting), friendly
>
> **contact: John McGuire, 19 Currie Street, Edinburgh   tel. 87696354**

Please answer the advertisement and write a letter to Mr McGuire. In the letter:
- introduce yourself and talk about your family situation,
- talk about your hobbies and interests,
- describe your experience with kids.

Write 100 – 130 words on a separate sheet of paper.

Writing a review of a restaurant or hotel

Ein *review* ist eine Bewertung oder ein Erfahrungsbericht zu einem Restaurant oder Hotel (oder einem Buch, Film, Kleidung, elektronischen Gerät). Der Text sollte sachlich und im Präsens (*simple present*) oder im Imperfekt (*simple past*) formuliert werden. In der Einleitung liefert man Hintergrundinformationen, z. B. den Namen des Restaurants/Hotels und evtl. die Adresse oder Angaben zur Lage. Anschließend nennt man Personen, mit denen man dort war, und gibt an, wie oft man dort war. In einer Hotelbewertung sollte man angeben, ob man privat oder beruflich gereist ist, allein oder mit der Familie und welchen Zimmertyp man gewählt hat. Im Hauptteil werden positive Aspekte und negative Punkte aufgeführt. Hier sollte auch der Internetauftritt des Restaurants oder Hotels bewertet werden: Entsprechen die Angaben im Netz der Realität? Am Ende formuliert man seine eigene Meinung und erklärt, warum man das Restaurant oder Hotel weiterempfiehlt oder warum nicht.

INFO review

Words and phrases

– *Last week/month me and my family/ friend visited …*	Letzte(n) Woche/Monat besuchten ich und meine Familie / mein Freund …
– *We travelled to … and stayed in …*	Wir reisten nach … und wohnten im …
– *It was a vacation / business trip.*	Es war eine Urlaubs-/Geschäftsreise.
– *The waiter / concierge / service …*	Der Kellner / Portier / Service …
– *The hotel was near …*	Das Hotel war in der Nähe von …
– *The food/service/room/ pool area / family activities was/were …*	Das Essen / der Service / das Zimmer / der Pool / Freizeitaktivitäten war/waren …
– *Positive/Negative aspects are …*	Positive/Negative Aspekte sind …
– *It is important to mention that …*	Es ist wichtig zu erwähnen, dass …
– *My experience with this restaurant/ hotel is/was …*	Ich habe die Erfahrung mit diesem Restaurant / Hotel gemacht, dass …
– *I can/can't recommend …*	Ich kann das … (nicht) empfehlen.

So könnte eine BEISPIELAUFGABE aussehen:

Look at the picture and write a hotel review. List the basic information (date of stay, duration, type of room, holiday or business trip, people you travelled with). List three positive and two negative aspects of the hotel (picture). Give a recommendation in the end and explain the number of stars you are giving (1 – 5). Write about 100 words on a separate sheet of paper.

> **Facts about your trip**
> • date: 15th to 22nd of May
> • duration: one week
> • people: travel with husband/wife and two kids
> • room: family
> • trip: holiday

Writing a blog or a diary entry

Das Wort Blog ist die Abkürzung von Weblog, was sich wiederum aus den beiden englischen Wörtern *web*, für Netz, und *log*, für Logbuch beziehungsweise Tagebuch, zusammensetzt. Also bedeutet der Begriff „Netztagebuch" oder „Netzlogbuch". Ein Blog ist eine tagebuchartige Website, die fortlaufend um kurze Einträge zu einem bestimmten Thema ergänzt wird und die Möglichkeit zum Kommentieren bietet. Die Texte sind im Allgemeinen zwischen 500 und 2000 Wörter lang und beschäftigen sich oft mit aktuellen Themen, die anhand von Beispielen aufbereitet werden. Als Autor oder Autorin sollte man sich die Frage stellen, warum jemand sich für den Blogeintrag interessieren könnte und den vollständigen Text lesen will. Dieser sollte neben wichtigen Informationen auch mögliche Lösungen und Tipps für die jeweiligen Probleme anbieten. Du kannst in einem Blogeintrag einen anderen Text kommentieren, etwas über dich mitteilen, eine persönliche Frage stellen oder eine Tatsache schildern. Der Stil sollte informell sein: Verwende also informelle Vokabeln, interagiere mit den Lesenden, stelle Fragen und gib Tipps. Gliedere deinen Text in Einleitung, Hauptteil und Schluss. Schon die Einleitungssätze, die sich auf einen anderen Blogeintrag oder ein bestimmtes Thema beziehen, sollten den Leser fesseln. Beachte folgende Hinweise:

1. Nenne zu Anfang deinen Namen, Datum, Ort und evtl. die Uhrzeit.
2. Wähle einen interessanten Titel, der über das Thema des Blogeintrags informiert. In der Einleitung solltest du das Thema auf interessante Art und Weise vorstellen und dich eventuell auf einen anderen Eintrag beziehen.
3. Im Hauptteil geht es um deine Meinung. Was denkst du über das Thema? Welche Erfahrung hast du damit? Nenne Beispiele.
4. Zum Schluss kannst du deine Meinung kurz zusammenfassen, dich bei den Leserinnen und Lesern bedanken oder um Kommentare bitten.

INFO blog

Words and phrases

– *Did you know that …?*	Wusstest du, dass …?
– *Have you heard of …?*	Hast du gehört, dass …?
– *Have you ever thought about …?*	Hast du mal daran gedacht …?
– *Shouldn't we …?*	Sollten wir nicht …?
– *What's it like in your country/school/family?*	Wie ist das in deinem Land/deiner Schule/Familie?
– *I recently came across …*	Vor Kurzem habe ich …
– *I couldn't believe that …*	Ich konnte nicht glauben, dass …
– *This post will …*	Dieser Eintrag ist/wird …
– *On the one hand …, on the other hand …*	Einerseits …, andererseits …
– *Considering the fact that …*	In Anbetracht der Tatsache, dass …
– *Regarding the fact that …*	Diese Tatsache berücksichtigend …
– *As you can imagine …*	Wie du dir vorstellen/denken kannst …
– *In retrospect …*	Im Nachhinein …
– *A study shows that …*	Eine Studie zeigt, dass …
– *Thank you for reading my blog.*	Danke fürs Lesen.
– *I look forward to your comment.*	Ich freue mich auf deinen Kommentar.

AUFGABENSTELLUNG

Read the following blog entries and comment on one of them. In your blog comment you should:
- find a good title for your comment,
- describe the situation with corona vaccines in your family/school,
- discuss your own opinion and say why you would or wouldn't recommend the vaccination.
- Write about 120 words on a separate sheet of paper.

Blog about corona vaccines

1. There is no doubt that the available vaccines[1] are safe and effective, and that the possibility of a strong reaction to the protection[2] given by the vaccine against the deadly coronavirus is low. I am vaccinated. It was the right decision for me. I am glad I did it. All members of my family have received the vaccine. We feel safer with it. Now life feels more normal.   5
(13th of December 2020, Asaya Lazaar, Washington State)

2. The new vaccines are expected to be safe and effective. Scientists used a decade of modern research which was fast-tracked[3] during this pandemic. Results of Pfizer and Moderna vaccines are very promising and show a good safety profile. I would encourage all to take it as the first step to defeating 10 this pandemic. I did it last week. Half of my class in school got the vaccine.
(15th of December 2020, Rashid Kaan, New Delhi)

3. In the first week of December, regulatory authorities[4] announced the start of a large-scale[5] vaccination campaign with Sputnik V. It started on Saturday, December 5th in Moscow and in areas outside. The first to be vaccinated were 15 doctors, teachers and social workers. In Moscow, five thousand people have signed up for vaccination in the next days. I am going to be one of them. I can't wait to get the vaccine. My mother and my sister will go too.
(18th December 2020, Yevgeni Zarkov, Moscow)

4. Take the vaccine if you have no health problems. No matter what, the truth 20 is that millions of people died from this dangerous virus. Don't wait to see what happens. Act now and get the vaccine. There is no guarantee that you will not get the virus but the vaccine offers protection against it. My father took our whole family to the doctor to be vaccinated.
(21st of December 2020, Jason Dias, Perth)   25

Annotations:

1 **vaccines** – Impfstoffe, 2 **protection** – Schutz, 3 **fast-tracked** – im Schnellverfahren,

4 **regulatory authorities** – Zulassungsbehörden, 5 **large-scale** – groß angelegt

Writing a report (Bericht) *or an article* (Zeitungsartikel)

Man schreibt einen **Bericht** häufig über vergangene Geschehnisse oder sich ständig wiederholende Aktivitäten (z. B. Tagesablauf). Auch der Bericht oder Artikel wird **sachlich** geschrieben, enthält also **keine eigene Meinung.** Der Text sollte die **W-Fragen** (Wer? Wie? Wann? Wo? Warum?) beantworten. Für Berichte, die über **Vergangenes** informieren, benutzt man das *simple past.* **Tägliche Gewohnheiten** werden mit dem *simple present* ausgedrückt.

Im Vergleich mit dem Bericht weist der **Artikel** zusätzliche Merkmale auf. Zum einen benötigt er eine **spannende Überschrift,** die das Interesse des Lesers weckt. Eine **ansprechende Einleitung** informiert den Leser über das Thema des Artikels, beantwortet die wichtigsten Fragen (W-Fragen) und motiviert zum Weiterlesen. Im Hauptteil gibt man detaillierte Informationen und Erklärungen oder schildert ein Ereignis. Das Ende mündet in eine Aussage oder Frage zum Hauptthema.

INFO reports and articles	
Words and phrases (simple past)	
– *The incident happened on (date) ... at (time) ...* – *It was caused by ...* – *... was/were involved* – *As a result ...* – *As a consequence ...*	Das Ereignis geschah am (Datum) ... um (Uhrzeit) ... Es wurde verursacht durch ... ... war/en beteiligt/betroffen Als Folge davon ... Als Konsequenz daraus ...
Words and phrases (simple present)	
– *He often/sometimes/never/usually goes ...* – *Most of the time he works ...* – *Normally he doesn't like ...* – *He loves ...ing ...* – *She hates ...ing ...* – *On Mondays he ...* – *Once/twice a week he ...*	Er geht oft/manchmal/niemals/gewöhnlich ... Meistens arbeitet er ... Normalerweise mag er ... nicht. Er liebt es zu ... Sie hasst es zu ... Montags ... er ... Einmal/zweimal in der Woche ... er ...

(Denk immer daran: *He, she, it* – das „s" muss mit!)

AUFGABENSTELLUNG

Your friend Karsten has just returned from an exchange trip to England. He tells you about his stay in an English family and his visit to London.
Write a report and cover all the points in your notes.
Use a separate sheet of paper.

Notes:

Ten days in England – Eurostar train through the Channel Tunnel / very exciting – guest family at railway station – very nice / one daughter Peggy, my age – food good /especially breakfast and fish and chips – day trip to London – shopping for hours – the London Eye – wonderful experience – Peggy and I good friends – my English much better.

Writing an e-mail

Bei dieser Textsorte muss man wie bei Briefen zwischen einer E-Mail an einen Freund *(informal)* und an eine Firma *(formal)* unterscheiden. Während der Ton in einer Mail an einen Freund vertraut und persönlich ist, schreibt man einer Firma sachlich und formgerecht. Viele Jugendliche achten in ihren elektronischen Nachrichten an Freunde nicht mehr auf die Regeln der Rechtschreibung. In der Abschlussarbeit musst du in beiden Fällen Rechtschreibfehler vermeiden. Für die E-Mails gelten ähnliche Regeln wie für einen Brief. Die Anrede und das Datum platziert man genauso, lässt jedoch die Adressen weg, da der Adressat mit der Nachricht auch die E-Mail-Adresse des Absenders erhält. Alle anderen Teile der E-Mail entsprechen denen eines Briefes. Sieh dir die Hinweise zum Brief, die entsprechenden Redewendungen und den Musterbrief nochmals an, bevor du mit der Schreibaufgabe zur E-Mail beginnst.

AUFGABENSTELLUNG

Last weekend you went on a class trip to an amusement park. Write an e-mail to your e-pal in London and tell him/her all about:

- the one-hour bus trip
- the fun rides in the park
- food and drinks

Write about 60 words. Count your words!

To:	minniemouse@yahoo.com
From:	Mohammed Tayci
Subject:	Class Trip

Hello my friend,

Last weekend was very funny. I went to the amusement park with my class. The rollercoaster was so funny. I hope we go together to the amusement park. The food was also tasty like the drinks. I ate some fish and chips and i drank some cola zero. It cost 10 pounds it was amero. This was my trip

Number of words: 63

50

Writing a description (Beschreibung)

Bei einer Beschreibung kommt es besonders auf genaue Details an. Dabei ist es unerheblich, ob es um eine Person, einen Gegenstand, ein Bild oder einen Vorgang geht. Die Sätze sollten im Präsens (siehe Hinweis unten im Kasten) geschrieben und sachlich formuliert sein und mit möglichst präzisen Ausdrücken die Fakten darstellen.

Im Kasten findest du viele nützliche Wörter und Ausdrücke, die du bei Beschreibungen von Dingen, Personen und Bildern verwenden kannst.

INFO description	
Words and phrases for things	
– Size: small, tiny, big, ... – Shape: round, square, oval, ... – Colours: red, blue, ... – Form: cylinder, cube, sphere, pyramid, ... – Texture: hairy, rough, smooth, ...	Größe: klein, winzig, groß, ... Form: rund, eckig, oval, ... Farben: rot, blau, ... Form: Zylinder, Quadrat, Kugel, Pyramide, ... Oberfläche: haarig, rau, glatt, ...
Words and phrases for people	
– Size: small, tall, big, short, heavy, fat, slim, ... – Character: nice, (un)friendly, helpful, smart, intelligent, aggressive, ... – Looks: colour of eyes, colour of hair, young/old, clothing, handsome, pretty, beautiful, healthy, ...	Größe: klein, groß, schwer, dick, schlank ... Charaktereigenschaften: nett, (un)freundlich, hilfs-bereit, schlau, intelligent, aggressiv, ... Aussehen: Augenfarbe, Haarfarbe, jung/alt, Klei-dung, gut aussehend, hübsch, schön, gesund, ...
Words and phrases for pictures	
– The picture shows ... – In the picture you can see ... – On the left/on the right there is/are ... – In the foreground/in the background there is/are ... – The person on the left/on the right is ...ing ... – The children in the background are ...ing ...	Das Bild zeigt ... Im Bild kann man ... sehen. Links/rechts ist/sind ... Im Vordergrund/im Hintergrund ist/sind ... Die Person links/rechts ... gerade ... (Tätigkeit) Die Kinder im Hintergrund ... gerade ... (Tätigkeit)
Useful prepositions:	
– behind, in front of, next to, inside (of ...) – outside (of), through, under, over – on top of, at the top/bottom of ...	hinter, vor, neben, innerhalb, außerhalb, durch, unter, über, auf, am oberen/unteren Ende von ...

(Gefühle und Darstellungen auf Bildern werden im *simple present* beschrieben. Wenn man beschreibt, was jemand gerade tut, dann benutzt man das *present progressive*.)

AUFGABENSTELLUNG

You have lost your sports bag in school. The next day you ask the janitor, who wants you to answer his questions about your bag. Describe your bag and its contents.

This is what my bag looks like:

_____

_____

_____

_____

These things are in the bag:

_____

_____

_____

_____

Filling in a form

Das Ausfüllen eines Formulars ist eine sehr beliebte Schreibaufgabe für die Abschlussprüfung. Meistens musst du deine persönlichen Angaben wie Name, Adresse, Telefonnummer, E-Mail, Alter, Nationalität, Geburtsort und -tag oder Ähnliches eintragen. Es ist wichtig, dass du darauf achtest, was von dir verlangt wird und dass du die richtige Information in die entsprechende Zeile schreibst oder das auf dich zutreffende Kästchen ankreuzt. Die folgenden Vokabeln könnten in einem Formular vorkommen:

INFO filling in a form

Words and phrases	
– *Personal information*	Informationen zur Person
– *Title (Mr/Mrs/Ms/Prof./Dr.)*	Anrede (Herr/Frau/Prof./Dr.)
– *First/last name*	Vor-/Nachname
– *Country of origin*	Geburtsland
– *Postal address*	Vollständige Adresse
– *Nationality*	Nationalität
– *Date/place of birth*	Geburtsdatum/-ort
– *Signature*	Unterschrift

AUFGABENSTELLUNG

Imagine you are planning a trip to Edinburgh, Scotland in May 2023. You want to fly on Saturday (20th May) and come back on Tuesday (23rd May). You want to stay in a youth hostel for three nights. You check out the website online and find a form to reserve a bed. Fill in all the required details to get a bed in a single room for three nights. You do not want to spend more than £ 75 for the room.

Edinburgh Youth Hostel

Personal information (Please tick or write clearly in CAPITAL LETTERS!)

1. Title: ☐ Mr ☐ Mrs ☐ Ms ☐ Prof. ☐ Dr. ☐ other (please specify): _____

2. First name: _____ 3. Last name: _____

4. Age: _____ 5. Postal address: _____

6. Nationality: _____ 7. Telephone: _____

8. E-mail: _____

9. Preferred accommodation:

	Single room	Double room
Price category A	£15 – 20 ☐	£10 – 15 ☐
Price category B	£20 – 25 ☐	£15 – 20 ☐
Price category C	£25 – 30 ☐	£20 – 25 ☐

10. Date of arrival: _____ 11. Date of departure: _____

12. Signature: _____

Giving your own opinion (die eigene Meinung darstellen)

In vielen der oben genannten Textsorten musst du deine eigene Meinung zu einem Thema (z. B. Rauchen, Alkoholmissbrauch, Schuluniformen etc.) in schriftlicher Form darlegen. In diesem Fall ist es wichtig, dass du vor dem Schreiben deine Gedanken und Argumente ordnest (das wichtigste Argument an den Schluss stellen!) und die Vor- und Nachteile deutlich unterscheidest. Schreibe deine eigene Meinung immer im *simple present* und verstärke sie anhand von Beispielen oder Zitaten aus dem Text. Die folgenden Redewendungen helfen dir beim Formulieren deiner Sätze.

INFO giving your opinion

Words and phrases

– advantage/disadvantage	Vor-/Nachteil
– pros and cons	Das Für und Wider
– First of all/second/third/finally, …	Erstens/zweitens/drittens/letztendlich …
– In my opinion …	Meiner Meinung nach …
– I think …	Ich denke …
– In my experience …	Meiner Erfahrung nach …
– I believe …	Ich glaube …
– The evidence shows …	Die Beweise/Argumente zeigen …
– I can imagine that …	Ich kann mir vorstellen, dass …
– It is obvious that …	Es ist offensichtlich, dass …
– Firstly, … secondly, …	Erstens … zweitens …
– On the one hand, …, on the other hand, …	Auf der einen Seite …, auf der anderen Seite …
– Finally, …	Schließlich, abschließend …
– The reason for this is that …	Der Grund dafür ist, dass …
– For example, …	Zum Beispiel …
– In other words, …	Mit anderen Worten …
– So, all in all I think …	Alles in allem denke ich daher …
– Summing up it can be said that …	Zusammenfassend kann man sagen, dass …

AUFGABENSTELLUNG

Your class is having a discussion about school uniforms. A lot of kids have arguments for and against this new idea. The teacher asks you to go home and write a short text about your own opinion.

Find arguments and answer the following questions:
- What do you think about school uniforms in general?
- How do the majority of your friends feel about them?
- Would it be a good idea to introduce school uniforms at your school?

Write about 100 – 120 words on a separate sheet of paper. Count your words.

Number of words: _____

Interpreting tables and charts (Tabellen und Diagramme interpretieren)

Diagramme und Tabellen gibt es in verschiedenen Varianten: Tabelle *(table)*, Tortendiagramm *(pie chart)*, Balkendiagramm *(bar chart)* und Kurvendiagramm *(line graph)*. Wenn du ein Diagramm beschreibst, achte auch auf die Verwendung der richtigen Zeitform. Stellt das Diagramm Fakten dar, die sich auf die Gegenwart beziehen, dann verwendet man das *simple present.* Wenn es um Fakten geht, die in der Vergangenheit liegen, dann schreibt man im *simple past.* Stellen die Zahlen einen Bezug von der Vergangenheit bis heute dar, dann nutzt man das *present perfect.*

In der Einleitung beschreibst du, was das Diagramm aussagt (Hauptaussage). Achte auf den Titel des Diagramms. Es ist auch wichtig zu sagen, wo du das Diagramm gefunden hast (Quelle).
Im Hauptteil beschreibst du, was die Tabelle (die Zahlen, Fakten, Daten) zu einem bestimmten Thema aussagt. Am Ende ziehst du eine Schlussfolgerung *(conclusion)* und schreibst in einem Satz, was die wichtigste Erkenntnis ist, die man aus dem Diagramm entnehmen kann.

INFO charts and tables

Words and phrases	
– *The chart/table is about …*	In der Tabelle geht es um …
– *The chart/table deals with …*	Die Tabelle beschäftigt sich mit …
– *The chart/table shows …*	Die Tabelle zeigt …
– *The chart is devided into … parts.*	Das Diagramm ist in … Teile aufgeteilt.
– *It compares the … with …*	Es vergleicht die … mit …
… has the largest number of …	… hat die größte Anzahl von …
… has the second largest … number of …	… hat die zweitgrößte Zahl an …
… is as big as …	… ist so groß wie …
… is bigger than …	… ist größer als …
… is twice as big as …	… ist doppelt so groß wie …
… is more/less than … a third/half of …	… ist mehr/weniger als … ein Drittel/halb so groß
– *The number … goes up/increases/decreases by …*	Die Zahl … geht nach oben/steigt an um …
– *The number does not change …*	Die Zahl verändert sich nicht …
– *So we can say that …*	So können wir sagen, dass …
– *The conclusion we come to is …*	Die Schlussfolgerung, zu der wir kommen, ist …

So könnte eine BEISPIELAUFGABE aussehen:

Look at the bar charts and write a short text about each.
You can start like this:

The bar chart is about …

On page 107/108 you can find two examples of a bar chart.

C 4.2 Hinweise zur Grammatik

Die Grammatik der englischen Sprache wird in der Abschlussprüfung nicht ausdrücklich abgefragt. Bisher wurde nur in einer Abschlussprüfung ein Lückentext angeboten, der mit Verben, Präpositionen, Konjunktionen u. a. ausgefüllt werden sollte. In den letzten beiden Jahren wurden solche Aufgabenformen nicht mehr verwendet. Trotzdem musst du bestimmte Grammatikthemen besonders zum Schreiben von Texten beherrschen. In den angeleiteten Schreibaufgaben im Teil D werden diese nochmals angesprochen und anhand von Übungen wiederholt. Du kannst jedoch andere Möglichkeiten nutzen, um deine grammatischen Fähigkeiten zu verbessern und dich auf die Prüfung vorzubereiten. Im Internet gibt es viele Seiten, die dir neben zahlreichen Aufgaben und Tests auch einen Überblick über die Regeln und die Anwendung anbieten. Du kannst allein oder mit Freunden die wichtigsten Zeitformen *(simple present, present progressive, simple past, present perfect, going-to-future, will-future)* wiederholen und anhand der Schreibaufgaben in diesem Buch anwenden und festigen.

TIPP Internetseiten (Grammatik)
– www.englisch-hilfen.de
– www.ego4u.de
– https://englishlive.ef.com/de-de/
– www.englisch-lehrbuch.de
– www.insiders-english.de
– https://onlineuebung.de/englisch
– www.englisch-jetzt.de/englischjetztlinkverzeichnis.html
– www.englisch-lernen-online.de

C 4.3 Wortschatzarbeit

Der Wortschatz, also die Wörter einer Sprache, könnte man als das Skelett der Sprache bezeichnen. Ohne ein gutes Vokabelwissen hast du Probleme beim Verstehen von Hör- und Lesetexten. Beim Schreiben fällt es dir schwer, deine Gedanken in Worte zu fassen. Um das zu vermeiden, gibt es Möglichkeiten, deinen Wortschatz zu erweitern oder einfach zu aktivieren. Sicherlich ist dir schon aufgefallen, dass du sehr viele englische Wörter verstehst, sie aber in deinem eigenen Sprachgebrauch kaum benutzt. Dein sogenannter **passiver Wortschatz** (Wörter, die du verstehst) ist sehr viel größer als dein **aktiver Wortschatz** (Wörter, die du verstehst und auch selbst beim Schreiben und Sprechen verwendest). Du musst also nicht unbedingt neue Wörter lernen, sondern nur deinen passiven Wortschatz aktivieren. Außerdem gibt es einfache Schritte, mit denen du dein Vokabelwissen auch um neue Wörter erweitern kannst. Hierzu gibt es verschiedene **Trainingsmöglichkeiten,** die dir im Folgenden vorgestellt werden.

1. Wortfamilien: Eine Wortfamilie ist eine Gruppe von Wörtern, die alle den gleichen Wortstamm haben. Häufig unterscheiden sie sich in der Wortart, sodass du Verben, Adjektive und Substantive zusammenstellst. Wenn du diese Wortfamilien beherrschst, kannst du die Vokabeln z. B. beim Schreiben von Texten flexibel einsetzen.

Beispiel: *to explore, exploring, explored (verb), the explorer (person), exploration (noun), exploratory (adjective)*

2. Wortfelder: Ein Wortfeld besteht aus Wörtern, die inhaltlich miteinander verbunden sind. Sie gehören alle einem bestimmten Thema an.

Beispiel: *classroom objects – pen, pencil, ruler, chair, desk, blackboard, chalk, sponge, pencil case, school bag, ballpoint pen, felt-tip etc.*

Bilde aus deinen Vokabeln Wortfelder, denn so kann sie sich dein Gehirn besser abspeichern. Später kannst du dann Gruppen von Wortfeldern bilden (z. B. *school – classroom objects – clothing – subjects – colours)*, die sinngemäß zusammenhängen. So kannst du dir die Themen der einzelnen Tests erschließen und dein Vokabelwissen gezielt erweitern.

3. Mindmapping: Du kannst dir den Wortschatz zu bestimmten Themen auch anhand einer Mindmap (Gedankenkarte) oder eines *word webs* (Wortnetz) erschließen. Du kannst mit einem *word web* anfangen und zuerst nur deine Ideen sammeln. Anschließend ordnest du deine Gedanken in einer Mindmap anhand von Überschriften oder Themen.
Beispiel:

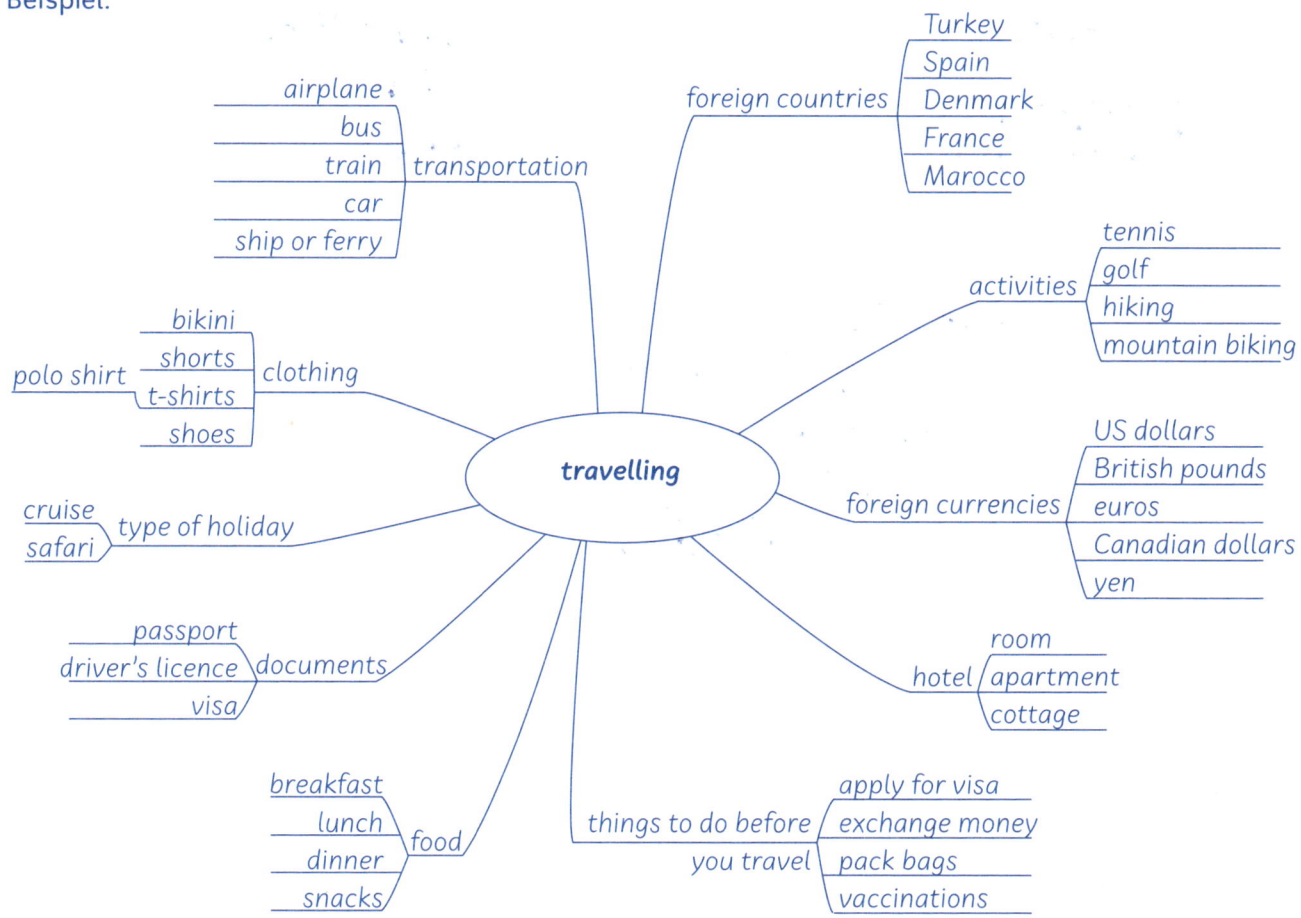

C 4.4 Aufgabenformate zur Wortschatzarbeit

Obwohl es in der Abschlussarbeit keine Aufgaben zum Wortschatz gibt, bieten wir dir hier trotzdem eine Auswahl an. Die Übungen können dir beim Aktivieren deines Wortschatzes helfen und beziehen sich auf die oberen drei Strategien (Zusammenstellen von Wortfamilien, Wortfeldern, Mindmaps).

AUFGABENSTELLUNG

Find words or expressions which mean almost the same.

1. (to) improve _____

2. (to) attempt _____

3. weird _____

4. correct _____

5. frightened _____

6. cruel _____

7. grade _____

8. awesome _____

9. huge _____

10. hard _____

Write down the opposite of the word.

1. polite ~~ambitious~~ rude impolite
2. (to) disagree _agree_
3. happy ~~sad~~ unhappy
4. healthy _unhealthy_
5. expensive _cheap_
6. minority _majority_
7. egal _Illegal_
8. married _divorced_
9. low ~~faster~~ high
10. peace _war_

Read the definition and name the word.

1. to make better _Improve_
2. someone from another country _foreigner_
3. to buy and sell products _trade_
4. a large group of people _crowd_
5. the area outside a town or city _countryside_
6. the exchange of information, ideas _____
7. the people living next-door to you _____
8. someone who writes books _____
9. to write your name on a document _____
10. the title of a newspaper story _____

Write a definition for the following words.

1. The Channel _____
2. queue _____
3. plumber _____
4. career _____
5. punishment _____
6. height _____
7. health _____
8. battery _____
9. hostage _____
10. jealousy _____

Complete the following chart of word families.

Verb	Noun	Adjective
(to) improve		
	conquest	
		influential
(to) attract		
	interest	
		damaging
(to) protect		

Find the keyword for the following words.

1. couch, chair, table, bookshelf _____

2. green, blue, yellow, red _____

3. teddy bear, doll, train set _____

4. backpack, suitcase, bag, satchel _____

5. pants, shirt, tie, skirt, shorts _____

6. bread, butter, milk, yoghurt _____

7. mechanic, hairdresser, taxi driver _____

Make a mind map or a word web for the following topic: Business and Trade.

Nun hast du die wichtigsten Arbeitstechniken, Strategien und Aufgabenformate kennengelernt. Versuche nun, nach der Bearbeitung der Aufgaben in diesem Kapitel die Checkliste auszufüllen.

CHECKLISTE nach der Bearbeitung der Aufgaben Teil C

Aufgabe	Zeit	Was hat mir geholfen?	Fehlerquellen
Hörübung Part 1: Pictures			
Hörübung Part 2: Summer camp			
Hörübung Part 3: New job			
Hörübung Part 4: Radio program			
Leseübung Part 1: Fripp Island			
Leseübung Part 2: Houses			
Leseübung Part 3: Texts 1–5			
Leseübung Part 4: Problems for students at university			
Mediation Part 1: Bus tours			
Mediation Part 2: School rules			
Writing: A letter			
Writing: A review			
Writing: A blog entry			
Writing: A report			
Writing: An e-mail			
Writing: A description			
Writing: Filling in a form			
Writing: Giving your opinion			

Im nächsten Teil bearbeitest du typische Aufgaben und bekommst dazu viele Tipps und Hilfestellungen.

Teil D Angeleitete Prüfungsaufgaben

Die folgenden angeleiteten Übungen sollen dich auf die Teile E und F vorbereiten, in denen du die Aufgaben selbstständig bearbeitest. Im Teil F findest du die Originalprüfung aus dem Jahr 2022. Alle Hörverstehensaufgaben in den folgenden Übungen befassen sich mit dem Thema **„School in Britain".**

Die einzelnen Aufgaben sind mit Erläuterungen versehen und erinnern dich an die einzelnen Arbeitsschritte, die du in Teil C kennen gelernt hast. Lies zuerst die Aufgabenstellung durch und schau dir die Fragen an. Bevor du dann die Aufgabe löst, solltest du die Lösungshilfen zu Rate ziehen, denn dort findest du auch Hinweise, in welchen Schritten du die Aufgabe lösen kannst. Bei der Abschlussprüfung hast du 120 Minuten Zeit, um alle vier Bereiche zu bearbeiten. Für die folgenden Aufgaben wirst du wegen der Zwischenschritte und Erklärungen mehr Zeit brauchen, doch das Training lohnt sich. Bearbeite die Aufgaben in aller Ruhe, behalte aber die Zeit besonders bei den Hörübungen im Auge. Damit du nicht viel mehr Zeit brauchst, findest du hier nur zwei Hörübungen.

D I. Hörverstehen

Schools in Great Britain

Aktiviere deinen Wortschatz. Vervollständige zum Thema „Schools in Britain" die folgende **Mindmap.**

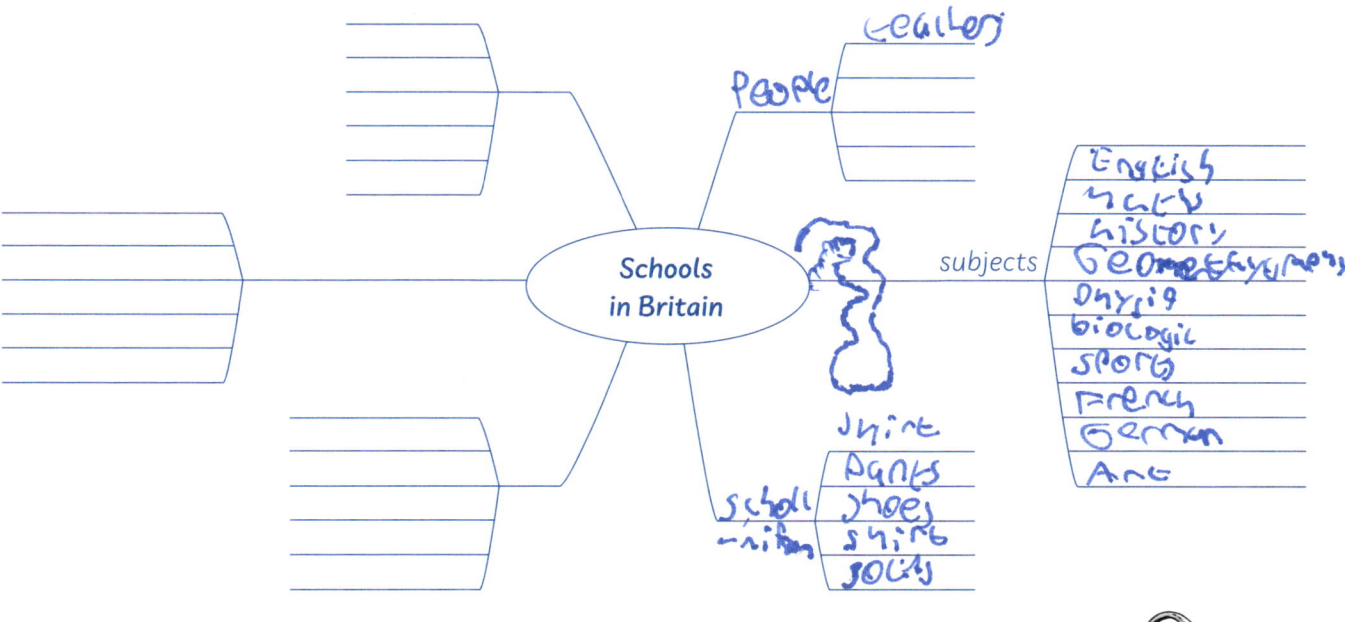

Part 1 – Questions 1 – 7

 Track 5

Vor dem Hören solltest du dein Vorwissen aktivieren. Das Thema „Schools in Britain" gibt dir Hinweise auf den Inhalt der Hörtexte. Lies die Aufgabenstellung und die Lösungshilfen durch, stelle Vermutungen an und löse anschließend die **Aufgabe.**

AUFGABENSTELLUNG

- You are going to hear seven extracts from different classes at school.
  Find out which subject is being taught in each extract.
- First look at the list of subjects below.
- Then listen to the seven extracts.
- Choose the right subject for each extract and put the number in the chart below.
- There are more subjects than you need.

subject	extract no.
Art	
English	
Geography	
PE	
History	
French	
Home Economics	
Maths	
Biology	

Wenn die Höraufgabe zu Ende ist, vervollständige deine Antworten mithilfe deiner Notizen.

Lösungshilfen

Das Thema für alle Aufgaben in diesem Hörtest ist „Schools in Britain". In dem ersten Hörtext wirst du mit einzelnen Fächern konfrontiert. Ein Lehrer oder eine Lehrerin spricht über den Inhalt seines oder ihres Fachs oder du hörst einen Dialog aus einer Unterrichtsstunde. Anhand dieser Hörtexte kannst du auf das Unterrichtsfach schließen. In der Tabelle stehen neun Fächer, du hörst aber nur sieben Beschreibungen, d. h., dass zwei nicht genannt werden. Diese Zeilen in der Tabelle bleiben leer. Wenn du dir die Namen der Fächer ansiehst, verbindest du mit jedem ganz bestimmte Inhalte beziehungsweise Vokabeln. „Art" (Kunst) befasst sich mit Bildern, Farben etc. Hier könntest du in der Beschreibung Vokabeln wie *paint, pictures, colours, style* usw. hören. Ähnliches gilt für die anderen Fächer. Anhand dieser typischen Vokabeln kannst du die Fächer erkennen. Trage deine Antworten in die Tabelle ein.

Beantworte zur Vorbereitung folgende Fragen:
Welche Gesprächssituation wird hier präsentiert?

_____

_____

_____

_____

Worüber wird gesprochen?

_____

_____

_____

_____

Auf welche Begriffe/Inhalte musst du achten?

_____

Nutze dein Allgemeinwissen und überlege, welche Unterschiede zwischen dem deutschen und dem britischen Schulsystem bestehen. Wenn dir keine Unterschiede einfallen, dann schreibe nur die Informationen auf, die dir zu Schulen in Großbritannien einfallen.

_____

_____

_____

_____

_____

Bevor du die Übung bearbeitest, lies dir die **Aufgabenstellung** genau durch. Höre bei allen Texten bis zum Ende zu, auch wenn du die Antwort schon kennst. Mache dir nun zu folgenden Fragen Notizen: Was sollst du aus den Hörtexten heraushören? Was musst du bei dieser Aufgabe beachten?

_____

_____

_____

_____

Konzentriere dich nun beim ersten Hören auf die Texte. Achte gezielt auf die gesuchte Information und mache dir kurze **Notizen** zu den einzelnen *extracts*. Schreibe Wörter oder auch Satzteile auf, die für die Lösung wichtig sind. Manchmal genügen ein oder zwei Wörter.

Extract 1 _____

_____

Extract 2 _____

_____

Extract 3 _____

_____

Extract 4 _____

_____

Extract 5 _____

_____

Extract 6 _____

_____

Extract 7 _____

_____

Helfen dir die Notizen beim Lösen der Aufgaben? Höre dir die Texte noch einmal an und fülle die Tabelle aus.

Part 2 – Questions 8 – 12

 **Track 6**

Beim folgenden Hörtext handelt es sich erneut um das Thema „Schools in Britain". Lies die Aufgabenstellung und die Lösungshilfen und beantworte anschließend die Fragen.

AUFGABENSTELLUNG

Naomi's school

You are going to hear an interview with Naomi, who is talking about her school.

- First read the questions.
- Then listen to the interview.
- Tick the correct answer.
- There is only one correct answer per question.

8. Naomi is from …
  - **A** Germany. ☐
  - **B** Scotland. ☐
  - **C** Wales. ☐

9. How old is Naomi?
  - **A** 9 ☐
  - **B** 11 ☐
  - **C** 13 ☐

10. One of the subjects Naomi studies is …
  - **A** Biology. ☐
  - **B** German. ☐
  - **C** Science. ☐

11. For lunch, Naomi eats …
  - **A** sandwiches. ☐
  - **B** roast dinner. ☐
  - **C** pizza. ☐

12. Naomi …
  - **A** gets a lot of homework. ☐
  - **B** doesn't get a lot of homework. ☐
  - **C** doesn't get any homework. ☐

Lösungshilfen

Die Gesprächssituation ist in diesem Fall ein Interview zwischen der Schülerin Naomi und einem Journalisten, der ihr Fragen zu ihrer Schule in England stellt. Sie sprechen zu Beginn über Naomi persönlich und anschließend über ihre Vorlieben und Gewohnheiten in Bezug auf die Schule. Die Fragen werden der Reihe nach besprochen, sodass es während des Hörens wichtig ist, dass du auf die entsprechenden Fragen (*"How old are you, Naomi?"*) oder die Antworten (*"I am …"*) achtest. Höre konzentriert zu und lass dich nicht aus der Ruhe bringen, denn du kannst dir den Text ja zweimal anhören.

Beantworte zur Vorbereitung folgende Fragen:
Welche Gesprächssituation wird hier präsentiert?

_____

_____

_____

_____

Worüber wird gesprochen?

_____

_____

_____

_____

Auf welche Begriffe/Inhalte musst du achten?

_____

_____

Bevor du die Übung bearbeitest, lies dir die **Aufgabenstellung** genau durch. Höre bei allen Texten bis zum Ende zu, auch wenn du die Antwort schon kennst.
Mache dir nun zu folgenden Fragen Notizen: Was sollst du aus dem Interview heraushören? Was musst du bei dieser Aufgabe beachten?

_____

_____

_____

Kreuze nun die Antworten der Fragen 8 – 12 an. Deine Notizen helfen dir dabei.

Part 3 – Questions 13 – 17

 **Track 7**

Der folgende Text handelt vom Thema „Internet bullying". Lies die Lösungshilfen, achte genau auf die Aussagen im Hörtext und kreuze „true" oder „false" an.

AUFGABENSTELLUNG

- Listen to the following text about Internet bullying.
- For questions 13 – 17 tick the correct answer.

	true	false
13. Internet bullying has been around a long time.	☐	☐
14. It is easy to find out who is behind the actions.	☐	☐
15. The teenagers spread rumours or gossip.	☐	☐
16. In the past only a small group of people would know about lies like this.	☐	☐
17. Modern technology makes bullying worse.	☐	☐

Lösungshilfen

Der Sprecher in diesem Hörtext berichtet über das Thema „Internet bullying". Das Sprechtempo entspricht einem Muttersprachler und ist eher schnell. Er berichtet über Jugendliche, die Gerüchte oder Lügen über andere Kinder im Internet verbreiten. Dieses Problem spielt sicherlich auch in deinem Alltag eine gewisse Rolle, sodass dir viele der genannten Tatsachen bereits bekannt sind. Der Wortschatz bezieht sich auf technische Geräte *(video, picture)* und bestimmte Situationen, die mit dem Thema im Zusammenhang stehen.

Notiere dir Vokabeln, die du deiner Meinung nach im Text erwarten kannst:

lies, rumours, _____

_____

_____

Welche typischen Situationen verbindest du mit „Internet bullying" in und außerhalb der Schule?

_____

_____

_____

Bevor du die Übung bearbeitest, lies dir die Aufgabenstellung genau durch. Höre den Text bis zum Ende an, auch wenn du die Antwort schon kennst. Die Aussagesätze kommen im Hörtext der Reihe nach vor. Mache dir nun zu folgenden Fragen Notizen: Was sollst du aus dem Hörtext heraushören? Was musst du bei dieser Aufgabe beachten?

Konzentriere dich beim Hören auf den Text. Achte gezielt auf die gesuchte Information und mache dir eventuell kurze Notizen (einzelne Wörter oder Satzteile) zu den einzelnen Aussagen, die dir bei der Lösung helfen können, wenn du unsicher bist. Wenn du die Antwort nicht weißt, kreuze auf jeden Fall eine Antwort an.

Part 4 – Questions 18 – 23

AUFGABENSTELLUNG

Listen to the text on Internet bullying again and complete the sentences in the chart.

0.	**Example:** Internet bullying is a new kind of ...	*harassment*
18.	They publish humiliating pictures and ...	
19.	Everybody laughs about you ...	
20.	Today technology makes it possible to share something with the ...	
21.	One in four students has been bullied online in ...	
22.	It is very distressing for the ...	
23.	The bullies change their names and ...	

Lösungshilfen

Bei dieser Aufgabe sollst du die Sätze aus der Tabelle, die wortwörtlich im Hörtext vorkommen, beenden. Häufig fehlt ein Wort oder auch mehrere. Diese Aufgabe verlangt von dir sehr genaues Zuhören, da du die fehlenden Wörter verstehen und dann in der Fremdsprache aufschreiben musst.

Wie schon erwähnt, spricht der Sprecher sehr schnell. Die meisten Wörter sind sehr gut herauszuhören, da sie am Ende eines Satzes stehen. Wenn du das Wort oder die Wörter beim ersten Durchgang nicht genau verstehst, notiere dir mit Bleistift das Wort, das du verstanden hast. Beim zweiten Hören kannst du deine Notizen überprüfen. Zum Teil kann man sich schon beim Durchlesen der Sätze denken, wie der Sprecher die Sätze beenden wird. Daher könntest du dir Möglichkeiten auf Deutsch notieren und die Wörter später im Wörterbuch nachschlagen (du darfst in der Abschlussprüfung ein zweisprachiges Lexikon benutzen). Vielleicht kommt dir eines der nachgeschlagenen Wörter vom Hören bekannt vor.

Wenn du Wörter aus den Sätzen nicht kennst, solltest du versuchen, ihre Bedeutung aus dem Kontext heraus zu erschließen. Schlage nur in Ausnahmefällen Wörter nach. Du hast in der Abschlussprüfung sehr wenig Zeit dafür.

Die folgenden Wörter solltest du aus dem Kontext erschließen können.
Notiere weitere Wörter wenn nötig.

a new kind –	*publish –*	*humiliating –*
share –	*distressing –*	

Überlege beim folgenden Beispiel, welches Wort den Satz beenden könnte und schreibe es auf. Überprüfe anschließend, ob deine Idee richtig war oder nicht. Probiere diese Technik auch mit anderen Sätzen aus der Übung aus.

Beispiel: *They publish humiliating pictures and …?* _____

Bevor du die Übung bearbeitest, lies dir die Aufgabenstellung genau durch. Höre beim Text bis zum Ende zu, auch wenn du die Antwort schon kennst. Die Sätze kommen im Text der Reihe nach vor. Mache dir nun zu folgenden Fragen Notizen: Was sollst du aus dem Hörtext heraushören? Was musst du bei dieser Aufgabe beachten?

_____

_____

Konzentriere dich beim Hören auf den Text. Achte gezielt auf die gesuchte Information und mache dir eventuell kurze Notizen (einzelne Wörter oder Satzteile) zu den einzelnen Sätzen, die dir bei der Lösung helfen können, wenn du unsicher bist.

D II. Leseverstehen

In Teil C ging es im Kapitel 2 (S. 31) um Leseverstehen. Dort wurde genau vorgestellt, welche **Aufgabenformate** es gibt und welche **Arbeitstechniken** und **Strategien** dir das Lesen von unbekannten Texten erleichtern. Hier werden noch einmal die wichtigsten Punkte zusammengefasst.
Zunächst solltest du dich damit beschäftigen, was von dir erwartet wird und wie du die Aufgabe lösen willst. Dies wird dir leichter fallen, wenn du vor der Beantwortung der Fragen folgende Schritte durchgehst.

Vorwissen aktivieren
Hat der Lesetext ein **Bild,** so kann es dir das Thema des Texts verraten. Schau dir auch den **Titel** bzw. Überschrift an und stelle weitere Überlegungen zur **Herkunft** und **Art** des Textes an und schreibe kurze Notizen. Automatisch fallen dir viele Wörter ein, die zu diesem Thema gehören. Überlege, welche **englischen Begriffe** dir einfallen und notiere sie.

Aufgabenstellung beachten
Bevor du mit der Arbeit anfängst, lies die **Aufgabenstellung** und die Fragen genau. Schreibe auf, welche Informationen du herausfinden sollst.
Lies den Text und **markiere Textstellen** und **Wörter** (Schlüsselwörter), die für das Beantworten der Fragen wichtig sind.

Wörter erschließen
Wenn du einen dir unbekannten Text liest, so wirst du auf Wörter treffen, die du nicht kennst. Das ist ganz normal und muss dich nicht beunruhigen. Häufig ist es nicht so wichtig, jedes einzelne Wort zu verstehen, um die Aufgabe zu lösen.

Wende dich nun den Aufgaben zum Leseverstehen zu. Gehe so vor wie bei den Hörverstehensaufgaben: Lies zunächst die Aufgabenstellung und die Fragen, dann die Lösungshilfen und löse anschließend die Aufgabe.

Part 1 – Questions 1 – 5

AUFGABENSTELLUNG

- Read the four texts about different places and festivals in England.
- Then answer questions 1 – 5 below.
- For each question, tick the correct answer.

York

York was established by the Romans and soon became England's second most important city. It has witnessed wars, peace agreements and prosperity throughout its 2,000 years of existence. King George VI emphasized the central role York has played throughout the years when he commented that: „The history of York is the history of England". Come and visit the fascinating museums, enjoy walking along our old cobbled streets or find out about our excellent restaurants and shops.

Blackpool illuminations

Said to be the 'greatest free show on earth', this spectacular light show started in 1879 and has since grown into a spectacular event using over a million lights: There are lasers, neon, lightbulbs, fibre optics, searchlights and floodlighting. The three-dimensional scenes are particularly popular. The show will be on for 66 days and nights. It is expected to attract over 3.5 million visitors to Blackpool.

Over 15,000 people are expected to enjoy Blackpool's biggest night of the year 'The Big Switch On Show' live, from a specially built arena in the heart of the UK's most famous holiday destination.

Nottingham Goose Fair

Experience the 700-year-old Nottingham Goose Fair when it returns to town for five days from 2nd to 6th October at the Forest Recreation Ground. There will be a number of new attractions that have not been seen in Nottingham before. Altogether there will be more than 500 attractions, among them a variety of Roller Coasters, Water Rides, Giant Wheels, Bombers and Dodgems. There is something for everyone at this historic fair – for thrill-seekers and families who love the still popular old-time rides. And when you need a snack you can enjoy local Nottinghamshire food including mushy peas and mint sauce as well as food from around the world.

The Forest Recreation Ground is easily accessible by bus or tram. Use the Nottingham City Council journey planner to find the best route for you.

York Food and Drink Festival

From 20 to 29 September, the ancient city of York hosts this celebration of fine food and drink in and around some of the city's most historic places. From native award-winning goats' cheese to Yorkshire seafood, it's all about presenting local ingredients and local talent. The numerous producers present the best of the region's ingredients and culinary skills and there is a huge variety of events taking place throughout the festival.

Visit different tents that serve delicious beer, try food from different areas, take part in cookery classes or just walk from stall to stall. There is plenty of vegetarian and vegan food on offer at York Food and Drink Festival. Most stalls have vegetarian/vegan alternatives.

		true	false
1.	a) The illuminations in Blackpool take place in the summer.	☐	☒
	b) The rides in Nottingham give you a variety of different types.	☒	☐
2.	a) More than a million lights will be used to light up the night in Blackpool.	☒	☐
	b) In York you can try different kinds of beer and cheese.	☒	☒
3.	a) The Goose Fair in Nottingham lasts ten days.	☐	☒
	b) About 50 thousand people will witness the lights in Blackpool.	☐	☒
4.	a) George VI said that the history of York represented the history of England.	☒	☐
	b) York is best known for its seafood.	☐	☒
5.	a) York was founded over 2,000 years ago.	☒	☐
	b) In Nottingham you can eat local food and dishes from around the world.	☒	☒

Lösungshilfen

Mache dir zunächst wieder Notizen zur Vorbereitung:
Kannst du aus dem Titel oder den Überschriften herausfinden, worum es sich handeln könnte?

_____

_____

Welche englischen Begriffe fallen dir zum Thema ein?

_____

_____

_____

Schau dir die Aufgabenstellung genau an. Schreibe auf, worauf du genau achten musst.

_____

_____

Markiere Schlüsselwörter.
Im Text sind einige Wörter unterstrichen. Sie könnten dir unbekannt sein. Anhand der Hilfen solltest du ihre Bedeutung verstehen können, ohne sie im Wörterbuch nachschlagen zu müssen. Schreibe die deutsche Bedeutung in die entsprechende Spalte. Du kannst weitere Wörter in die leeren Zeilen eintragen.

unknown word	word family	sentence in English	German word
witnessed (verb)	The witness (person)	He witnessed the murder and went to the police.	Zeuge
prosperity (noun)	(to) prosper (verb)	The company prospered and became successful.	wohlssend
(to) host (verb)	host (person)	He **hosted** a party for his birthday and invited about 50 people.	Gastgber

ingredient (noun)		When you bake a cake you need different **ingredients** like eggs, milk, sugar, flour.	*Zutat*
culinary (adjective)		something to do with the kitchen/ cooking food	*kulinarisch*
variety (noun)	vary (verb) various (adjective)	School dinners vary from good to awful.	*Varietät*

Nun kannst du die Aufgabe lösen.

Lösungshilfen zu den einzelnen Punkten:

Du wirst die Informationen in den Texten finden. Aber du wirst die Antworten nicht immer direkt aus den Texten übernehmen können. Als Beispiel nehmen wir 1.: Die Aussage bezieht sich auf Blackpool. Die Aussage zu a) „The Illuminations in Blackpool take place in the summer" ist falsch, doch wirst du im Text nicht den Satz finden: „The Illuminations take place in autumn." Im Text steht der Monat (oder die Monate) und du musst daraus schlussfolgern, dass September bis November der Herbst ist und nicht der Sommer. Wenn du die Vokabeltabelle oben vollständig bearbeitet hast, sollte dir das Verstehen der Texte keine Probleme bereiten. Lies dir die obigen Sätze genau durch und versuche, die notwendigen Informationen zu finden.

Part 2 – Questions 6 – 10

In diesen Fragen geht es um Touristenattraktionen. Lies zunächst die Aufgabenstellung und die Lösungshilfen und löse dann die Aufgabe.

AUFGABENSTELLUNG

- Decide which attraction (A–G) would be the most suitable for the tourists below (6 – 10).
- Write the correct letter behind the number in the box.

6.	**Jonathan** I'd really like to learn more about the history of the sights that I visit. Zoos and big <u>estates</u> are really boring. I want to learn more about our country and its history, especially about the people who lived here before all the immigrants came.	☐
7.	**Lucy** I love gardens and flowers. I can look at plants and exotic flowers for hours. I especially love the small Bonsai trees. I can walk for miles on trails if there are beautiful trees and plants to see.	☐

8.	**Aaron** When I travel as a tourist I want to have fun. I like adventures, cool rides and entertainment. Museums are really boring and I don't really care about history or nature. My friends and I went to Disney World last summer so I want to visit something similar and just enjoy myself.	☐
9.	**Susan** I am a <u>geology</u> major so I love all kinds of rocks and rock formations. When I travel I like to explore caves and mines underground. I have been to Europe and Asia and I have visited a lot of caves there but I haven't seen our local ones here in the USA.	☐
10.	**Ernest** I love history. I've read a lot of books about the history of the United States. What I find most interesting are the lives of our former presidents. I have been to <u>several</u> homes and have seen original rooms and <u>furnishings</u>. For me history comes alive that way.	☐

A North Carolina's first **Wild West Adventure Theme Park** <u>featuring</u> a three mile steam-powered train ride with a live train robbery for the passengers. It will be an adventure you will never forget. Shopping, live entertainment, amusement rides, a Deer Park, and gold panning. Open May through October 9 am to 6 pm.

B The **Blowing Rock** is North Carolina's oldest travel attraction. It's been visited since 1933. Put on your hiking boots and enjoy spectacular views, gardens and gift shops while <u>strolling</u> along our walking trails. Take pictures of breathtaking colors, flowers and wild life. Open all day in the summer.

C Discover the beautiful **Biltmore Estate** in Ashville, North Carolina. Experience the breathtaking beauty of America's largest home and century-old gardens. Explore Antler Hill Village & Winery, estate shopping , dining and outdoor activities. For a complete escape, stay at our four-star inn.

D The **North Carolina Arboretum** offers 63 acres of cultivated gardens within a 434 acre estate. You can enjoy 10 miles of hiking and biking trails, and the finest Bonsai collection in the Southeastern U.S. Ongoing <u>exhibits</u> of science, art and culture are featured in the Baker Exhibit Center, which also serves as the visitor information center. Located on the Blue Ridge Parkway at Milepost 393.

E Come to the **Indian Reservation** at Cherokee, North Carolina. Experience trails of legend and adventure in the homeland of the Cherokee Indians. Learn more about the history of the American Indians and their life then and today. See their dances and beautiful artwork at the Cherokee Welcome Center in Cherokee.

F **Luray Caverns** are Eastern America's largest and most popular caverns. A U.S. Natural Landmark featuring the world's only Stalagpipe Organ. Come and enjoy the beautiful world of caves. Visit a concert or follow a tour and listen to the stories of our tour guides. The brilliant lighting in the different caves invites our visitors to take splendid photos of this natural wonder.

G Be inspired by **Monticello**, a true American original. Guided tours of Thomas Jefferson's exceptional mountain-top home offered daily. Come and enjoy the original rooms and furnishings of this great man, the third President of the United States. Look at the garden and grounds, walk the trails and learn more about the house's history.

Lösungshilfen

Vorwissen aktivieren

Automatisch fallen dir sicherlich viele Wörter ein, die zu diesem Thema gehören. Überlege, welche **englischen Begriffe** du kennst und notiere sie.

_____

_____

Aufgabenstellung beachten

Bevor du mit der Arbeit anfängst, lies die **Aufgabenstellung** und die **Fragen** genau. Schreibe auf, welche Informationen du herausfinden sollst.

_____

_____

Lies den Text und **markiere Textstellen** und **Wörter** (Schlüsselwörter), die für das Beantworten der Fragen wichtig sind.

Wörter erschließen

Folgende Wörter aus dem Text könnten dir unbekannt sein, sie sind im Text unterstrichen. Anhand der Hilfen solltest du ihre Bedeutung verstehen können, ohne sie im Wörterbuch nachschlagen zu müssen. Schreibe die deutsche Bedeutung in die entsprechende Spalte in der Tabelle.

unknown word	word family	sentence or phrase in English	German word
estate (noun)	family estate	A family estate is a big house with a lot of land.	
geology (noun)	–	same word in German	
several (adjective)	–	I did not go to the movies alone. I went with several others – like five people.	
furnishings (noun)	to furnish (verb)	The things in a room like chairs, tables, pictures etc. are the furnishings.	
to feature (verb)	feature (noun)	The movie featured a train robbery sequence.	
to stroll (verb)	stroll (noun)	to walk slowly: They strolled through the gardens.	
to exhibit (verb)	exhibition (noun)	You can exhibit paintings or old furniture.	

Bei dieser Aufgabe geht es um fünf Personen, die eine Sehenswürdigkeit besuchen wollen. In den einzelnen Texten werden die Attraktionen und die Wünsche der Personen dargestellt. Aus der Aufgabenstellung kannst du entnehmen, dass du entscheiden sollst, welche Person welche Sehenswürdigkeit besuchen könnte. Jonathan zum Beispiel liebt Geschichte und möchte mehr über die Vergangenheit seines Landes und der dort lebenden Menschen herausfinden. Welche Attraktion käme für ihn in Frage? Du schreibst den entsprechenden Buchstaben in das Kästchen.

Part 3 – Questions 11 – 16

Lies die Aufgabenstellung, den Text und die Lösungshilfen, bevor du die Aufgabe bearbeitest.

AUFGABENSTELLUNG

Read the text and complete the sentences.

Where do our clothes come from?

Across the world, hundreds of free trade zones have been created, especially in developing countries. These are industrial areas where factory owners pay no tax, there is no minimum wage and there is very little safety for the workers. Twelve-hour shifts are the norm and trade unions are often illegal. Here are reports by our correspondents in China. 5

News from China:
Despite the very quick growth of the Chinese economy in recent years, more than 482 million people in China – that is 36% of the population – live on less than $2 a day. They live in villages in the country and because of extreme poverty they have to look for jobs in the cities. There are about 150 million 10 workers in China who have to leave the country and live in poor neighbourhoods in big cities. Because of these conditions those people do not receive any help or protection from the government because pensions, housing and education is tied to a person's place of birth. People who have to move away from their home to find a job, have to live with bad working conditions such 15 as long working hours, no pensions or contracts and dangerous health risks. There is no movement to form trade unions and organisations who represent the workers' rights are watched by the Government who control them regularly. International companies and national factory owners take advantage of this situation. They don't want the workers to know their own rights and 20 since the Chinese government is unwilling to change these conditions, the difficult situation continues. One example for an industry abusing the workers is the textile production.
China is the world's biggest clothing exporter – in 2016 it produced 34 % of the world's clothing exports. China's industry depends on a lot of the above- 25 mentioned migrant workers. They represent the majority of the working population but they do not receive any state benefits. Most of these workers are women earning extremely low wages – the average monthly salary including overtime is 1,690 yuan; that is $270. Migrant workers have to work long hours, often seven days a week, and face discrimination. Living condi- 30 tions are poor – imagine having to share a small room with up to six people! Because of the chemicals they often work with, there is a high health risk. In 2009 alone, about one million workers were injured at work and about 20,000

suffered from diseases due to their working conditions. One of the biggest
35 risks to the health of textiles workers is sandblasting, a technique used to
treat jeans so that they have a worn look. Sandblasting exposes workers to
a dangerous chemical which can damage their breathing passages. This can
cause a serious disease which can lead to the death of the workers. Although
sandblasting was banned in 1966, it continues to be used in China ignoring
40 the serious health risks. Companies avoid facing the responsibility for creating
these conditions by having a large legal department which can fight off any
claim by the workers. On top of that the official state trade union in China
has failed to take action for the workers who fall ill and can't work anymore.
Humanitarian organisations are trying to help the migrant workers to defend
45 their rights and raise the workers' awareness of the illegal conditions they
are working in and the abuse by the employers.

Lösungshilfen

Lies den Text und markiere die Textstellen und Wörter (Schlüsselwörter), die für das Bearbeiten der Aufgaben wichtig sind. Schreibe die richtigen Zeilenangaben für die Antworten in die Tabelle. Nur dann erhältst du die volle Punktzahl für diese Aufgabe.

Du sollst die Sätze beenden und die Zeilen aus dem Text angeben, in denen die Antworten zu finden sind. Es kann sein, dass sich die Antwort über mehrere Zeilen erstreckt (z. B. Zeile 5, 6, 7 oder 5–7).

Wörter erschließen

Folgende Wörter aus dem Text könnten dir bekannt sein. Anhand der Hilfen solltest du ihre Bedeutung verstehen können, ohne sie im Wörterbuch nachschlagen zu müssen. Schreibe die deutsche Bedeutung in die entsprechende Spalte.

unknown word	word family	sentence in English or phrase	German word
to trade (verb)	trade (noun)	to buy or sell goods from another company	
trade union (noun)	–	organisation for workers, makes sure that the workers have fair wages or good working conditions	
tax (noun)	to tax (verb)	In Germany we have a 19% sales tax on every product we buy.	
migrant (adjective)	migration (noun)	some birds migrate in the winter – they fly south	
protection (noun)	protect (verb)	to keep someone safe	

Der Titel verrät dir, von welchem Thema der Lesetext handelt. Die Arbeitsbedingungen in der Textilindustrie sind in vielen Ländern menschenunwürdig. Diese Tatsache ist in Europa kein Geheimnis und viele Menschen entwickeln dafür ein Bewusstsein. Sie achten beim Kauf ihrer Kleidung darauf, wo sie hergestellt wird und kaufen gezielt bei Unternehmen, die in Europa produzieren.

Da der Text sehr lang ist, musst du zwei unterschiedliche Aufgabenformen dazu bearbeiten. Hier sollst du Sätze beenden und die Zeilenangaben machen. Im anschließenden Part 4 (Seite 77) musst du Aussagen als richtig *(true)*, falsch *(false)* oder nicht im Text *(not in the text)* erkennen. Lies die unvollständigen Sätze und die Aussagen genau durch und konzentriere dich. Wenn du die Vokabeltabelle vervollständigt und die wichtigsten Textstellen markiert hast, sollte das Bearbeiten der Aufgaben kein Problem für dich sein.

Complete the following sentences and write down the correct line(s) from the text for the answer.

	line in the text
11. Migrant workers are people who _____	*line* _____
12. Government benefits are tied to _____	*line* _____
13. In 2016 China produced _____	*line* _____
14. The average monthly salary of a woman working in the textile industry _____ _____	*line* _____
15. The biggest health risk in the textile industry _____ _____	*line* _____
16. Humanitarian organisations are trying _____ _____	*line* _____

Part 4 – Questions 17 – 24

Die folgenden Fragen beziehen sich auf den gleichen Text wie die Fragen 11 – 16.

AUFGABENSTELLUNG

- Read the text and then look at the sentences.
- For each sentence, tick the correct answer: "true", "false" or "not in text".

	true	false	not in the text
17. Although the Chinese economy has grown in the past decade, a lot of people still live in poverty.	☐	☐	☐
18. Trade unions who protect workers' rights are being formed all over China.	☐	☐	☐
19. Private companies in China made billions of dollars in profits in the textile industry last year.	☐	☐	☐
20. The living situation for migrant workers working in the textile industry are usually really bad.	☐	☐	☐
21. The chemicals used in the sandblasting technique are not dangerous for the workers.	☐	☐	☐
22. The Chinese government still ignores the unsafe working conditions of these workers.	☐	☐	☐
23. Women who have worked in the textile industry may have breathing problems and lung damage.	☐	☐	☐
24. If the workers are not able to work anymore, the companies will give them a place to live.	☐	☐	☐

D III. Mediation (Sprachmittlung)

Die Sprachmittlung überprüft deine Fähigkeiten als Dolmetscher. In einigen Situationen sollst du für eine andere Person (oder für mehrere Personen) Informationen aus Fahrplänen, Anzeigen, Broschüren oder Dialogen in die jeweils andere Sprache übertragen. Diese Person spricht also entweder kein Deutsch oder kein Englisch. In anderen Situationen sollst du zwischen zwei Personen vermitteln, die sich nicht verständigen können.

Es kommt bei diesen Aufgaben nicht darauf an, die Details wortwörtlich zu übersetzen. Der Inhalt des Texts muss deutlich werden. Im Kapitel C 3 (S. 42) findest du ausführliche Erklärungen zum Thema und zu den Arbeitstechniken für die Sprachmittlung.

AUFGABENSTELLUNG

1. Sam's friend Thomas did a presentation on interesting post offices all over the world. Sam's English is not very good so he couldn't follow the presentation. Sam is asking him questions after class.

Read the text and answer Sam's questions.

Interesting post offices in the world

The world has a floating mosque and a floating market, but is there a floating post office? Yes, there is. It is located in the beautiful city of Srinagar in Kashmir, in the middle of tall snow-covered mountains. The building is on a big wooden houseboat in Dal Lake which is near the Dachigam National Park in India. When you look at it for the first time you might think that it is a regular boat. If you get closer you can see the official red and yellow sign for the Indian Post Office. This unique construction has an interesting style of architecture and is an important tourist attraction in the area. You won't believe the number of travellers who visit the post office to send a postcard to their family or get local stamps that show the image of Dal Lake, which is a natural wonder in Kashmir.

The floating post office was opened in the year 2011. This is an active post office and is visited by people from the area for posting letters. Other services offered here include internet facility and international phone calls. There is also a museum for international stamps in the back of the building. In the souvenir shop you can buy postcards, stamps, local products and greeting cards.

The Ochopee Post Office near the Everglades in Florida is the smallest post office in the United States. It is a tiny shed on U.S. Route 41 near Ochopee, Florida. It is located about 3 miles (5 km) east of the intersection of US 41 and State Road 29. The building used to be a storage facility for irrigation pipes of a near-by tomato farm. It was converted into a post office in 1953, after a fire which destroyed Ochopee's previous post office located in the Gaunt Company Store. The post office is currently fully functional, serving the surrounding populations of Miccosukee and Seminole Indians. The local post clerk is often asked for the famous Ochopee post mark.

Lösungshilfen

Hintergrundinformationen sind nicht notwendig, um die Aufgabe erfolgreich zu lösen. In einem Postamt kann man Briefmarken kaufen und Pakete verschicken. Daher kannst du das Wort *stamp* aus dem Kontext erschließen, wenn du es nicht kennst. Ähnliches gilt auch für die Wörter *post clerk* und *post office* (*post* wird häufiger im Britischen Englisch verwendet, während *mail* im Amerikanischen Englisch für alle Sendungen verwendet wird) und das Adjektiv *wooden* (das Nomen ist *wood*).

Wenn du bestimmte Wörter nicht aus dem Kontext erklären kannst, musst du sie nachschlagen (z. B. *shed, floating, wonder*), um die Informationen richtig wiedergeben zu können. Lass dich nicht von den vielen Namen für Seen, Städte oder Menschengruppen irritieren.
Bevor du die Antwort formulierst, kannst du folgende Schritte erledigen:
Lies die Aufgabe durch und notiere das Thema und die Situation.

_____

_____

_____

Stelle eine Liste der wichtigen Wörter und Informationen aus der Anzeige zusammen und überprüfe, ob du alle verstehst. Versuche, unbekannte Wörter aus dem Kontext zu erschließen, und schlage sie nur im Wörterbuch nach, wenn es unbedingt nötig ist.

Words: _____

_____

_____

_____

_____

Information: _____

_____

_____

_____

_____

_____

Beantworte nun Sams Fragen.

1. Wo genau befindet sich das Postamt in Indien?

_____

2. Wann wurde das Postamt eröffnet?

_____

3. Welche Dienste bietet das Postamt an?

_____

4. Was passierte mit dem alten Postgebäude in Florida?

_____

_____

5. Welche Funktion hatte das jetzige Gebäude vorher?

_____

AUFGABENSTELLUNG

2. You are in a clothes store and want to buy some socks. While you are looking for them you overhear a conversation between a salesman and a customer.

Salesman:	Kann ich Ihnen helfen?
Customer:	Sorry, I don't speak German. Do you speak English?
Salesman:	Nein, kein Wort.

You hear this and decide to help.

You:	Hallo. Kann ich Ihnen helfen? Ich spreche Englisch.
Salesman:	Können Sie sie fragen, ob ich ihr helfen kann?
You:	_____
Customer:	Yes, great. I am looking for a pair of jeans.
You:	Sie sucht eine Jeans.
Salesman:	Möchte sie eine bestimmte Marke?
You:	_____
Customer:	No, I don't care.
You:	Die Marke ist ihr egal.
Salesman:	Welche Größe hat sie und welche Farbe möchte sie?
You:	_____
Customer:	I take size 29 waist and 30 inch inseam. I would like dark blue jeans.
You:	Sie hat die Größe 29/30 und sie möchte eine dunkelblaue Jeans.
Salesman:	Wir haben Jeans in dieser Größe und Farbe von Lovis oder Hers im Angebot für 75 Euro.
You:	_____
	_____
Customer:	I will take the Lovis. Thank you for your help.
You:	Sie nimmt die Lovis und dankt Ihnen für Ihre Hilfe.

Lösungshilfen

Bei dieser Aufgabe musst du Sätze auf Englisch in einen Dialog einsetzen und ihn vervollständigen. Achte auf die Hinweise im Dialog, denn sie können dir bei der Lösung helfen. Der erste Satz ist eine dir bekannte Redewendung und sollte dir keine Schwierigkeiten bereiten. Wenn du die unbekannten Vokabeln nachgeschlagen hast, solltest du auch bei der zweiten Frage keine Probleme haben. Die Vokabeln für die Größe und Farbe kannst du der Antwort der Kundin entnehmen. Im letzten Satz könnte nur die Kombination „im Angebot" ein Stolperstein sein, aber wenn du an die Werbeschilder in den deutschen Geschäften beim Schlussverkauf denkst, fällt dir die Redewendung bestimmt schnell ein.

Bereite dich wieder in kleinen Schritten auf die Aufgabe vor.
Lies dir die Aufgabe durch und notiere das Thema und die Situation.

_____

_____

Schreibe die Vokabeln, die du nicht kennst, in die folgende Tabelle und schlage sie im Wörterbuch nach:

German	English
bestimmte Marke	
Größe	
im Angebot	
	waist

Formuliere nun die fehlenden Sätze auf Englisch und setze sie in den Dialog ein.

D IV. Schreiben

Um dir das Verfassen eines Texts zu erleichtern, wirst du in diesem Kapitel in einzelnen Arbeitsschritten durch die Aufgaben geführt, die du bearbeiten sollst. Die Schritte helfen dir beim Fokussieren deiner Gedanken auf das Thema des Texts, beim Formulieren deiner Ideen und beim Überarbeiten deines Texts.

Bevor du dich an das Schreiben von Texten herantastest, sollst du im Folgenden einige Übungen bearbeiten, die dir helfen, von vornherein Fehler zu vermeiden und einen besseren Text zu schreiben.

INFO types of mistakes

1. grammar – Grammatikfehler (z. B. falsche Zeitform)
2. spelling – Rechtschreibfehler
3. punctuation – Zeichenfehler
4. word order – Wortstellung
5. vocabulary – Vokabelfehler (ein falsches Wort eingesetzt)

a) There are several **mistakes** (grammar, spelling, punctuation, word order, vocabulary) in the following text. Underline them and rewrite the sentences correctly.

Facts about Alaska

in 1945 was Juneau the capital of Alaska. In 1953 was found oil fields in alaska. The population of Alaska is 600,000. In 1959 was Alaska the 69 state of the USA. Alaska is the biggest State of the USA. On some days in Alaska it gave no daylight and on some days in Alaska it gave only daylight and no night. In 1867 buy the USA Alaska from Russia. In 1926 become Alaska a state flag

_____

_____

_____

_____

_____

_____

_____

b) Read the following text about a visit to a museum and fill in **connecting words** where necessary.

Last week I went to the museum of natural history.

_____ I am not really interested in museums

_____ I really liked this one. They had a map in

the entry hall _____ the tourists could find information

about the different exhibits and continents _____ you could

visit. We had a tour guide _____ he was not very good. He

always spoke in the same monotonous voice _____ he did not seem excited about the animals in the

museum. The different continents and their animals were really interesting, _____ some areas of the

museum were boring _____ you had to read a lot of information, _____ you could

also rent a pair of headphones. Instead of reading everything by yourself you could also walk _____

listening to the explanations on the tape. I really liked the dinosaurs best _____ there was a lot

of action, _____ was exciting. The dinosaurs moved and made noises _____ the

whole scene seemed real _____ scary. Some kids were at the controls, _____ were

easy to operate _____ you just had to move the lever up and down. _____ the adults

laughed, _____ the smaller kids were really scared_____ started crying. _____

I went to the restaurant _____ enjoyed a cup of coffee. _____ the souvenir

shop was very expensive, I bought a small dinosaur _____ I wanted to take home with me.

_____ visiting this museum was such a good idea and I had _____ such a good time, I will

go again.

> **TIPP** connecting words
>
> *after, also, although, and, because, besides, but, for, however, instead, in general, in short, moreover, or, on the other hand, otherwise, so, that, too, which, while, yet*

Nach diesen Vorübungen kannst du nun mit den Schreibaufgaben beginnen. In der Prüfung besteht diese Aufgabe aus mehreren Teilen. Aus diesem Grund findest du auch hier zwei Abschnitte: „Writing Part 1" und „Writing Part 2". Wie bei den anderen Aufgaben solltest du zunächst die Aufgabenstellung, den Text und die Lösungshilfen lesen, bevor du deinen Text schreibst.

Writing Part 1

AUFGABENSTELLUNG

Read the text and write an e-mail to the author of the article. Name arguments **for** and **against** digital learning tools and state **your own opinion** at the end of the e-mail. Write at least 130 words.

Lösungshilfen

In dieser Aufgabe sollst du Argumente und Gegenargumente zum Thema „Sind digitale Geräte gefährlich?" sammeln. Sicherlich hast du in den letzten Jahren von vielen Seiten gehört, dass digitale Medien nicht nur positiven Einfluss auf unser Leben haben. Die Coronapandemie hat dieses Problem verstärkt und so noch mehr Aufmerksamkeit auf dieses Thema gelenkt. Vielleicht hast du schon eigene Erfahrungen gemacht, dir eine eigene Meinung zu dem Thema gebildet und kannst auch ohne den Text Argumente finden. Stelle Überlegungen zur Nutzung von digitalen Medien an und male dir aus, wie dein Alltag ohne digitale Instrumente aussehen würde. Könntest du dir das vorstellen? Welche Nachteile würden für dich dadurch entstehen? Welche Vorteile siehst du? Denke daran, dass nicht nur die Menge der Argumente ausschlaggebend ist, sondern auch deine Darstellung, die du anhand von Beispielen und Zitaten aus dem Text untermauern kannst. Überlege dir, in welcher Zeitform du die E-Mail schreibst und verbinde deine Sätze mit *connecting words*. Anhand der Hinweise zur Überarbeitung deines Textes kannst du viele Fehler vermeiden. Nähere dich der Lösung der Aufgabe in Einzelschritten. Dann fällt es dir leichter, einen zusammenhängenden Text zu schreiben. Bevor du den Text liest, solltest du folgende Schritte erledigen.

Schritt 1: Orientiere dich! Lies dir die Aufgabenstellung zum Schreiben eines Texts genau durch und unterstreiche wichtige Hinweise.

Schritt 2: Gib mit eigenen Worten wieder, was du tun sollst.

_____

_____

_____

TIPP Schritt 1: sich orientieren

1. Lies die Aufgabenstellung genau durch.
2. Unterstreiche die wichtigsten Hinweise auf das, was du in der Aufgabe tun sollst.
3. Überlege dir, worum es in dem Text geht und was dir die Überschrift verrät!

Schritt 3: Notiere stichpunktartig, was dir die Überschrift verrät. Wovon könnte der Text handeln?

_____

_____

Erst nach diesen Schritten solltest du den Text lesen.

Are digital tools dangerous? A study

The lives of many children and teenagers are influenced more and more by new technological devices[1], including smartphones and tablets. The coronavirus pandemic happened in a time of vast[2] scientific progress[3] and global digitalization. The infection control measures[4] that were implemented[5] in many countries had psychological and behavioral[6] effects on teenagers. Children 5 and teenagers had to stay at home, schools and day care centres were closed. This led to spending more time with and using technological tools. The goal of this study is to look at health and social outcomes of smartphone overuse among children and teenagers during the COVID-19 pandemic. It analyzes patterns[7] and reasons for using digital tools, as well as the eventual presence 10 and degree of addiction[8] to digital devices.

184 school-age (6 – 18 years) children and teenagers anonymously answered questions during the second wave of the COVID-19 pandemic. The test was electronically (email, WhatsApp) explained and sent by their doctors either directly to older children (middle and high school), or indirectly, through the 15 help of teachers, to younger ones (primary school). [...] The questions asked information about the frequency[9] and reasons for smartphone use. The answers also included parental behaviour and showed the eventual occurrence[10] and degree of addiction.

[...] The study showed more frequent smartphone use among children and 20 teenagers during the COVID-19 pandemic, compared to the pre-epidemic period. This may be related to the social distancing[11] measures implemented during the months of the pandemic. The present survey also showed the changing patterns and reasons for the use of smartphones among young people. Smartphones were used for social contacts, learning and entertainment. 25 Finally, a significant increase of overuse and addiction was noted. This led to many health and social problems (not enough sleep, bad eating habits, weight gain, no exercise, social isolation, loss of hobbies, bad grades in school). Doctors, teachers and parents should recognize the risks related to inappropriate[12] overuse of smartphones. They should pay attention to the possible 30 negative effects, in order to notice early signs and symptoms that may lead to addiction. They must avoid these effects by preventing and/or lowering the huge impact of smartphone overuse on children and teenagers' health. Parents should make sure that their children keep up a daily routine (regular study hour, time for TV etc.), exercise regularly during the day, keep in touch 35 with their friends and spend time listening to music, playing real games or reading books.*

Annotations:
1 **device** – Gerät, 2 **vast** – riesig, 3 **progress** – Fortschritt,
4 **infection control measure** – Maßnahme zur Infektionskontrolle, 5 **implemented** – eingeführt,
6 **behavioral** – Verhaltens-, 7 **pattern** – Muster, 8 **addiction** – Abhängigkeit,
9 **frequency** – Häufigkeit, 10 **occurrence** – Auftreten, 11 **social distancing** – Kontaktreduzierung,
12 **inappropriate** – unangemessen

Source: adapted from https://ijponline.biomedcentral.com/articles/10.1186/s13052-021-01102-8

Lösungshilfen

Schritt 4: Lies dir den Text durch und unterstreiche wichtige Textstellen. Nutze unterschiedliche Farben für Argumente dafür (grün) und dagegen (rot). Schreibe unbekannte Wörter in die Tabelle und schlage sie wenn notwendig im Wörterbuch nach.

Englisch	German

Schritt 5: Schreibe Argumente und Gegenargumente zum Thema in die folgende Tabelle. Versuche, unterschiedliche Perspektiven zum Thema zu berücksichtigen. Versetze dich in die Rolle von Eltern und Lehrern hinein, die die Gefahr einer Abhängigkeit von digitalen Geräten erkennen und dies verhindern wollen.

arguments for digital tools	arguments against digital tools

Schritt 6: Notiere Zitate aus dem Text, die du für deine E-Mail benutzen möchtest.

_____

_____

_____

Schritt 7: Schreibe deine eigene Meinung in Sätzen. Beginne mit der Redewendung: *In my opinion, …*

_____

_____

_____

Gliederungspunkte	Formulierungshilfen
1. Bezug auf den vorliegenden Text mit kurzer Angabe zum Inhalt	*I've read your article in which …* *In your article "…" it says that …/you report that…/ you refer to the problem that …*

2. in einem Absatz Argumente dafür formulieren, in einem zweiten Absatz Gegenargumente zum Ausdruck bringen	*I agree … with …* *An argument for …/against …* *I disagree … for the following reasons …* *It may be true that …, but …*
3. eigene Meinung äußern und begründen	*In my opinion, …* *I believe that …* *I think that …*

Schritt 8: Schreibe deine E-Mail in das folgende Feld. Vergleiche deinen Text nach der Überarbeitung mit dem Beispiel im Lösungsheft.

To:	*jsmith@yahoo.com*	︿
From:		
Subject:		

Dear Mrs Smith,

Number of words: _____

1. **Text inhaltlich überprüfen:**
   - Sind deine Sätze vollständig?
   - Wurden in deinem Text alle Teile der Aufgabenstellung berücksichtigt?
   - Hast du deine Argumente und Gegenargumente in einem eigenen Absatz formuliert?
   - Hast du Zitate zur Verstärkung deiner Argumente in deinen Text eingebaut?
   - Wird deine eigene Meinung am Ende der E-Mail deutlich?
   - Stimmt die Zeichensetzung?
   - Hast du die formalen Vorgaben für die E-Mail eingehalten?
   - Überprüfe deine Verben: Stehen sie in der richtigen Zeitform?
2. **Text sprachlich überarbeiten:**
   - Hast du unnötige Wiederholungen vermieden?
   - An welchen Stellen kannst du Verbindungswörter einsetzen, um zwei Sätze miteinander zu verbinden?
   - Hast du unterschiedliche Satzanfänge gewählt?
3. **Die Rechtschreibung überprüfen:**
   - Welche Wörter musst du nachschlagen?
   - Achte auf Flüchtigkeitsfehler (unvollständige Wörter, Buchstabendreher etc.).

Writing Part 2

Auch bei der zweiten Form der Schreibaufgabe solltest du in kleinen Schritten vorgehen und die Lösungshilfen beachten, bevor du den Text verfasst.

AUFGABENSTELLUNG

An invitation

A new fast-food restaurant is going to open in your hometown. You would love to go and be one of the first people in your class to try the food. You want to invite the exchange student from the USA who is in your class. Her name is Heather. Write an invitation to her.

- Invite her to come with you.
- Tell her what restaurant you want to go to and why.
- Suggest a good place and time to meet.
- Write about 60 – 70 words. Count them at the end.

Lösungshilfen

Bei dieser Aufgabe handelt es sich um die Textsorte Einladung. Sie hat Ähnlichkeit mit einem informellen Brief (s. S. 45), doch lässt man die Adressen weg. Die Anrede und Schlussformel bleibt bestehen. Die Notizen zu den einzelnen Teilen der Aufgabe sollten dir helfen, deine Sätze zu formulieren.

Schritt 1: Lies dir die Aufgabenstellung genau durch und unterstreiche wichtige Hinweise.

Schritt 2: Gib mit eigenen Worten wieder, was du tun sollst.

_____

_____

Schritt 3: Notiere stichpunktartig, was dir die Überschrift verrät.

_____

_____

Schritt 4: Mache dir Notizen zu den einzelnen Teilaufgaben. Schreibe bestimmte Redewendungen (Deutsch oder Englisch) auf, die du verwenden willst und schlage sie wenn nötig nach.

Invite her to come.

_____

_____

Tell her what restaurant you want to go to and why.

_____

_____

Suggest a good place and time to meet.

_____

_____

Schritt 5: Formuliere nun deine Notizen um und schreibe die Einladung.

> ✎ **Invitation** ✎

Writing Part 3 – A diary entry

Last month Sharon had an exciting weekend. She visited her friend Kristina in Berlin. Sharon wrote in her diary during her visit.

- Write Sharon's diary entry for Saturday and Sunday. Use the words in the box below.
- Write about 80 words on a separate sheet of paper. Use the simple past.

Saturday: cloudy weather / visit Museum of Natural History / see dinosaurs / shopping / new T-shirt / coffee at a music café / meet famous actor	**Sunday:** get up late / walk in the park / eat fast food / cinema / exciting film / train back home / nice dinner with family / talk / very tired / go to bed late

Number of words: _____

Lösungshilfen

In dieser Aufgabe sollst du einen Tagebucheintrag schreiben. Dieses Aufgabenformat gehört in Teilen zu „reports and articles", denn auch im Tagebuch berichtet der Erzähler über Dinge, die in der Vergangenheit geschehen und bereits abgeschlossen sind. Daher schreibt man einen solchen Text im *simple past*. Im Vergleich zu einem Zeitungsartikel oder Bericht ist ein Eintrag in ein Tagebuch jedoch ein sehr persönlicher Text, der neben den Tatsachen auch eigene Eindrücke und Gefühle enthält. Vielleicht ist dir das Schreiben in ein Tagebuch vertraut oder du kannst dich in eine Person hineinversetzen, die die gemachten Erfahrungen und Erlebnisse eines aufregenden Tages berichtet.

Lies die Aufgabenstellung genau durch und unterstreiche wichtige Hinweise. Gib mit eigenen Worten wieder, das du tun sollst.

In den Kästchen stehen bereits Informationen zu den beiden Tagen, die du benutzen sollst. Mit diesen Satzteilen kannst du kurze und einfache Sätze bilden und sie mit *connecting words (and, but, or, when, because)* und Wörtern, die eine Reihenfolge ausdrücken *(later, first, then, after, next, before, when)* anordnen.

Wichtig sind die persönlichen Kommentare von Sharon, die man anhand von Adjektiven *(great, wonderful, perfect, good, bad, awful, terrible)* und Verben *(like, love, hate, enjoy)* ausdrücken kann.
Schreibe zwei oder drei positive oder negative Eindrücke auf.

Example: I really **loved** the museum. It was very **interesting.**

Formuliere nun den Tagebucheintrag und nutze die Tipps aus den Lösungshilfen.

CHECKLISTE nach der Bearbeitung der Aufgaben Teil D

Aufgabe	Zeit	Was hat mir geholfen?	Fehlerquellen
Hörübung Part 1 Subjects			
Hörübung Part 2 Interview			
Hörübung Part 3 Internet bullying			
Hörübung Part 4 Internet bullying			
Leseübung Part 1 Festivals			
Leseübung Part 2 Tourist attractions			
Leseübung Part 3 Clothes Part 1			
Leseübung Part 4 Clothes Part 2			
Mediation Part 1 Post offices			
Mediation Part 2 Dialogue			
Writing Part 1 E-mail			
Writing Part 2 Invitation			
Writing Part 3 A diary entry			

Nun hast du eine ganze Prüfungsaufgabe geschafft. In Teil E findest du Aufgaben zum selbstständigen Üben. Es gibt weniger Lösungshilfen, denn du fühlst dich bestimmt schon viel sicherer.

Teil E Aufgaben zum selbstständigen Üben – mit Hilfestellung

In diesem Kapitel findest du wieder Aufgaben zu den Bereichen Hörverstehen, Leseverstehen, Sprachmittlung und Schreiben. Dieses Mal gibt es aber weniger Lösungshilfen, denn du sollst ja immer selbstständiger arbeiten. Hier findest du eine Prüfung, die genauso lang ist wie die Originalprüfung.

TIPP Vorbereitung

1. Such dir einen ruhigen Arbeitsplatz, an dem du ungestört arbeiten kannst.
2. Du benötigst mindestens 25 Minuten für die vier Höraufgaben. Es ist sinnvoll, alle vier Aufgaben nacheinander zu bearbeiten, da dies die Prüfungssituation simuliert.
3. Starte die Audio-Dateien auf www.finaleonline.de und folge den Anweisungen in den Aufgaben.

E I. Hörverstehen

TIPP one – two – three

1. Lies die Aufgabenstellung und Erläuterungen genau durch. Um welches Thema bzw. um welche Situation geht es?
2. Welche Informationen werden im Text erfragt (Zahlen, Uhrzeit, Geldbetrag)?
3. Überlege, welche Wörter und Vokabeln dir bei dieser Aufgabe/Frage/diesem Bild einfallen?

TIPP beim Hören

1. Lass dich durch das Thema des Hörtexts, die Geschwindigkeit, die Vokabeln oder die Aussprache nicht aus der Ruhe bringen.
2. **Bleib ruhig** und konzentriert bei der Sache.

Part 1 – Questions 1 – 6

 Track 8

AUFGABENSTELLUNG

- You will hear six short conversations or texts.
- There is one question for each conversation or text.
- For questions 1–6, put a tick under the right answer.

1. What job does Peter do?

A ☐

B ☐

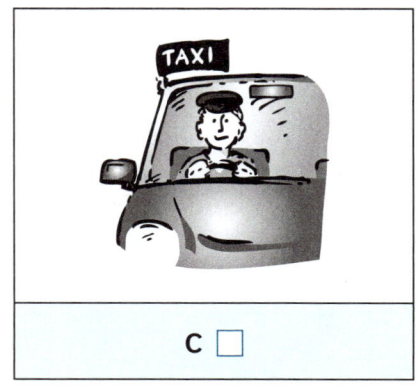

C ☐

2. What pet does Mary get?

A ☐

B ☐

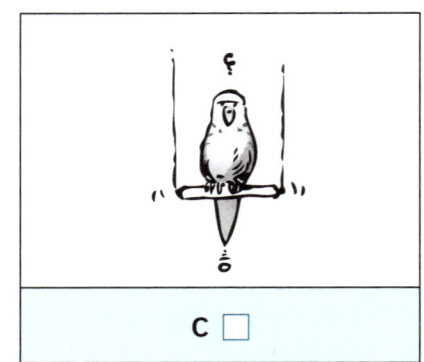

C ☐

3. What type of sports does Mike do in his free time?

A ☐

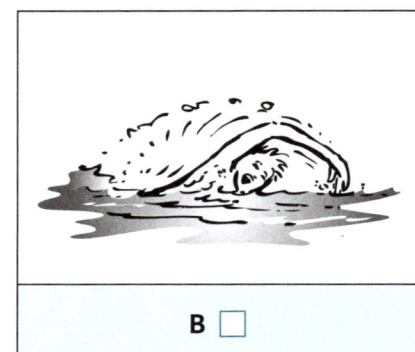

B ☐

C ☐

4. How much does she pay for the jeans?

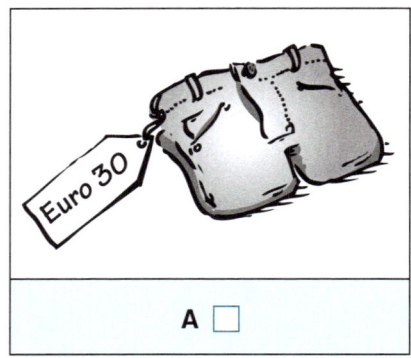

A ☐

B ☐

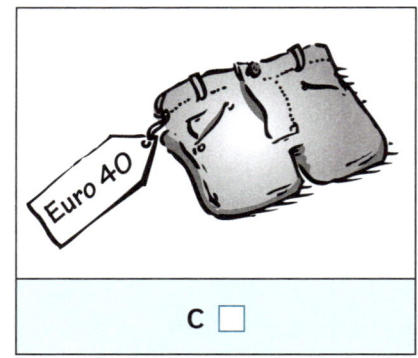

C ☐

5. When does his flight leave from Chicago?

A ☐

B ☐

C ☐

6. Which body part did Linda hurt in her accident?

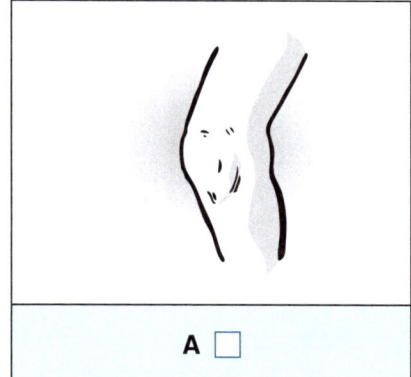

A ☐

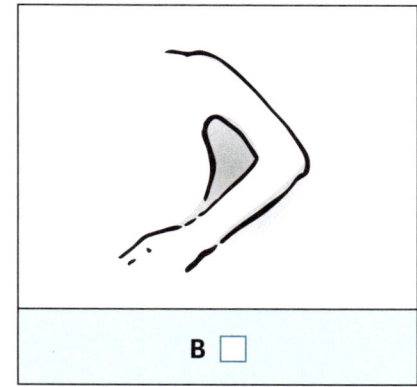

B ☐

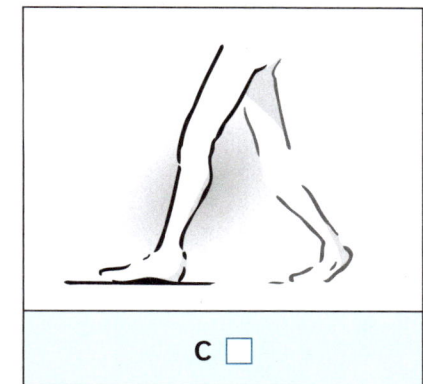

C ☐

Die Situationen, die dir in den Höraufgaben Part 1 bis Part 4 präsentiert werden, sind alle eindeutig und sollten dir daher keine Schwierigkeiten bereiten. Befolge die einzelnen Arbeitsschritte, die du in Teil C kennengelernt hast (S. 23) und überlege sehr genau, welche Informationen du heraushören musst. Die Akzente der Sprecher sind unterschiedlich. Lass dich dadurch nicht verwirren. Konzentriere dich auf den Inhalt und die zur Auswahl stehenden Bilder oder Antwortmöglichkeiten.

Part 1 – Questions 7 – 12

 Track 9

AUFGABENSTELLUNG

- Listen to Tim and Jeff talk about their dream jobs.
- For questions 7–12 tick A, B or C.

7. Tim wants to be a fisherman, because	A	he likes fish.	☐
	B	he likes the ocean.	☐
	C	he can't swim.	☐

8. To be a fisherman is dangerous, because	A	you can hook yourself.	☐
	B	of bad weather.	☐
	C	seamonsters might eat you.	☐

9. Jeff wants to be a writer, because	A	you make a lot of money.	☐
	B	it's an exciting job.	☐
	C	you can write anywhere you like.	☐

10. Tim thinks fire is dangerous, because	A	it's hot.	☐
	B	it's boring.	☐
	C	people are careless.	☐

11. Tim likes working	A	in a team.	☐
	B	indoors.	☐
	C	at night.	☐

12. Jeff wants to be an astronaut, because	A	they are famous.	☐
	B	he wants to go to the moon.	☐
	C	he likes the food.	☐

Part 3 – Questions 13–18

 **Track 10**

AUFGABENSTELLUNG

- You will hear an engineer talking about a bridge he has built.
- Listen and complete questions 13–18.

13. location of the bridge _____

14. construction began _____

15. construction ended _____

16. bridge crosses river _____

17. the bridge's span _____

18. height above water _____

Part 4 – Questions 19–23

 **Track 11**

- Listen to Heidi talking about her school in Mongolia.
- Listen and answer questions 19–23.
- Decide whether each sentence is true or false. Put a tick in the correct box "true" or "false".

	true	false
19. In Mongolia school is split into three different types like in Germany.	☐	☐
20. A typical class lasts 45 minutes.	☐	☐
21 School starts at 9 a.m.	☐	☐
22. The elementary school has classes in the afternoon.	☐	☐
23. Sometimes teachers have to teach both levels – elementary and secondary school.	☐	☐

E II. Leseverstehen

Part 1 – Questions 1–5

- Read the short texts about sights in Washington DC. Then answer questions 1–5 below.
- For each question, tick the correct answer.

Arlington Cemetery: Arlington National Cemetery is the largest military cemetery in the United States of America. More than 400,000 soldiers who died fighting for their country (in the USA they are called veterans – people who worked as soldiers in the Army, the Navy or the Air Force) are buried
5 here. You can find really old graves from the American Civil War (1861–1865), the First World War (1914–1918), the Second World war (1939–1945) and other conflicts. There are about 30 funerals every weekday. It is a popular tourist attraction. It is open to the public 365 days a year, and you can see the Tomb of the Unknown Soldier and the J.F. Kennedy Eternal Flame.

10 **Dulles International Airport:** This airport serving the capital city of Washington is located 26 miles west of Washington outside the city. There are many popular airlines at this airport like Aer Lingus, Air France, American Airlines, British Airways, Delta Air Lines and many more offering a full range of domestic and international flights. You can get to the airport with your
15 choice of ground transportation like taxis, rental cars, shared ride van service

and bus service. If you want to take your own car, there are several parking lots for short and long term parking. Check the airport webpage for prices.

Lincoln Memorial: You can find the Lincoln Memorial in downtown Washington DC near the Reflecting Pool, a big square pond at the end of the National Mall. The best way to see the memorial is from the east, by the Washington 20 Monument and the National World War II Memorial. The Lincoln Memorial honours President Abraham Lincoln, the 16th United States president. He fought the Civil War against the Southern States to end slavery. In the middle of the memorial is a huge statue of Abraham Lincoln in a sitting position. You can find his famous Gettysburg Address inscribed in the south wall of the 25 Memorial. The Lincoln Memorial is open for visitors every day of the year, 24 hours a day.

The White House: This famous building has been the home of every U.S. president except George Washington. You can find it on Pennsylvania Avenue. The construction of the building began in October 1792 and was finished in 30 1800. The first president to live in the White House was John Adams. In 1902, President Theodore Roosevelt decided that the nickname for the house would now be its official name, the White House. If you want to tour the building you have to plan ahead and book a tour at least three months in advance. Security checks are standard, and you are not allowed to take anything into the White 35 House like food items, cameras or drinks. All White House tours are free.

Source: based on data from https://washington.org

	true	false
1. a) Dulles International Airport is located 35 miles outside of Washington DC. b) About 400,000 people are buried in Arlington.	☐ ☐	☐ ☐
2. a) The President of the United States lives in the White House. b) President Lincoln was against slavery.	☐ ☐	☐ ☐
3. a) From Dulles Airport you can fly to national and international locations. b) At Arlington you can see J. F. Kennedy's grave.	☐ ☐	☐ ☐
4. a) At Lincoln Memorial you can find his address to the slaves in the north wall. b) Visitors are not allowed in the White House at all.	☐ ☐	☐ ☐
5. a) The first president to live in the White House was George W. Bush. b) Abraham Lincoln was killed in the American Civil War.	☐ ☐	☐ ☐

Lösungshilfen

Die Aufgabenformen im Leseteil sind entsprechend den Abschlussarbeiten aus den letzten Jahren gewählt. Sie sind dir schon aus den vorangegangenen Kapiteln bekannt. Das gibt dir Sicherheit im Umgang mit dem Format der Aufgaben. Arbeite ruhig und konzentriert, lies dir alle Ankreuzmöglichkeiten genau durch und unterstreiche anschließend die entsprechenden Informationen dazu im Text. So kannst du im Part 2 zum Beispiel die Vorlieben von Meike, Max, Jenny, Marc und Peter unterstreichen und so die folgenden Texte *(job offers)* leicht zuordnen.

Part 2 – Questions 6–10

AUFGABENSTELLUNG

- Decide which job offer (A–G) would be the most suitable for the people below (6–10).
- Write the correct letters behind the numbers.

6. Meike, Germany Oh, I would love to work in a big city. I would love to help people in need or take care of animals. I am good at foreign languages and maybe that could help me in my job, too. I know that in the USA there are many people from different countries.	☐
7. Max, Austria I am really good at building or repairing things. I would love to participate in an environmental project, because I think it is very important to do something for nature and animals. I hate cold weather, though, so I would like to work somewhere warm and sunny.	☐
8. Jenny, Belgium I love kids, so working with them would be a lot of fun. I have a small group of girls I work with in my sports club here at home, but I really want to help kids and make a difference in their lives. I really don't care about the location. I just want to work in another country.	☐
9. Marc, France I am an outdoor kind of guy. I love skiing, hiking and all other activities that you can do in the mountains. For me an activity in the mountains would be perfect. I have heard a lot about the National Parks in the USA and would really like to learn more about the park system.	☐
10. Peter, Poland I like animals. I have done volunteer work in a zoo and I learned a lot about exotic animals from other countries. I took care of animals that were hurt and also worked with school classes. I showed the kids around and explained details about the animals to them. That was a lot of fun. I would like to do something like that again.	☐

A

California Conservation With this job you can work on two different projects in the Golden State of California. You will get involved in activities such as planting new trees, trail reconstruction, building renovation and flood prevention. If you like to work in a group of young people and like the sunny weather, apply for this location.

B

Rebuild New Orleans Here you can really help repair some of the damage caused by Hurricane Katrina. We will all help rebuild homes and public buildings and roads in New Orleans. You don't need any special experience. We have experts that will show you what to do. Come and bring the music back to this place.

C

Florida Wildlife Sanctuary Here you can help care for all kinds of animals that have been abandoned by their owners. You will work with leopards, bears and wolves for example, but also with birds, lizards and snakes. You should like animals and feel comfortable around them. You will live near the place where the animals are kept, but also close to beaches and the Everglades National Park.

D

Island Wildlife Protection Program A lot of tourists are unaware of the threat that they pose to the local animals. We want to educate them to make coexistence possible. You will learn about the living conditions and daily routine of all the island animals like alligators, deer etc. and do information workshops for the tourists who come to stay on these islands.

E

Appalachian Trail conservation The Appalachian Trail is used by millions of hikers every year. You will walk the trail with a group of people and make necessary repairs to signs or trails and do clean-up if necessary. You will sleep in tents or little cottages along the way. You should have hiking experience, be physically fit and like the outdoors.

F

Colorado Conservation You can help protect some of Colorado's most beautiful lakes, mountains and national parks. You will build stone walls and create trails that won't spoil the scenery, you will do water testing to ensure the quality and protect the fish. At night you will camp under the stars and enjoy nature.

G

Daycamp for kids You will work with kids who come from different ethnic backgrounds. Most of them come from families that speak a different language at home. The kids will learn English in the morning and do fun activities in the afternoon. You will be a counselor for the kids, organize activities and make them feel comfortable.

Part 3 – Questions 11–17

AUFGABENSTELLUNG

- Read the text, then look at the statements.
- For each statement tick the correct answer: "true" or "false" and give the line/lines in which you find the information.
- For a correct answer you must fill in both: true or false and the line(s).

Ellis Island – History

From 1892 to 1954, over twelve million immigrants entered the United States through the portal of Ellis Island, a small island in New York Harbor. Ellis Island is located in the upper bay just off the New Jersey coast, within the shadow of the Statue of Liberty. Through the years, this gateway to the New
5 World was enlarged from its original 3.3 acres to 27.5 acres.
Before being designated as the site of the first federal immigration station by President Benjamin Harrison in 1890, Ellis Island had a varied history. The local Indian tribes had called it "Kioshk" or Gull Island. Due to its rich and abundant oyster beds and plentiful and profitable shad runs, it was
10 known as Oyster Island for many generations during the Dutch and English colonial periods. By the time Samuel Ellis became the island's private owner in the 1770s, the island had been called Kioshk, Oyster, Dyre, Bucking and Anderson's Island.

Prior to 1890, the individual states regulated immigration into the United States. Castle Garden in the Battery served as the New York State immigration 15 station from 1855 to 1890 and approximately eight million immigrants, mostly from Northern and Western Europe, passed through its doors. These early immigrants came from nations such as England, Ireland, Germany and the Scandinavian countries and constituted the first large wave of immigrants that settled and populated the United States. Throughout the 1800s and in- 20 tensifying in the latter half of the 19th century, political instability, restrictive religious laws and deteriorating economic conditions in Europe began to fuel the largest mass human migration in the history of the world. It soon became apparent that Castle Garden was unprepared to handle the growing numbers of immigrants arriving yearly. 25

The federal government intervened and constructed a new federally-operated immigration station on Ellis Island. The new structure on Ellis Island, built of "Georgia pine" opened on January 1, 1892; Annie Moore, a 15 year-old Irish girl, accompanied by her two brothers entered history and a new country, as she was the very first immigrant to be processed at Ellis Island on January 30 2. Over the next 62 years, more than 12 million were to follow through this port of entry.

While there were many reasons to emigrate to America, no reason could be found for what would occur only five years after the Ellis Island Immigration Station opened. During the evening of June 14, 1897, a fire on Ellis 35 Island, burned the immigration station completely to the ground. Although no lives were lost, many years of federal and state immigration records dating back to 1855 burned along with the pine buildings that failed to protect them. The United States Treasury quickly ordered the immigration facility to be replaced under one very important condition. All future structures built on 40 Ellis Island had to be fireproof. On December 17, 1900, the new Main Building was opened and 2,251 immigrants were received that day.

	true	false	line(s)
11. Ellis Island is located in New Jersey near the Statue of Liberty.	☐	☐	_____
12. Ellis Island was known as Oyster Island because the flag had an oyster on it.	☐	☐	_____
13 Castle Garden was the immigration station in New York from 1890 to 1930.	☐	☐	_____
14. The immigrants came to America for reasons such as political instability in their own countries.	☐	☐	_____
15. The new facility on Ellis Island was built because the numbers of immigrants increased.	☐	☐	_____
16. The fire in 1897 was small and was put out quickly.	☐	☐	_____
17. After the fire the buildings on Ellis Island were constructed to withstand fire.	☐	☐	_____

Part 4 – Questions 18–24

Find out which words are missing in the text. Tick the correct word A, B, C or D in the grid below.

The Botanical Garden at Edinburgh

History

Edinburgh Botanical Garden was (18) ... in 1670 at St. Anne's Yard, near Holyrood Palace. It is the second oldest botanical garden in Britain after Oxford's. The first plant collection used as the basis of the garden was a private one which was (19) ... by a second collection of eight or nine hundred plants. The
5 original place for the garden proved too small. In 1676 grounds belonging to Trinity Hospital were leased from the City Council: this second garden was sited just to the east, down from the High Street. In the early 1820s the garden moved west to its present (20) ... next to Inverleith Row. The Palm House, which remains the tallest in Britain, was built in 1858. The Botanical Garden's
10 main site in Edinburgh is a very important player in a worldwide network of institutions trying to make sure that biodiversity is preserved. Located one mile from the city centre it covers 70 acres (28 ha). The Royal Botanical Garden of the City of Edinburgh is actively involved in and coordinates numerous (21) ... both in the UK and internationally. The three main important themes
15 of scientific work are: Scottish biodiversity, plants and climate change.
The Royal Botanical Garden of Edinburgh is a place where you can look at and study plants and see their diversity. It is a (22) ... tourist attraction in the beautiful city of Edinburgh. It is about 350 years old and was intended as a garden for growing medicinal plants. Today it is a place of peace, quiet and
20 relaxation. Tourists come here to see the delicate (23) ... and enjoy the collection of plants which consists of more than 13,302 species. You can bring your own food and have a picnic or eat in the local restaurants and try (24) Scottish dishes. The large garden, which opens daily at 10a.m. and closes at 4 p.m., is a green oasis much like Central Park in New York City. Tourists can visit
25 ten glass houses with more than 3000 exotic plants from all over the world. You can also visit the Botanical Cottage and the library. The view of the city of Edinburgh from the garden grounds is magnificent just like the colourful flowers you can see in the garden.

18.	A found	B founded	C find	D has found
19.	A met	B calculated	C cleaned	D enlarged
20	A location	B tense	C gift	D past
21.	A numbers	B figures	C projects	D triangles
22.	A popular	B expensive	C difficult	D cool
23.	A streets	B chocolate	C stones	D flowers
24.	A similar	B typical	C physical	D cooking

E III. Mediation (Sprachmittlung)

Part 1

What do these signs mean? Write on a separate sheet of paper.

1

2

3

Lösungshilfen

Mediation bedeutet nicht, dass du die Texte wortwörtlich übersetzt. Du musst sie in die andere Sprache übertragen, also die Bedeutung wiedergeben. Verschwende nicht zu viel Zeit mit dem Nachschlagen vieler Vokabeln. Versuche, sie aus dem Kontext zu erschließen. Du solltest die Informationen so kurz wie möglich zusammenfassen. Ganze Sätze sind nicht notwendig – du kannst auch kurze Stichworte schreiben.

Part 2 – Eine neue Sportart: Discgolf in Berlin

AUFGABENSTELLUNG

The American exchange student in your class, Sam, has been at your school for three weeks. He is very interested in all types of sports, especially new ones. He has found information about discgolf online. His German is not that good yet, so he asks you for help. You answer his questions.

Bist du gerne an der frischen Luft und bewegst dich? Dann ist Discgolf vielleicht genau das Richtige für dich. Wir sind immer auf der Suche nach neuen Mitgliedern für unseren Verein. Also, komm vorbei und probiere diese tolle Sportart aus. Was ist dabei wichtig? Du solltest einen Frisbee zielsicher werfen können. Eine gute Wurftechnik erleichtert den Einstieg, aber natürlich trainieren wir das mit dir intensiv, sodass du immer besser wirst.

5

Was ist Discgolf denn eigentlich?

Discgolf ist ein Frisbeesportspiel, bei dem versucht wird, von einem festgelegten Abwurfpunkt (Tee) mit möglichst wenigen Würfen des Frisbees Körbe zu treffen. Es wird nach den gleichen Regeln wie im Golfsport gespielt. Im Discgolf wird kein Ball geschlagen, sondern ein Frisbee geworfen. Wer am Ende die wenigsten Würfe für den Kurs braucht (wie beim Golf spielt man auf 9 oder auf 18 Körbe), hat am Ende gewonnen. Man kann es als Einzel- oder Mannschaftssportart spielen. In unserem Verein können Männer, Frauen und auch Jugendliche trainieren, die Lust auf diese neue Sportart haben. Wir freuen uns sehr auf dich und werden dich in unserem Verein herzlich empfangen.

10

15

Schnuppertermin:

Wir bieten interessierten Menschen jeden Donnerstag ab 18 Uhr eine Einführung in das Discgolf an. Mitzubringen sind: bequeme Kleidung, Sportschuhe und Spaß. Die Frisbees bekommst du von uns. Bitte melde dich zum Schnuppertermin an, damit wir dich auch entsprechend begrüßen können. Wende dich telefonisch oder per E-Mail an:
Herrn Horst Meier
Tel: 030 / 152637
horst.meier@discgolf-verein-berlin.de

20

25

Trainingslager im Ausland:

Berühmte Golfplätze gibt es auf der ganzen Welt. Viele von diesen wurden inzwischen zusätzlich für das Discgolf umgerüstet. Wir suchen uns jedes Jahr einen neuen aus, organisieren die Reise dorthin und führen dort ein Trainingslager durch. Im letzten Sommer haben wir die 18 Körbe in St. Andrews in Schottland gespielt. In diesem Jahr soll es in den Süden gehen, in die Schweiz. Dort gibt es einen Golfplatz in den Bergen, den wir bespielen wollen. Dort findet ein Freundschaftsturnier mit einigen Schweizer Vereinen statt.

30

Sam: I've found this internet webpage about discgolf. It sounds really interesting. I've never heard about this type of sport before. Can you tell me how you play this game?

You (1):   _____

              _____

Sam: That sounds cool. Who can play in this club?

You (2):   _____

              _____

Sam: Sam: What do I need to bring?

You (3):   _____

              _____

Sam: Do they do any other activities?

You (4):   _____

              _____

Sam: How do I sign up? ?

You (5):   _____

              _____

You: Do you want me to contact the club?

Sam: Yeah, that would be great. Can you ask how long the sessions are and where they meet? My host parents want me to be home at 9 p.m. My family only has one car so they might not be able to drive me there or pick me up depending on how far it is. So I also need to know about public transportation. Can I get there by subway or bus?

You: I'll write a short email to Horst Meier and find out for you
          Du schreibst Horst Meier vom Discgolf-Verein eine kurze E-Mail:

          Sehr geehrter Herr Meier, ich habe einige Fragen zum Discgolf-Verein: _____

          _____

          _____

          _____

          Vielen Dank für Ihre Antwort. Mit freundlichen Grüßen _____

E IV. Schreiben

Part 1 – Change of perspective

AUFGABENSTELLUNG

Read the following blog about "Trunk or treat" and imagine you are Ben (32). Write a blog entry
(100 words) explaining the different arguments for and against it. Give your own opinion at the end.
The phrases in the box on p. 54 can help you.
Write down all the ideas on arguments for and against "trunk or treat" in the following table.
You can add your own ideas if you want.

Arguments for "trunk or treat"	Arguments against "trunk or treat"
– easy for parents, don't have to walk around the neighborhood	– not really typical of Halloween
– safe for kids – no traffic	

Trunk or treat – What is it?

At Halloween, children in the US and Great Britain traditionally dress up
in costumes and walk around their neighborhood. They knock on doors of
houses and say "Trick or treat". The door opens and the kids get candy from
all their neighbors. Trunk or treat is a new idea for children who live in small
5 villages or busy neighborhoods. People park their cars in a school or church
parking lot[1] and decorate the trunk. Children go from car to car and get candy.

Here are some different opinions:
Steven (35) writes: "I live in a small town in Iowa. My tea shop is on Main Street
downtown. For Halloween the police close the road to traffic in the evening.
10 People can then park their cars in two rows, one on each side of Main Street.
All the people here get really excited about decorating their trunk. There are
trunks decorated with pumpkins, spiders and ghosts. The kids walk from car
to car and get candy. It's like a Halloween party for everybody in Main Street.
There's food, music for the parents and candy for the kids. It's safe and it's
15 also a chance for everybody to meet. This new idea brings people together
in our community."
Dana (24) thinks: "There are no sidewalks in my neighborhood so you are right
out there in traffic, which is really dangerous. Trunk-or-treating here started
at some local churches and schools where people know and trust each other. I
20 think a mother heard about it from a friend and liked the idea, so she suggested
it to her church. It's a safe way for kids of all ages to get candy and have fun."
Michelle (29), however, says: "I really don't understand how people can say
that trunk or treat is a great idea. It's simply boring to walk around a parking

lot and get candy. Parents could just go and buy candy for their kids. That is basically the same thing. Parents are just lazy. They don't want to walk around and spend time with their kids. Yes, some neighborhoods are dangerous, but in a normal town you get to know your neighbors. Then your kids can go trick and treating safely."

Phil (30) answers: "I disagree with Michelle. I have three kids and I am not too lazy to walk around with them. The problem is that our next-door neighbor lives two miles down the road. We live in a nice house in a small village but the walk from one house to the next in the dark is really scary."

Sarah (13) adds: "I love trick-or-treating for Halloween. It's so cool to walk from one house to the next, knock on doors, do tricks and get candy. Two years ago, we moved to a big city. We tried to do trick or treat last year but it was too dangerous. We have no sidewalks and the streets are really busy so our school organized trunk or treat which was OK."

Carol (71) has the last word: "Well, Halloween really is about walking around the neighborhood, knocking on doors and getting candy. I think it's important for kids who are old enough to go out with their friends, dress up like adults and walk from door to door. These kinds of situation are a good test for adulthood. When they grow up, they have to make decisions for themselves. We can't protect them from everything."

Annotation: 1 parking lot – Parkplatz

Lösungshilfen

In dieser Aufgabe geht es um einen Perspektivenwechsel. Du sollst die Meinung von Ben vertreten. Notiere die Argumente der anderen Personen im Blog für und gegen „trunk or treat" in der Tabelle. Überlege anschließend, welche Meinung Ben vertritt. Im Text solltest du einen Absatz für „pro" und einen für „kontra" schreiben und am Ende Bens Meinung darstellen.

Part 2 – Writing an e-mail: couch surfing

AUFGABENSTELLUNG

Your best friend Sally from Manchester has just spent two weeks in Australia. She did not have a lot of money and did **"couch surfing"** (read explanation below this paragraph). In her last e-mail she wrote that couch surfing was just amazing. People in Australia opened their homes to her and offered her a place to stay for free. She met very interesting and nice people who showed her around in Melbourne and Adelaide. She made friends and wants to go back soon.

Couch surfing: Menschen aus anderen Ländern stellen im Internet ihre Wohnung oder eben ein Sofa zum Übernachten zur Verfügung. Als Reisender wählt man einen Zielort aus und kann sich per E-Mail anmelden und um Aufnahme bitten. Die Gastgeber suchen sich ihre Gäste im Internet aus und bieten ihnen eine kostenlose Bleibe bei sich an. Häufig entstehen Freundschaften.

- Write an e-mail to Sally, ask questions and give your opinion about couch surfing.
- Write about 75 words.

To:	Sallyp@xyz.com
From:	
Subject:	

_____

_____

_____

_____

_____

_____

_____

_____

_____

_____

_____

_____

_____

_____

Lösungshilfen

Achte bei der E-Mail auf die Aufgabenstellung. Überlege, welche Fragen du Sally stellen könntest und welche Meinung du in Bezug auf das „couch surfing" vertrittst. Begründe deine Meinung und schreibe, was dir daran gut und/oder nicht so gut gefällt.

Part 3 – Interpreting charts: charts about the coronavirus

AUFGABENSTELLUNG

Look at the following two charts. They give you information about "people vaccinated by age in Germany" (1) and opinions against vaccination in the general population (2). Look again at p. 55, "Interpreting tables and charts". Use the words and phrases and write a text for each chart on a separate sheet of paper – 60 – 80 words.

1 Vaccinations[1] defined by age groups

(8th of January 2022)

Germany

age group	one vaccination	two vaccinations	booster
age 12–17	60.8%	54.3%	8.5%
age 18–59	77.8%	79.8%	42.0%
age over 60	88.3%	87.4%	65.3%

Bavaria

age group	one vaccination	two vaccinations	booster
age 12–17	62.2%	55.6%	8.2
age 18–59	75.7%	78.7%	40.4%
age over 60	86.2%	85.4%	66.1%

Berlin

age group	one vaccination	two vaccinations	booster
age 12–17	60.1%	54.7%	9.3%
age 18–59	79.2%	80.7%	41.4%
age over 60	91,00%	90.3%	71.1%

Annotation:

1 vaccination – Impfung

Source: based on data from ZDFheute, Mainz, https://www.zdf.de/nachrichten/politik/corona-impfung-daten-100.html

2 Opinions about vaccination

Here are several reasons why people don't want to be vaccinated (%):

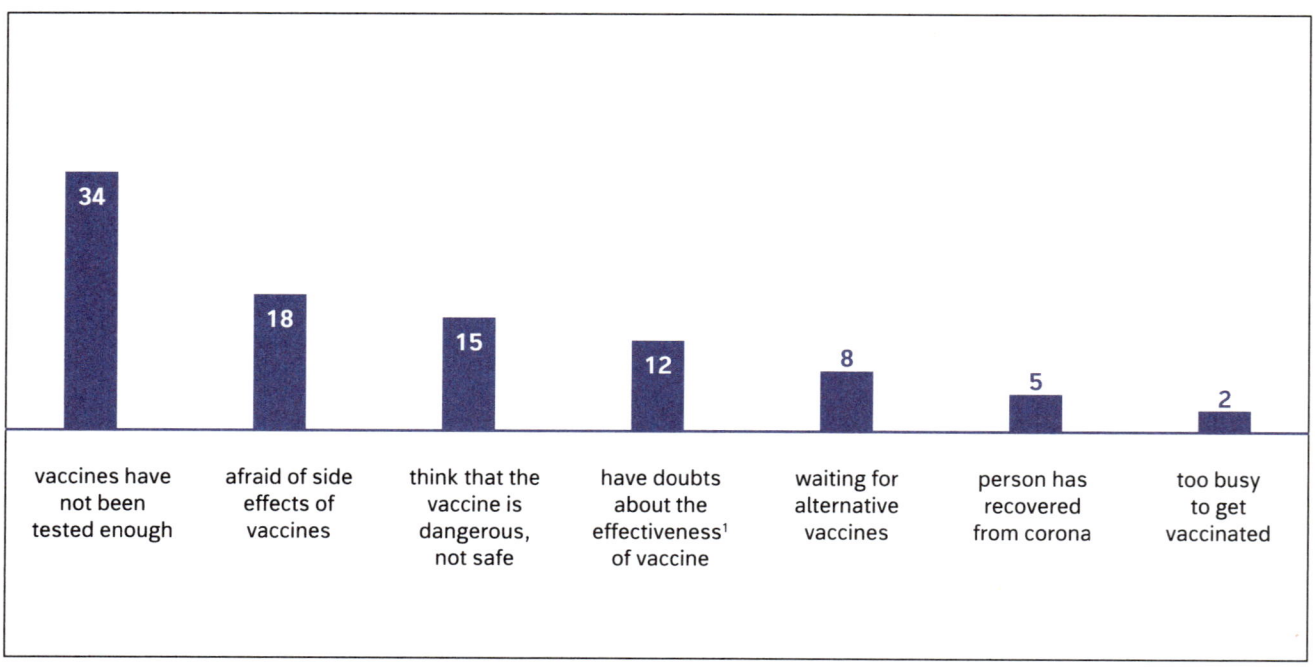

Annotation:
1 effectiveness – Wirksamkeit

Source: based on data from Impfdashboard, Robert Koch-Institut, https://www.bundesgesundheitsministerium.de/fileadmin/Dateien/3_
Downloads/C/Coronavirus/Befragung_Nichtgeimpfte_-_Forsa-Umfrage_Okt_21.pdf

CHECKLISTE nach der Bearbeitung der Aufgaben Teil E

Aufgabe	Zeit	Was hat mir geholfen?	Fehlerquellen
Hörübung Part 1 Pictures			
Hörübung Part 2 Dream jobs			
Hörübung Part 3 Facts about a bridge			
Hörübung Part 4 High school in Mongolia			
Leseübung Part 1 Sights in Washington DC			
Leseübung Part 2 Job offers			
Leseübung Part 3 Ellis Island			
Leseübung Part 4 The Botanical Garden			
Mediation Part 1 Signs			
Mediation Part 2 Discgolf in Berlin			
Writing Part 1 Change of perspective			
Writing Part 2 Couch surfing			
Writing Part 3 Interpreting charts			

Abschlussarbeiten 2022

Sekundarabschluss I – Realschulabschluss

Englisch 20.05.2022

Quelle der Aufgabenstellung

Niedersächsisches Kultusministerium
Einige der Abbildungen weichen aus lizenzrechtlichen Gründen von der Darstellung in der Original-Prüfungsarbeit ab.

I. Listening

Part 1 – Questions 1–7

 Track 12

AUFGABENSTELLUNG

- Listen to seven short recordings.
- For each recording, there is a question with three pictures.
- Choose the correct picture and put a tick in the box *A*, *B* or *C* below it.

Example:

0. What is the man going to buy?

SUN MILK 30	sunglasses	MAGAZINE
A ☐	B ☐	C ☑

1. Where does the band meet for the final rehearsal?

 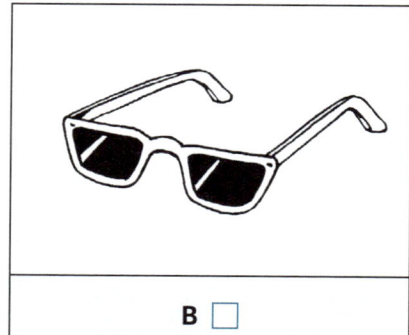 

A ☐	B ☐	C ☐

2. Which dog is missing?

A ☐

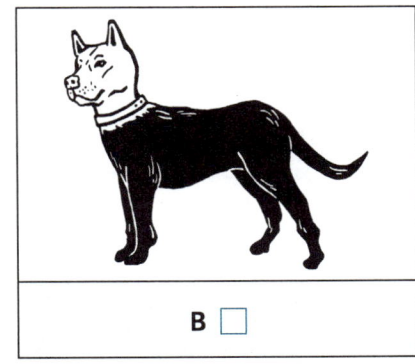

B ☐

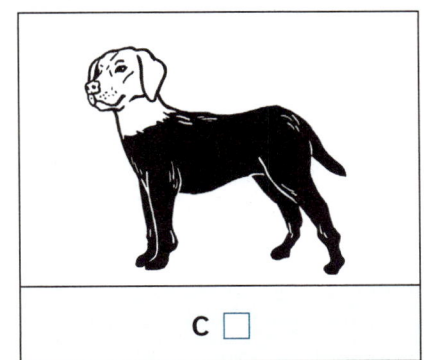

C ☐

3. When does the main boarding start?

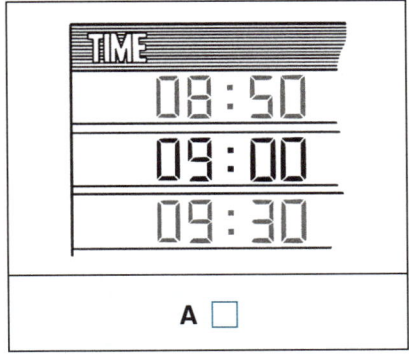

A ☐

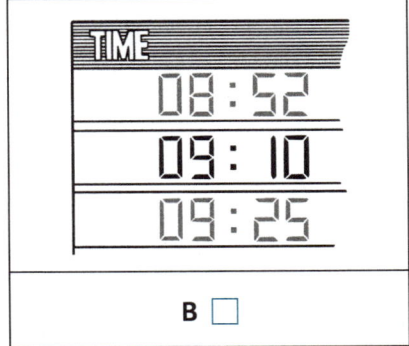

B ☐

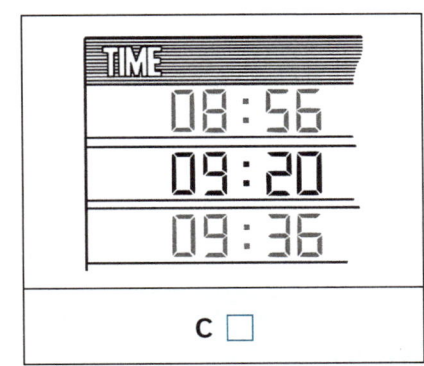

C ☐

4. Where will the party be?

A ☐

B ☐

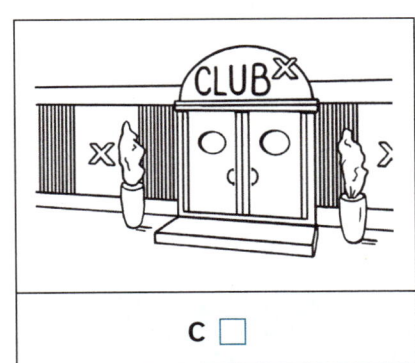

C ☐

5. What's the weather forecast for Friday?

A ☐

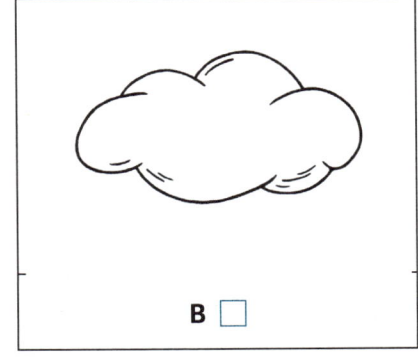

B ☐

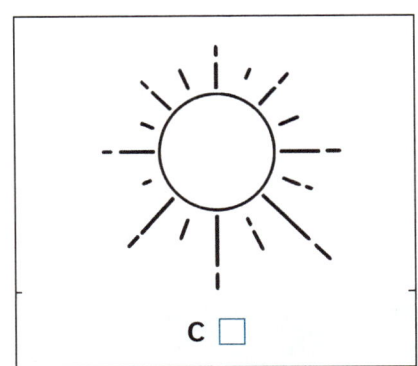

C ☐

6. How much flour are they adding to the pancake batter?

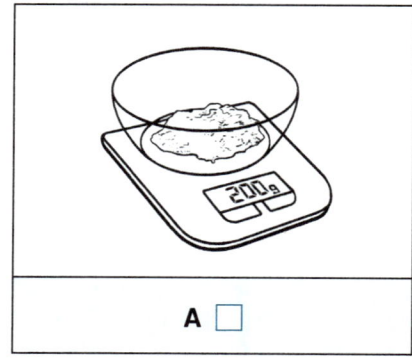 A ☐

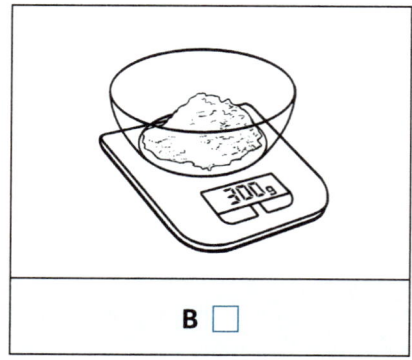 B ☐

 C ☐

7. Where is the couple going on holiday?

 A ☐

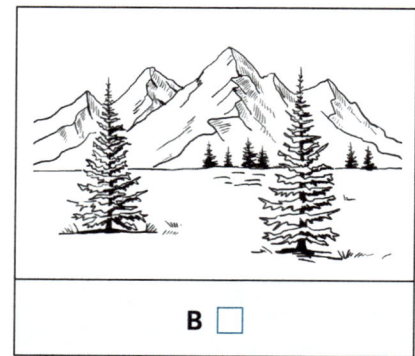 B ☐

 C ☐

/ 7 P.

Part 2 – Questions 8–13: Robin's New Life in New York City

 **Track 13**

- Listen to Anne and Robin talking online about Robin's new life after he's moved from a small town in Oregon to New York City.
- For each question, tick the correct box *a, b* or *c.*

8. Robin's new home ...
a) has a backyard. ☐
b) is near a skatepark. ☐
c) is across the street from his school. ☐

9. At the moment, Robin mostly ...
a) skates in the park. ☐
b) explores New York City. ☐
c) works on his basketball skills. ☐

10. Robin ...
a) loves the skyscrapers and sights. ☐
b) enjoys the atmosphere of the city. ☐
c) thinks the city is too noisy for him. ☐

11. Robin's new school ...
a) is smaller than his old school. ☐
b) has a bad name in the city. ☐
c) offers many activities. ☐

12. Rubio and Jalen have ...
a) played basketball with Robin. ☐
b) skated with Robin. ☐
c) shown Robin around the city. ☐

13. Anne is going to visit Robin ...
a) during spring break. ☐
b) when school is out in June. ☐
c) after her summer job. ☐

/ 6 P.

Part 3 – Questions 14–20: Staying at a Youth Hostel

 **Track 14**

- You are on a class trip in Copenhagen. The youth hostel manager tells you what you have to know about your stay.
- Fill in the missing information.
- The first question is an example.

Quelle Foto: stock.adobe.com, Dublin: joyt

Name of the youth hostel?	**0.** *Danhostel Copenhagen*
Location of students' and teachers' rooms?	**14.**
Where do I find my room number?	**15.**
Breakfast time and location?	**16.**
Who to inform in case of food allergies?	**17.**
Consequence of smoking?	**18.**
What should you do before going bowling?	**19.**
WiFi-password?	**20.**

/ 7 P.

Part 4 – Questions 21–26: Interview with an Influencer

 Track 15

AUFGABENSTELLUNG

- You will hear a radio interview with the social-media influencer Emma D.
- Decide whether each statement is true or false and put a tick in the correct box.
- The first question is an example.

Quelle Foto: stock.adobe.com, Dublin: fizkes

No.	Emma D...	true	false
0.	is like most other influencers.	☐	☑
21.	is sponsored by brands.	☐	☐
22.	creates new outfits.	☐	☐
23	says that fashion trends repeat themselves.	☐	☐
24.	says that her followers start buying lots of new clothes.	☐	☐
25.	already sells her clothes online.	☐	☐
26.	sells clothes for men and women.	☐	☐

/ 6 P.

II. Reading

Part 1 – Questions 1–6: Short Texts

AUFGABENSTELLUNG

- Read the texts (1–6) below and the statements *a*, *b* and *c* next to them.
- Decide which of the statements is the correct one for each text.
- Put a tick in the box next to the correct statement.

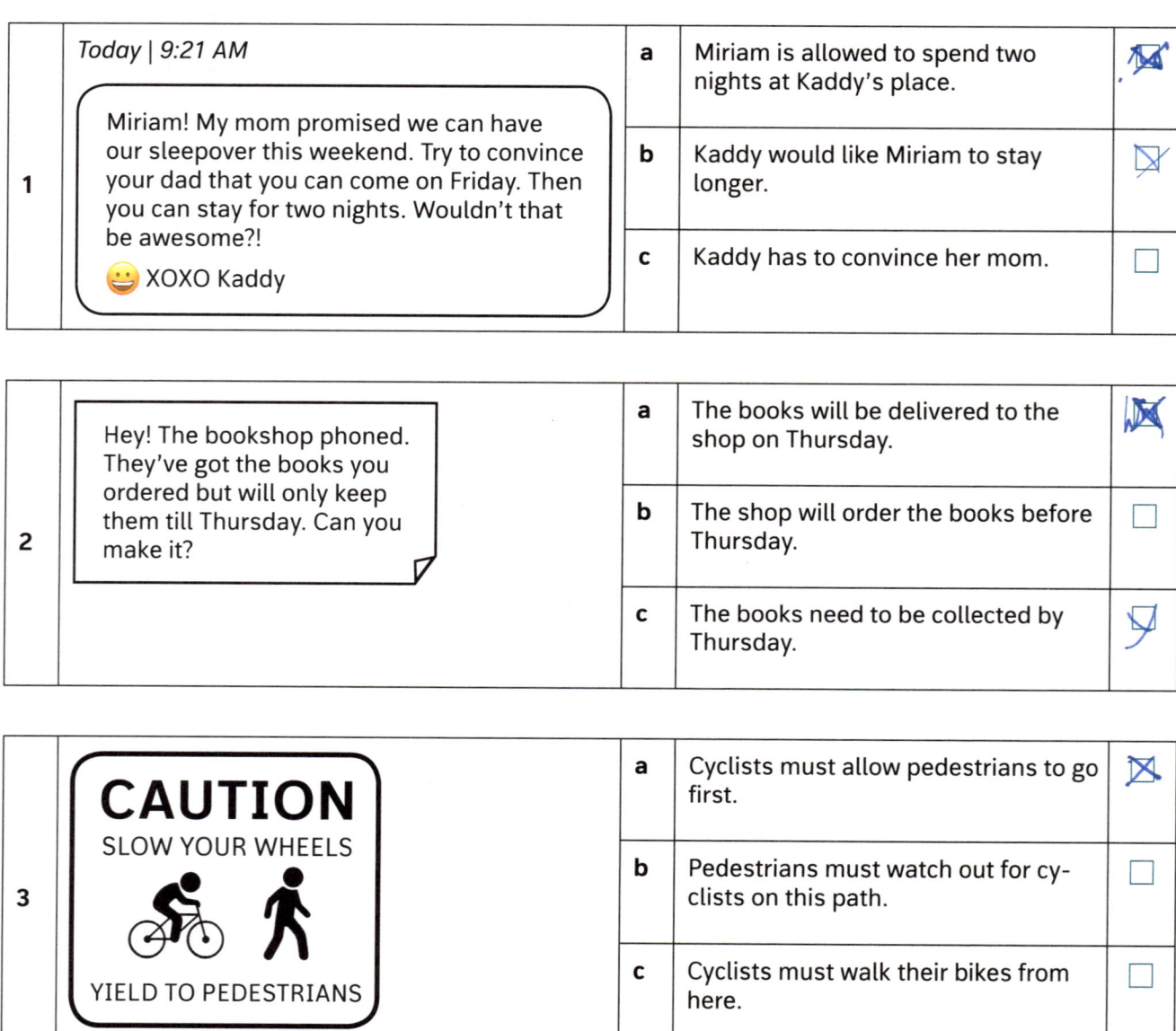

1	Today | 9:21 AM Miriam! My mom promised we can have our sleepover this weekend. Try to convince your dad that you can come on Friday. Then you can stay for two nights. Wouldn't that be awesome?! 😄 XOXO Kaddy	**a** Miriam is allowed to spend two nights at Kaddy's place.	☒
		b Kaddy would like Miriam to stay longer.	☒
		c Kaddy has to convince her mom.	☐

2	Hey! The bookshop phoned. They've got the books you ordered but will only keep them till Thursday. Can you make it?	**a** The books will be delivered to the shop on Thursday.	☒
		b The shop will order the books before Thursday.	☐
		c The books need to be collected by Thursday.	☑

3	**CAUTION** SLOW YOUR WHEELS YIELD TO PEDESTRIANS	**a** Cyclists must allow pedestrians to go first.	☒
		b Pedestrians must watch out for cyclists on this path.	☐
		c Cyclists must walk their bikes from here.	☐

4	**WAITER WANTED!** Standing on the front lines, our waiters are vital to the guest experience. Can you handle such responsibility? Our waiters should: • Always be friendly and attentive • Be flexible. Working hours are not 9 to 5. • Be experienced but it's no requirement.	a	People skills are most important for the job.	☒
		b	People work regular hours.	☐
		c	Work experience is necessary for the job.	☒

5	THESE SEATS MUST BE VACATED FOR SENIORS AND DISABLED PERSONS	a	Only elderly and physically challenged people may sit here.	☐
		b	This seat has to be offered to elderly or physically challenged people.	☒
		c	Elderly and physically challenged people will vacate this seat for you.	☐

6	*Today | 7:21 AM* Hey Sam! Do you remember the backpack I had yesterday? I don't know where it is. Did I leave it in your flat? 🤞 It's not mine. I borrowed it and gotta give it back today! 😱 Thx, Bob	a	Bob has to return a backpack.	☒
		b	Bob is looking for a backpack he can borrow.	☒
		c	Bob left the flat with the backpack.	☐

Quellen Grafiken: Aufgabe 1: stock.adobe.com, Dublin: pixelliebe; Aufgabe 6, oben: stock.adobe.com, Dublin: Stalvalki; Aufgabe 6, unten: stock.adobe.com, Dublin: pixelliebe

/ 6 P.

Part 2 – Questions 7–13: An Interview with a Londoner

- Read the answers Alexa has given in an interview about her hometown, London.
- On the next page there are eight questions.
- Decide which question is most suitable for each answer.
- For texts 7–13 write the correct letter (A–H) in the box next to the number.
- There are more questions than answers. Each letter can only be used once.

✓	**7.** D	I don't think there's a language that isn't spoken here. No matter where you come from, you fit right in. The city is one big melting pot of different cultures, languages, and accents. At first, I thought it was British accents everywhere, but it turns out I was wrong.
✓	**8.** B	People are always in a rush, so when they bump into you, they won't always apologize. I'm not criticizing Londoners because technically this doesn't mean that Londoners are rude. It just means that everyone has their own business to get to. They don't want to be late for their business meeting or class. Personally, if I were in a hurry in such a big, crowded city, I would do the same.
H	**9.** A	It is as appetizing as it sounds and looks. The best thing about it is: it's cheap! Usually, London is an expensive place to live, but it's a matter of where you go. Of course, right in the city where all the tourists go, you can't save any money. I enjoy some of the great Indian places in the suburbs.
A	**10.** E	It really depends on the neighbourhood. [...] Theatres are a big thing – not just cinemas, but theatres where they produce plays. [...] But the places people go to a lot are London's parks. They are huge! People go there to hang out with their friends, have a picnic, or just go outside and enjoy the weather. [...] You can also find a gym at every corner, but they're expensive.
✓	**11.** C	They say the weirder the better! You could walk into a fancy restaurant in pyjamas and they would still serve you. [...] People start their own trends all the time. So, at one point, you just give up on trying to follow them. You begin to become more creative with your choices. [...] Store-wise you find a lot of designer brands. That's why tourists think clothes are expensive here.

| 12. | F | Like in most countries in the western world, the majority of the population is Christian. With London being so international, there is a lot more variety in religions than in most other cities in the world. Overall, London isn't much of a religious place but Christmas is a very big deal. |
| 13. | G | This may come as a surprise, but it isn't as big as it may seem in London. Sure, it's offered in some restaurants in the afternoon. And there are a couple of parlours that celebrate this British tradition. Actually, the amount of coffee shops found around this city is triple the number of tea parlours.* |

Quelle Text: adapted from: Chiara Bramante, The Teen Magazine, 01.09.2020, https://www.theteenmagazine.com/interviewing-a-londoner-what-it-s-like-to-live-in-london

Quelle Foto: iStockphoto.com, Calgary: Arsty

A	How do Londoners spend their leisure time?
B	Londoners are known for being polite. Is this true?
C	How do you feel about the fashion in London?
D	Would you say that London is an international city?
E	How do Londoners usually get around?
F	Is religion important in London?
G	Is teatime still a thing there?
H	What do you think of the food in London?

/ 7 P.

Part 3 – Questions 14–19: Who is Banksy?

- Read the following article about the artist "Banksy".
- For questions 14–19, tick the correct box *a, b* or *c*.
- For each question there is only one correct answer.

Every time a piece by Banksy appears people get very excited. His work can sell for over £1 million and is known all over the world.

But what do we really know about the mysterious artist?

We don't exactly know who he is. Banksy is a famous – but anonymous – British
5 graffiti artist. He keeps his identity a secret. It is assumed that he was born in Bristol around 1974. Although a lot of his art is produced in public places, he usually only reveals that it is his after it has appeared in his social media. [...] Banksy first got noticed for spray-painting trains and walls in his home city of Bristol during the early 1990s, before appearing in London. Street art and
10 graffiti can be seen as criminal damage, so in the beginning it is thought the artist stayed anonymous to keep out of trouble. At first his pieces were mainly in Bristol, but in the 2000s his artworks started appearing all over the UK and other parts of the world.

A lot of his art is done in a particular style which people can easily recognise,
15 because he chose to use a technique invented by the artist Blek le Rat to create his pieces: stencils – probably because it is a faster way to paint. [...] However, Banksy does more than just street art: he has produced drawings, paintings, and installation pieces. He even created his own theme park called Dismaland. Banksy's work is known for critical political messages, dealing with topics
20 such as homelessness, racism or pollution.

Though regarded as mindless vandalism by some, the majority think his work is very valuable. As a result, his pieces can go for thousands of pounds. [...] Banksy has often made clear that he doesn't like to sell his work for so much money. In late 2018 *Girl with Balloon* (2006), a copy of one of Banksy's most
25 popular wall paintings, partially destroyed itself with a hidden shredder at an auction just after being sold for $1.4 million. After that Banksy called the destroyed version *Love is in the Bin* and it was said to be the first work ever created during a live auction. But its destruction most likely raised the value of the painting.

30 Since many people consider street art to be vandalism, some of his work was painted over as soon as it appeared. Sometimes graffiti artists put their own work over it. That's why the owner usually covers it up with plastic sheeting to protect it. There is a debate about why Banksy's work can be protected as "art" when other graffiti artists are sometimes put in prison for doing the
35 same thing. [...]*

Quelle Text: adapted from: BBC, 14.02.2020, London, https://www.bbc.co.uk/newsround/51504255
Quelle Foto: Courtesy of Pest Control Office – Banksy, London

14.	We know	a	Banksy's real name.	☐
		b	that Banksy was born in Bristol.	☒
		c	that Banksy likes public places for painting.	☐
15.	Banksy started his career	a	in the 2000s.	☐
		b	by spraying trains and walls.	☒
		c	in London.	☐
16.	Banksy	a	creates street art called "Dismaland".	☐
		b	invented the stencil technique.	☐
		c	draws attention to political issues.	☒
17.	Most people think that his art is	a	worth lots of money.	☐
		b	criminal damage.	☐
		c	pointless.	☐
18.	Banksy's work "Girl with Balloon"	a	was sold just after its destruction.	☐
		b	probably lost value by its destruction.	☒
		c	was renamed after its destruction.	☐
19.	Other street artists	a	have painted over Banksy's work.	☒
		b	protect Banksy's works with plastic covers.	☐
		c	criticise Banksy for vandalism.	☐

/ 6 P.

Part 4 – Questions 20–26: Long-Lost Sisters Find Each Other

- Read the article about two sisters, Victoria and Alyss.
- For questions 20–26, tick the correct box true or false and give the line(s) of reference in the text.
- The first question is an example.

27-year-old Victoria Voorhees knew she was adopted as a two-month-old girl. That's why she decided to
5   take a WhoAmI-home DNA test to find out a bit more about her Hispanic background and genetic makeup. She was astonished when
10 the results revealed she had a sister and was sent a photo of a woman who looked very much like her.

As an adopted child, Victoria always dreamed of having an older sibling. But she couldn't believe her eyes when she first saw the photo of her sister. "At first, I was like: there's no way, that's impossible! Maybe they found someone
15 that has some similarities to me? But I know now that's not how it works." She sent her sister a message through the WhoAmI-app and rushed home to tell her parents.

28-year-old Alyss Ravae and Victoria chatted. Then they joined a video call with their biological mother for the first time. "I showed her some photos of
20 me growing up with my adoptive parents," says Victoria, "and she was happy but crying!"

Alyss says of her sister, "We live very parallel lives even though we were placed in very different situations."

It's not just their mutual love of Halloween, of Stephen King, of *It* and *The*
25 *Shining* that she was fascinated by; they both have bat tattoos on opposite feet but the same part of the ankle.

Alyss said: "When she sent me that picture of her tattoo, I literally just dropped my phone."

They also both have cats and make and sell pet portraits online.
30 Victoria said: "We both like hiking trails as well. I'm going to show her all the cool ones around here in Chicago!" To show everyone their similarities, the two sisters created a video for social media in which they demonstrate all the things they have in common. If you didn't know better, you'd think that these two people have spent all their lives together. Whereas in fact, they
35 have yet to meet in person. They are now planning to meet up for the first time as soon as possible.*

Quelle Text: adapted from: Good News Network, 04.06.2021, https://www.goodnewsnetwork.org/sisters-long-lost-matching-tattoos-victoria-chicago/

Quelle Fotos: iStockphoto.com, Calgary: Feverpitched

	According to the article, Victoria...	true	false	line(s)
0.	was adopted as a child.	☑	☐	_1–3_
20.	took a test to learn about her genes.	☐	☐	_____
21.	never wanted any siblings.	☐	☐	_____
22.	sent a message to her parents.	☐	☐	_____
23.	also got to know her biological mother.	☐	☐	_____
24.	was shown photos of her sister growing up.	☐	☐	
25.	and her sister have lived in similar circumstances.	☐	☐	
26.	and her sister have shared their similarities with the rest of the world.	☐	☐	_____

/ 7 P.

III. Writing – Set I

Part 1 – A Complaint: Empty Box

You ordered a pair of Bluetooth earphones online but all
you got was an empty box. Write a complaint to the online shop.

Include:
- the reason for writing
- how you feel
- what you want the online shop to do

Write about 80 words.

iStockphoto.com, Calgary: Hlystov, Pavel

Dear Hello,

Im very angry becaue

/ 10 P.

Part 2 – A Letter of Application: Au Pair Job

You have found the following advert for an au pair job in Stockholm, Sweden and decide to apply for it.
Write about 150 words.

stock.adobe.com, Dublin: Kneschke, Robert

> We are looking for an au pair that would enjoy spending time with our kids (boy and girl, aged 5 and 7), doing activities with them, speaking to them in English and fits in with the family.
>
> Tell us about yourself:
> • education, hobbies and interests
> • work experience
> • why you are the right person for this job

To:	contact@aupair4u.com
Subject:	Applying for an au pair job

content:	/ 9 P.	language:	/ 9 P.	total:	/ 18 P.

III. Writing – Set II

Part 1 – A Comment: My Parents are Forcing Me into Apprenticeship

AUFGABENSTELLUNG

You find the following post on a website and decide to leave a helpful comment.
Write about 80 words.

> *alex_06:*
> I'm just graduating from school and my parents are forcing me into an apprenticeship at their car dealership. I'd rather become a musician and don't care for cars at all. They say they're not going to support me in any other way. Can I make it without their support? What should I do?
>
> ⬆ 97 ⬇　　⬜ reply　　share ●●●

/ 10 P.

Part 2 – A Blog Entry: Time Travel into the Past

AUFGABENSTELLUNG

Imagine you had the chance to use a time machine
and travel back in time for a day.
Write a blog entry about that day.

In your text, include:
- what time you decided to travel to and why
- what you experienced on that day
- whether or not you can imagine going back to that time again and explain why

Write about 150 words.

stock.adobe.com, Dublin: Poggianati, Delphine

_____

_____

_____

_____

_____

_____

_____

_____

_____

_____

_____

_____

_____

_____

_____

_____

_____

_____

| content: / 9 P. | language: / 9 P. | total: / 18 P. |

Quellenverzeichnis

Textquellen

32 "Climate change is unfair": Anote Tong, TED Conferences LLC, New York, 10-2015, https://www.ted.com/talks/anote_tong_my_country_will_be_underwater_soon_unless_we_work_together/transcript?referrer=playlist-why_climate_change_is_a_human&language=en (adapted) [06.02.2023]

33 "In this perspective-shifting talk …": Danny Hillis, TED Conferences LLC, New York, 04-2017, https://www.ted.com/talks/danny_hillis_should_we_create_a_solar_shade_to_cool_the_earth (adapted) [06.02.2023]

37 "Houses": Todd Beuckens (publisher), https://www.elllo.org/english/Mixer101/T102-Dream-house.htm [06.02.2023]

84 "Are digital tools dangerous? A study": Gregorio Serra, Lucia Lo Scalzo, Mario Giuffrè, Pietro Ferrara & Giovanni Corsello, "Smartphone use and addiction during the coronavirus disease 2019 (COVID-19) pandemic: cohort study on 184 Italian children and adolescents", in: Italian Journal of Pediatrics, volume 47, Article number: 150 (2021), Springer Nature, https://ijponline.biomedcentral.com/articles/10.1186/s13052-021-01102-8 (adapted) [06.02.2023]

107 "Vaccinations defined by age groups": based on data from Michael Hörz, Moritz Zajonz, „Wie viele bisher gegen Corona geimpft wurden", ZDFheute, Mainz, 08.01.22; Impfdashboard, Robert Koch-Institut, https://www.zdf.de/nachrichten/politik/corona-impfung-daten-100.html [06.02.2023]

108 "Opinions about vaccination": based on data from forsa Politik- und Sozialforschung GmbH, Berlin, 18.10.2021, S. 6, „Befragung von nicht geimpften Personen zu den Gründen für die fehlende Inanspruchnahme der Corona-Schutzimpfung – Gründe gegen die Wahrnehmung der Impfung – spontane Nennungen", https://www.bundesgesundheitsministerium.de/fileadmin/Dateien/3_Downloads/C/Coronavirus/Befragung_Nichtgeimpfte_-_Forsa-Umfrage_Okt_21.pdf [06.02.2023]

118 "An Interview with a Londoner": Chiara Bramante, The Teen Magazine, 01.09.2020, https://www.theteenmagazine.com/interviewing-a-londoner-what-it-s-like-to-live-in-london (adapted) [06.02.2023]

120 "Who is Banksy?": BBC, Großbritannien, 14.02.2020, London, https://www.bbc.co.uk/newsround/51504255 (adapted) [06.02.2023]

122 "Long-Lost Sisters Find Each Other": Good News Network, 04.06.2021, https://www.goodnewsnetwork.org/sisters-long-lost-matching-tattoos-victoria-chicago/ (adapted) [06.02.2023]

Hörquellen

64 "Naomi's school": Todd Beuckens (publisher), http://www.elllo.org/english/0901/T931-Naomi-School.htm [06.02.2023]

93 "Cool Jobs": Todd Beuckens (publisher), www.elllo.org/english/0701/T749-Tim-GoodJob.htm [06.02.2023]

95 "School in Mongolia": Todd Beuckens (publisher), www.elllo.org/english/1001/1009-Mongolia School.htm [06.02.2023]

westermann

FiNALE
Prüfungstraining

Niedersachsen

Abschluss
10. Klasse Realschule
Englisch

2024

Lösungen

Katja Werthen-Giles

Mohammed.Tusi

Lösungsheft zu 978-3-07-172427-3

TRANSKRIPTE

Seite 27
Track 1: Five short conversations
1. What time does the movie start?
Bob: Hi Sally.
Sally: Hi Bob. How are you?
Bob: I'm fine. And you?
Sally: I'm fine, too. Do you know what happened to me yesterday? I won two tickets on a radio show. Would you like to go to the movies with me?
Bob: Sure. What time does the movie start?
Sally: Well, there are several shows today. The first one starts at 3 p.m. I think that's too early.
Bob: Yeah, me too. What time is the next one?
Sally: The next one begins at 5:30 p.m.
Bob: I have a dentist's appointment at 5 p.m. so that doesn't work for me. Is there a later time?
Sally: How about 8 p.m.?
Bob: That is perfect. Do you want to meet in front of the theater at 7:45?
Sally: That sounds great.
Bob: What is the title of the movie?
Sally: The title is 'Avatar'.
Bob: Cool. I heard that movie is fantastic!

Seite 28
2. What will the weather be like today?
Hello there. My name is Joe. Welcome to the weather report on WNEP Channel 16. There is some good news for today's weather. After all those thunderstorms and rain that we had yesterday, the weather will clear up today. This morning we will have cloudy skies, but no rain showers. Around noon the sun will come out and it will be nice all day. This morning will start out with cooler temperatures around 55° Fahrenheit but they won't stay there for long. As soon as the sun comes out it will warm up to 75° Fahrenheit. Along with the temperature, the humidity will go up to 80%. So, all in all it looks like we will have a very nice day. Enjoy it while it lasts, because in the next few days the weather will get worse with more rain and cooler temperatures.

3. What is the man going to eat in the restaurant?
Waitress: Hello Sir, how are you today?
Guest: Hello. I am fine, thank you.
Waitress: My name is Jerry and I'll be serving you today. What can I do for you?
Guest: I would like a cup of coffee, please.
Waitress: Do you take sugar and cream?
Guest: No, thank you. I like my coffee black. What is on your lunch menu?
Waitress: The soup of the day is tomato soup. As a main course we have three choices – lasagna, pizza and spaghetti. For dessert we have chocolate mousse and various cakes.
Guest: Do you have vegetarian lasagna?
Waitress: Yes, we do. Instead of meat we use fresh spinach and cheese.
Guest: What kind of pizza toppings do you have?
Waitress: We have spinach, mushrooms, sausage, olives, peppers, onions and pepperoni.
Guest: Do you have salads?

Waitress: We have a mixed salad with lettuce, tomato, cucumber and mushrooms and a Caesar Salad with chicken.
Guest: I think I'll have a pizza with mushrooms and spinach and the chocolate mousse for dessert.
Waitress: Thank you, sir. I'll bring your coffee right away.

4. Where is she going?
Mary's voice (answering machine):
Hello, you have reached Mary Waters. I am not at home right now, so please leave a message after the beep and I'll get back to you as soon as I can.
Travel agent:
Hi, Ms Waters. This is Mr Coburn, your travel agent. I just wanted to tell you that your tickets have arrived. You will leave from Washington Dulles Airport on the 25th June and fly to Brussels. You will arrive there the next day. From Brussels you will take a connecting flight to Madrid and catch a smaller aircraft there to go to Mallorca. On the island you will stay in a small hotel by the sea for two weeks. I hope the weather will be nice and that you enjoy your vacation.

5. What can you buy in the new store?
Ladies and Gentlemen,
There's a new store that will open up in your town next week. Its name is "Books, Presents and More" and here are some of the things you can buy there. This shop has a large variety of cards for every occasion like birthdays, weddings, births and anniversaries. You can buy toys and stuffed animals for your children and decorations for Christmas, Easter and Halloween. Candles, books and magazines are also available. We have a coffee shop right in our store where you can enjoy a hot cup of coffee while you read a book or a daily newspaper. For the opening week we've lowered all prices and will take 20% off if you buy something. Our store is open from 9 a.m. to 5 p.m. every day of the week. We hope to see you all on Monday morning at 9 o'clock.

Seite 29
Track 2: A summer job
Tim: Hi, Ms Sully. Nice to see you again.
Ms Sully: Hello, Tim. How are you?
Tim: I'm fine, thanks. Do you have a minute? I'd like to tell you about my summer job in a camp in the USA.
Ms Sully: Sure, Tim. I have time.
Tim: In the spring I found this homepage for a camp in Pennsylvania. They were looking for European counselors to work there in the summer. I applied and got the job. It started at the beginning of June and lasted for two months until August. You had to work five days a week and had two days off depending on your weekly schedule.
Ms Sully: So what did you do there, Tim?
Tim: I planned and organized different activities for the kids. For example games, movie nights, canoeing, hiking and so on. I really liked working with the children. Some of them had never been in the country before and didn't know what a cow looked like.
Ms Sully: Where did you stay?
Tim: We had our own room in a big house with a lot of bedrooms. All the counselors stayed there.

Ms Sully: And did you get paid?
Tim: Yes, we got $1,000 for the two months. That doesn't sound like a lot of money but they also paid for our flights and gave us a room and free food. But I didn't do it for the money. The experience with the kids was great and I met so many people from all over the world and made new friends. I want to buy a new computer with the money so that I can write e-mails to all my friends and Skype with them.

Seite 30
Track 3: A new job
Hi. My name's Susan and I am a student at the university here in town. I needed some extra money for books so in March I found a job working in a restaurant. I earn $6 an hour. I have to start at 10 a.m. because we have some guests who come in for a late breakfast. I have a short break from 1 to 1:30 p.m. when I eat something. In nice weather we have 15 tables outside. That means a lot of running around carrying drinks and food outside. I get good tips but at night my feet hurt a lot and I can't sleep.

Track 4: A typical school day in Germany and America
The school systems in the US and Germany are different. In the US, all the kids have the same schedule every day, so they have their subjects five times a week. In Germany, the students have eight to ten different subjects and most of them are taught only once or twice a week. In America all the kids have lockers for their books and clothing. In between classes they can put the books they don't need away and take the ones they need for the next class out. In Germany kids usually don't have lockers and carry all their books around the whole day. German students usually go home at 1 p.m. and have six to eight lessons a day. They do their homework at home and go to sports clubs and other activities in the afternoon. In the US many students play in the school band and learn an instrument there. School is over around 3 p.m. During the school day they have study hall whenever they don't have a lesson. They can do most of their homework there. After school the kids go to different clubs that offer activities like drama, chess, publishing the school newspaper or go to school sports programs that offer sports like basketball, football, baseball and tennis.

Seite 61
Track 5: School subjects
1.
Teacher: Today we're going to read about Shakespeare, one of the most famous writers in the world. He lived from 1564-1616 and wrote 37 plays. Which Shakespeare plays do you know?
Pupil: *Romeo and Juliet, Hamlet …*
Teacher: Very good. Now, Shakespeare wrote a long time ago, so the language he used was quite different from how we speak and write today. Let's have a look. Open your textbooks at page 63.

2.
Teacher: What do we need to make a pizza base?
Pupil: The base is made from flour and water with a little salt and possibly yeast to make it rise.

Teacher: Very good. What about the topping? What would you put on?
Pupil: Well, there's got to be tomato sauce and grated cheese. In addition to that, I would put on ham, mushrooms, pineapple and maybe some salami.

3.
Teacher: Earthquakes usually happen when two land masses meet. At this point there is a fault line, such as the San Andreas fault in California. When there is a sudden movement between the two blocks of land, the ground shakes and there can also be tidal waves. Some earthquakes are very strong. They destroy many buildings and kill hundreds or even thousands of people. Other earthquakes are so small that you hardly notice them. Earthquakes are measured using the Richter scale.

4.
Teacher: If a train is travelling from London to Manchester at 100 kilometres per hour and the two cities are 181 miles apart, how long does the journey take? How can we solve this problem?
Pupil: We have to convert the miles into kilometres first.
Teacher: Very good. 1 km is 0.62 miles. So how many kilometres are 181 miles?
Pupil: 290 kilometres.
Teacher: Excellent. So what do we do now?
Pupil: Well, if the train travels 100 kilometres in 1 hour, meaning 60 minutes, we have to work out how long it takes to travel 290 kilometres.
Teacher: And how do we do that?
Pupil: We take 290 kilometres times 60 and divide it by 100.
Teacher: And that makes?
Pupil: 174 hours.
Teacher: 174 hours? That's a very long journey.
Pupil: No, 174 minutes.

5.
Teacher: Edvard Munch was one of Norway's greatest painters. His most famous picture is called "The Scream". The two painted originals can be seen in Oslo, but there are many copies, too. People think that Munch must have been very depressed to paint such pictures, and it is true that he had an unhappy personal life.
Here you can see Munch's painting once more. I've also brought along some other pictures. Some are very famous, others perhaps less so. Have a look at them and choose one painting. Tell me about the atmosphere in this picture. How does the artist express this mood? Look at the composition, style and colours, of course.

6.
Teacher: Welcome everybody. Before we start with the warm-up, let me remind you that we'll be playing basketball later. Can somebody tell me more about the rules of the game?
Pupil: You have to bounce the ball on the ground all the time. If you stop, you must shoot, or pass the ball to someone else on your team.
Teacher: Yes, that's correct.

Pupil: You are not allowed to shove or push the players of the other team. If you do, it's a foul and the other team will get the ball.
Teacher: Yeah.
Pupil: If you throw the ball into the basket you normally get two points, but you can also get three points if you're behind a certain line, farther away from the basket.
Teacher: OK, those are the most important rules. We'll talk about them again later. Now start warming up. The game will begin in 15 minutes.

7.
Teacher: Today we'll talk about animals that live in our oceans. The latest oil spill in the Gulf of Mexico has made us all aware of environmental problems and how pollution affects the animals living in the ocean. What kind of animals do you know?
Pupil: I like whales.
Teacher: There are many different kinds of whales. Do you know any?
Pupil: I know Free Willy.
Teacher: Yes, the Orca whale or killer whale. What do they eat?
Pupil: I think they eat fish.
Teacher: Yes, that's correct but they also like seals and sharks. Do you know any other types of whales? Well, the largest whale on earth is the blue whale.

Seite 64
Track 6: Naomi's school
Dai: So Miss Naomi from … where is it you are from?
Naomi: Wales.
Dai: Wales, OK. So, and how old are you now?
Naomi: I'm eleven.
Dai: Eleven. OK, so that means you're in … What would that be, junior school? Secondary school?
Naomi: Junior school.
Dai: Junior school, OK. And so what grade is that in junior school?
Naomi: Six.
Dai: Oh, grade six. OK. So, tell me about your school. What kind of subjects do you study in junior school?
Naomi: We study Art and Maths and Science and English and Geography and History and RE.
Dai: RE? What's RE?
Naomi: Religious Education.
Dai: And you go to school from what time in the morning?
Naomi: About a quarter to nine and it starts at five past.
Dai: The first class is at five past?
Naomi: Yeah.
Dai: And then do you get a break?
Naomi: We get a break at half past ten and then lunch at twelve o'clock.
Dai: Oh, twelve o'clock, for how long?
Naomi: For an hour.
Dai: Oh, for an hour? How nice! And then – what do you do for lunch in Wales? Do they have (like) a cafeteria where they cook for you?
Naomi: Yeah, they have that and you can bring sandwiches.
Dai: Oh, so you can bring your own sandwiches instead?
Naomi: Yeah.
Dai: OK. What do you do?

Naomi: I normally bring sandwiches.
Dai: OK, is that because the dinners are no good, or …?
Naomi: They're OK, but I don't really like them as much as sandwiches.
Dai: Oh. OK, what kind of food do they serve in the canteen?
Naomi: They serve roast dinners and …
Dai: Roast dinners? What's a roast dinner?
Naomi: It's like, uh, meat and vegetables.
Dai: OK. It sounds very simple.
Naomi: Yeah, and pizza and chips and ham and all sorts of stuff.
Dai: Oh. OK, it sounds good. And do they give you lots of homework?
Naomi: No.
Dai: Oh really?
Naomi: No.
Dai: Oh, that's good to hear. So what's your favourite subject then in junior school?
Naomi: Art.
Dai: OK. Why is that?
Naomi: I don't know, I just like painting and drawing.
Dai: And then, what's the subject that you find most boring?
Naomi: Maths.
Dai: Maths? Oh, really? Yeah, I'm not a big fan of Maths. So I guess if you're in grade six, you'll be going on to your next school soon?
Naomi: Yeah, secondary school.
Dai: OK, and are you looking forward to that?
Naomi: Yeah.
Dai: OK, it was very nice talking to you and good luck in your next school.

Seite 66
Track 7: Internet bullying
Internet bullying is a new kind of harassment. Instead of calling somebody names or threatening a fellow student, the bullies hide behind websites and secret names which make it hard to find out who is behind these actions. These teenagers spread rumours and gossip or threaten other kids via the Internet. They publish humiliating pictures and videos that they usually took secretly without the people knowing about it. All of a sudden you are the talk of the school, everybody laughs about you behind your back, or avoids you because they heard that you cheat or lie.
If somebody made a joke or spread rumours about you in the past, only a small group of people would know about it. After a few days it would blow over and be replaced by something else happening. Today, wireless technology makes it possible to share pictures and other information with the entire world. Something small like a video taken at a private party can be doctored and changed, and later uploaded for millions to watch. Many kids are being threatened or harassed online. One in four students has been bullied online in Great Britain. It can be very distressing for the victims, especially because the bullies are hard to trace. They change their names frequently and hardly ever get caught.

Seite 91
Track 8: Six short conversations or text
1. What job does Peter do?
Hi, my name is Peter and I'll tell you how I chose my job. I love working with my hands so first I thought I'd be a cook because I also like eating. But standing in a kitchen all day long making food for other people didn't seem so wonderful after all. Then I thought a career where I could talk to and meet interesting people would be great, so I drove around with a friend of mine who is a taxi-driver. He said he likes it because he sits in his car all day and he loves driving. I thought it was really boring and decided that I want to make something with my hands that will last. So now I am an apprentice and work with wood and make furniture every day. I love my job.

Seite 92
2. What pet does Mary get?
Mary: Dad, I want a dog.
Father: Oh, remember Mary, a dog means a lot of responsibility. You have to feed the dog and take it for two or three walks a day. Do you think you'll have time for all this? You have soccer practice on Tuesday and drama club in school on Thursday.
Mary: What about a budgie? I can easily take care of a budgie. It sits in its cage all day long so that shouldn't take up a lot of time.
Father: Sorry Mary, but we can't get a budgie. Your mother is allergic to those birds.
Mary: Would a cat be OK? My friend Kelly has one and she's doing a lot of extra activities besides school. She is in my soccer club and also plays in a band.
Father: I guess that would be OK, but you'll take care of it.
Mary: Yes, dad. I'll name my cat Garfield.

3. What type of sports does Mike do in his free time?
Tim: Hi Mike. How are you?
Mike: Hello Tim. I'm fine, thank you. How about you?
Tim: Oh, I'm fine. Listen, do you want to go to soccer practice with me tonight? We need another player and I think you'd be great.
Mike: I am sorry, Tim, but I hate soccer. The only types of sport I really like are swimming and jogging.
Tim: I like swimming, too. Do you do that in your free time?
Mike: No, I'm on the school team so we swim twice a week after classes. I go jogging after school or at the weekend just for fun.

4. How much does she pay for the jeans?
Saleswoman: Hello, can I help you?
Girl: Yes, I'd like a black pair of jeans.
Saleswoman: What size do you wear?
Girl: I need a size 30 at the waist and a 32 for the length.
Saleswoman: We have a couple of different brands on sale. We have a pair of black "Lovis" for 50 euros, "Hers" for 40 euros and "New Navy" for 30 euros.
Girl: I'll try them on. Where's the changing room?
Saleswoman: It's right next to the winter clothes.
Girl: Thanks.
Saleswoman: So, do they fit?
Girl: The "Lovis" feel uncomfortable. The "Hers" are too tight but the "New Navys" fit perfectly. I'll take them.

5. When does his flight leave from Chicago?
Man: Hello, I'd like to confirm my flight for tomorrow.
Salesrep: You know that confirming your flight is not necessary anymore. You can just check in online and get your seat and all the information you need.
Man: Yes, I know that but I would like to do it on the phone.
Salesrep: No problem, sir. Can you give me your name and your flight number?
Man: Sure. My flight number is 091 and my name is John Elmhurst.
Salesrep: Yes, Mr Elmhurst. I can see your information on my screen. There has been a slight change in your departure time.
Man: What do you mean? I have a connecting flight from John F. Kennedy and can't be late for that flight.
Salesrep: Well, you had about four hours at JFK but with the new departure time you only have two hours. The old time was 2:35 p.m. but now your flight from Chicago leaves at 4:15 p.m.
Man: What about my flight from JFK?
Salesrep: That flight leaves on time at 8:20 p.m. You'll be in Barcelona the next morning at 8 a.m.
Man: Thank you for your help.
Salesrep: No problem, sir. Have a good flight.

Seite 93
6. Which body part did Linda hurt in her accident?
Carol: Hi Linda. How are you?
Linda: Hello Carol. I'm not doing so good. I had a car accident last week.
Carol: Oh, what happened?
Linda: Well, I was driving along Main Street and all of a sudden this truck cut me off and took my right of way. I had no chance to brake and crashed right into him. My car was totaled and I was taken to the hospital.
Carol: Were you seriously hurt?
Linda: Well, at first I thought I'd broken my arm because it really hurt, but in the hospital they told me there was nothing wrong with it. They X-rayed my leg because I had trouble walking. I guess I twisted my leg in the accident.
Carol: So, what did they find?
Linda: I tore all the ligaments in my knee. They operated on it and fixed everything, but now I have to wear a brace and go to physical therapy three times a week.
Carol: That's awful, Linda.
Linda: Yes, it is and I also have to buy a new car. This time I'll get a big truck, too. The driver of the other car didn't have a scratch.

Track 9: Cool jobs
Jeff: Tim, I'm a teacher, but you can have many, many jobs in the world. If you could pick any job, what do you think would be a cool job?
Tim: Well, to be honest, I think it would be pretty cool to be a fisherman.
Jeff: Fisherman!
Tim: Yeah. Believe it or not I really like the ocean. I like spending time in the ocean and I think if you go out on those boats and get away from the land, you really get in touch with the sea, and I just think that you get to work with your hands.
Jeff: Is it dangerous though?

5

Tim: Oh, it is dangerous. For sure. You can hook yourself. You can get caught in storms. It can be not so good.

Jeff: Do you get paid a lot of money?

Tim: Not so much, but that is not necessarily so important. You know. You can work with nature. You can catch your own food. Provide for yourself and I think that's really rewarding. How about you? What do you think would be a cool job?

Jeff: I think I would like to be a writer.

Tim: Why is that?

Jeff: Because a movie star would be good, or a rock star but there is too much fame. Too many people always want to talk to you or want your autograph, but I think a writer, you're doing something you love without all that pressure or media coming after you and you can sort of make your own time and do it where you like. You can write in the country in a cabin, or you can write in the city, anywhere you like, so I think it is a very flexible, rewarding job.

Tim: Yeah, you've got to have the skill for it though. Do you think you have that skill?

Jeff: No, I'm a terrible writer, but if I could have my pick of jobs, I'd like to be a writer. How about you? So, you would like to be a fisherman. Any other jobs you'd like to do?

Tim: Another job that I think might be cool is a fireman to tell you the truth. Again, you're kind of working with nature. I'd really like to be a sort of a slash-and-burn fireman. Someone that goes out when there's wildfires, things like that, 'cause you're working with nature.

Jeff: Those guys, the slash-and-burn firemen, they get to jump out of helicopters sometimes.

Tim: Some of them do yeah, but that's kind of the glamorous one. Yeah, I wouldn't mind just being the guy that's on the ground, and the nice thing about it is you work really, really hard and you get paid pretty well for the time you work but then you get a long time off.

Jeff: But, I'm a little bit scared of fires. You don't mind fire?

Tim: I don't mind fire so much. You know. It's hot and it can be really, really dangerous but I don't know, it's kind of exciting and I like the idea of being out there in nature and just working hard to survive and working in a team. I think it would be a good thing.

Jeff: I want to be an astronaut. I think an astronaut would be good.

Tim: Why is that? It's a dangerous job. A fireman's dangerous, but it sounds like an astronaut would be pretty dangerous as well.

Jeff: A little dangerous, but I'd like to go to the moon to see what's on the moon. I think it would be kind of neat to be on the moon and looking back at the earth. They call the earth the blue planet. I think it would be neat to sit up there and look back on the earth and it would be kind of neat I think.

Tim: Sounds like you like the ocean. You should think about being a fisherman.

Jeff: No way! No thanks.

Seite 94
Track 10: Interview with an engineer who just finished his first bridge (A radio program)

Speaker: Hello Jim. Thank you for coming.

Jim : It's nice to be here.

Speaker: You must be really excited, because you just finished your first big building project as an engineer. You built a bridge.

Jim: Yes, I did and you are right, I'm really excited.

Speaker: So, tell us more about this bridge. Where exactly is it?

Jim: Well, it's in Minneapolis, Minnesota's largest city, and it was built so that cars can cross the Mississippi River.

Speaker: And when did you start this project?

Jim: Construction started in the spring of 1964 and it was completed in the summer of 1967.

Speaker: What about the size of the bridge?

Jim: The bridge spans a width of around 1907 feet and was built about 115 feet above the water.

Speaker: Wow, that is quite a bridge. What else?

Seite 95
Track 11: School in Mongolia

Todd: So Heidi, you're from Mongolia. Could you talk a little bit about what high school is like in Mongolia?

Heidi: Oh sure. In Mongolia, we don't have elementary school, secondary school, or high school divided into three parts, but we have from 1st grade until 12th grade in one school so we don't really call them like high school or secondary school or elementary school. And for the high school, like, from the 8th grade until 12th grade, well, they study what other students study in different countries but nowadays they are focusing on more, like, English studies or different language studies.

Todd: How long is a typical class? Do you have, let's say, six classes a day, each class is one hour?

Heidi: We start school at 8:00 in the morning until 1:00 in the [after] noon and we have about six classes a day. Each class has like 45 minutes. So we finish at 1:00.

Todd: And then, what do you do in the afternoon?

Heidi: We go back.

Todd: You go home?

Heidi: Yes, 'cause in Mongolia we have two parts. In the morning, the high school students go to the school and from 1:30 the elementary school students go to the school so we share one class [between] two classes.

Todd: Oh, so you split the school?

Heidi: Yes.

Todd: So teachers sometimes have to teach both levels?

Heidi: Yes.

Todd: Wow! That's tough.

Heidi: Yeah.

Todd: So when you go home, do you usually … do you have family there waiting or do usually both parents work?

Heidi: In Mongolia, the mother and father they usually work and when I finish my school I just go back and make my own food, kids are taught to clean up the home and cook their food and wash their clothes and that's your work and usually the mothers don't do that kind of thing.

Todd: Oh, so the children have to do all that work?

Heidi: Yes.

Todd: Actually it's quite similar I think in the US pretty much. So what about your study load? Do you have a really heavy study load? Like, do you have two hours of homework a night or …?

Heidi: It really depends on the school but for me, like, I was studying in an international school so I had to study quite hard to get the level still. So for me, I studied at night, so I studied like 3 or 4 hours at night. So that's my study habit.
Todd: That's a lot.
Heidi: Not really, compared to other students.

ORIGINALPRÜFUNG 2022

Seite 110
Track 12: I. Listening

This is the Listening Part of the Final Examination 2022 Level B1 for schools in Lower Saxony. There are four parts to the test. You will hear each recording twice. For each part of the test there will be time for you to look through the questions. You must not speak during the test.

Part 1
Now look at part 1, questions 1 to 7.
Listen to seven short recordings. For each recording there is a question with three pictures. Choose the correct picture and put a tick in the box A, B or C below it.
Before we start, here is an example:

0. What is the man going to buy?
I'm going shopping now. Anything else we need for our holiday?
The sunscreen from our last trip should still work. I haven't got any sunglasses but I can borrow some of yours, can't I? Maybe something to kill the time at the airport.
Yes, that's a good idea. I'll stop by the newsagent's.

The picture with the magazine is correct. So there is a tick in box C.
Look at the three pictures for question 1 now.
Now we are ready to start. Listen carefully.

1. Where does the band meet for the final rehearsal?
Good morning, staff and students of Hilary High School. Our school band is ready to play at the school festival next Saturday.
The rehearsal this Tuesday will not be in the music room as usual due to ground works. The band meets in the gym on Tuesday and on Friday they meet in the Assembly Hall for the final rehearsal. I'm looking forward to the festival and music from our great school band.
Now listen again.

Seite 111
2. Which dog is missing?
This is Laughton Lost Animals Home, how can I help you?
Hello, my name is Jack Austin. Our dog Leo ran off yesterday morning. Maybe someone brought him in to you?
Let's see. Could you describe your dog, please?
It's a crossbreed with black fur and a white head, long hanging ears and a short tail. He wears a collar around his neck.
Right, I'll check for you. Can you call back in ten minutes?
Yes, of course. Thank you!
Now listen again.

3. When does the main boarding start?
Good morning to all passengers for Kansas City. This is the boarding announcement for flight AA 3421 to Kansas City. Your boarding starts at 9:20. For passengers with young children as well as passengers requiring special assistance boarding starts at 9:00.
Priority boarding starts at 9:10. Please have your boarding pass and identification ready. Thank you for your attention.
Now listen again.

4. Where will the party be?
You know what? I didn't get Ben's invite, but he told me I could come to his party. It's on Saturday, right? But where is it? At his house?
Yeah, it's at his place. I think he wanted to celebrate down by the river, but that didn't work out for some reason. He thought about renting a club, but too expensive and some folks would have been too young to get in.
Now listen again.

5. What's the weather forecast for Friday?
The weather forecast for this weekend doesn't look too promising, really. There is going to be some heavy rain and temperatures in the low sixties. If you're planning on having a BBQ, you might want to do that on Friday. It should still be dry. You shouldn't expect any sunshine, though.
Now listen again.

Seite 112
6. How much flour are they adding to the pancake batter?
OK, let's make pancakes. How much flour do we need? The recipe says 200 grams. But I don't think that would be enough for the five of us.
That's true. Let's make it 300 then. That'll leave 700 grams for David's birthday cake on Saturday.
Brilliant. So let's add the eggs and the milk.
Now listen again.

7. Where is the couple going on holiday?
Look, this website has some great holiday deals. You know, I've always wanted to go to a desert island.
And I cannot think of anything more boring. How would you feel about going to the mountains? I believe it's not that hot there. Or how about going to a big city by the sea? Look, there is Rio and there is Sydney.
Cities are probably one of the hottest places of all. You know, I'd love to go hiking again.
Me too. I think there's only one place where we can do that.
Now listen again.
This is the end of part 1.

Seite 113
Track 13: Part 2
Now turn to part 2, questions 8 to 13.
Listen to Anne and Robin talking online about Robin's new life after he's moved from a small town in Oregon to New York City. For each question tick the correct box A, B or C.
You now have 30 seconds to look at part 2.

Now we are ready to start. Listen carefully.

Hey, Robin, can you hear me?
Yeah, so nice to see you. How are you?
Good. How is life in New York?
It's crazy. You can't imagine.
Really? Hit me.
Well, we moved to the upper Westside in Manhattan so we don't have our own house with a backyard anymore, just an apartment. It felt kind of small at first but now I got used to it. The cool thing is there is a skate park across the street and my new school is only two blocks away, so no more endless bus rides twice a day.
A skate park? Nice. So you still skate a lot?
Not really. I've just been there once so far. I haven't had the time to explore the city yet. I really want to get on the basketball team. Pretty much all I do is work on my shot. Try-outs are next week.
What? You're living in the most amazing city in the world and haven't even checked it out yet?
Well, of course a little bit. This city is unbelievable. I mean the skyscrapers and sights aren't bad but it's the vibe of the city that really gets me. It's true what they say – this city never sleeps. There is always something going on in the streets. Everything is so loud here. It bothered me at first but now I don't really notice it anymore.
Really? I don't know. I think I prefer the peace and quiet here in Oregon. So, how's school?
Everything is so different, way bigger. Not like our tiny school back in Oregon but still the school has a good team spirit because there is a different assembly or team project every week. Also, it's supposed to be one of the better inner city schools. You can choose classes that I had never heard of before. It's great.
That's nice. Have you met some cool people to hang out with?
Yeah, I met Rubio and Jaylin on the basketball court in the park. Now we are practising together for the try-outs. And they told me they also skate. After we've hopefully all made the team, they are going to show me all the nice spots to skate in the city.
Sounds nice. When am I going to meet them?
You want to come visit? That's great. Come right away. Like New York's around the corner. But yeah, I think I can come see you in spring break. Or wait. I'll come over in summer. We'll have much more time then. School is out in June and I'll be counseling at a summer camp right after. But I'm free all of July and August.
Great. Book a flight. I can't wait to show you everything. Remember when I was so afraid of moving here. Now I really feel at home. You know I definitely miss you guys but we can always stay in touch and visit. So tell me, what's up in Teelake. Is Angie still with ...
Now listen again.
This is the end of part 2.

Seite 114
Track 14: Part 3
Lösungsvorschlag:
Now turn to part 3, questions 14 to 20.
You are on a class trip in Copenhagen. The youth hostel manager tells you what you have to know about your stay. Fill in the missing information. The first question is an example. You now have 20 seconds to look at part 3. Now we are ready to start. Listen carefully.

Hello everybody. Please listen up. Welcome to Danhostel Copenhagen. I'm Ole. I'm the hostel manager. I'd like to give you some useful information on your stay. So please note down the most important things. Your teacher told me he's going to test you later tonight. First, your rooms are on the second floor. And your teacher's rooms are on the first floor. The rooms are right below yours so your teachers are closer than you might think. You better watch out. You will all get one of those keycards. You can find your room numbers on them so that you don't accidentally knock on the wrong doors. Make sure you don't lose your card, as there is a 10 Euro deposit on it. I guess you'd like to get that back at the end of your stay. Breakfast is served on the top floor from 7:00 to 10:00. You can eat as much as you like but do not smuggle anything out. If you want to get some supplies for your trips, you can buy a lunch bag for 3 Euros at the entrance to the dining hall. Dinner is from 6:00 to 8:00. You can choose between two different meals – vegan and vegetarian. If you eat nothing but meat, you will go hungry. We are a meatless hostel. Please let the kitchen staff know if you're suffering from any intolerances or food allergies. Our chefs will be happy to provide you with tasty alternatives. For example, we offer some excellent gluten-free specials. In case you're still hungry at night, there is a snack machine on each floor. The quiet time starts at 11:00. That's when you have to stay in your rooms and also turn down the volume. Alcoholic drinks, smoking or other drugs are strictly prohibited. If you break this rule, you will be expelled immediately. If you get bored in the evening, you can use the bowling alley in the basement. We've got six lanes. If you don't only want to watch other people bowl but have a go yourself, you should make a reservation in advance. Bowling is extremely popular at the moment. Maybe that's because it's free. The shoes however are not. The rent is 5 Euros for a pair. And you're not allowed to bowl without them. On departure day, make sure to clean your room. Remove the sheets from your bed and put them into the laundry container, which you'll find on your floor on the day of your departure. Now enjoy your stay and if you have any questions, let me know. Oh, right the WiFi-password: DHC – all in capital letters, 2022 in numbers. So DHC2022. Have a great stay.
Now listen again.
This is the end of part 3.

Seite 115
Track 15: Part 4
Now turn to part 4, questions 21 to 26. You will hear a radio interview with the social media influencer Emma D. Decide whether each statement is true or false and put a tick in the correct box. The first question is an example. You now have 30 seconds to look at part 4.
Now we are ready to start. Listen carefully. You will hear the recording twice.
Good morning listeners. With me today is a person some of you might already know. If so, you've come across her photos and stories on Instapic. Her name is Emma D. and you can find her under her username at Emma under-

score D and perhaps you have noticed that she is unlike most other influencers. Hi Emma, it's a pleasure to have you on the programme today.

Good morning. Thanks for having me.

For those who don't know you, what do you do differently than most other influencers out there?

Well, most other influencers are sponsored by brands. It's their job to promote their products. The latest fashion, the newest makeup, the coolest technology and all the stuff that people care about. I on the other hand like used clothes and accessories and want to show what you can do with them. For example, followers send me clothes they don't wear anymore and I turn them into new outfits and post them on my site.

I happen to be one of your followers and I have to admit it's really hard to believe that it's all second hand. What inspired you to completely focus on second hand?

The thing is, trends are never completely new. Big sunglasses – that was a trend in the eighties and now people are wearing them again. So why buy new ones if it's all been there before? Many people throw their stuff away because they think it's not fashionable anymore. I think that's idiotic. I followed other influencers and thought that they're not sending the right message. We live in a throw-away society and I really don't like that.

I absolutely agree. What do you think? How did you become so successful and gained so many followers?

I think many people have realized that if we continue living the way we do at the moment we will need more than one planet. Things have to change and people know it. And it's a fact – following the latest trends and buying loads of new clothes is not something that makes you happy in the long run. It only satisfies you for a short while but I show my followers how to be creative and make a lot out of a little. And they tell me that they find it inspiring. They begin to appreciate the things that they already have. It actually makes them happy and that makes me happy in return. And last but not least, they are saving a lot of money.

That's an interesting point. But speaking of money. Can you actually make a living off of it?

Well, I can't live from my postings but that's not my goal. I'm running a local secondhand shop. Many of my followers go there to buy what they see online or trade in their old clothes. Also, I want to start selling these clothes online too. At fair prices, of course.

So you're using and reselling clothes for women only?

Well, most of my followers and customers are women but most clothes can be worn by men and women. It's just a matter of how you want to design your outfit. There is nothing gender-specific in what I do.

Emma D., thank you for sharing your thoughts with us. I hope your ideas go viral and other influencers start listening and trying to make the world a better place, too. Coming up in our programme is Steven, who reads out children's books online. Stay tuned.

Now listen again.

This is the end of the listening part.

Good luck for the rest of your examination.

LÖSUNGEN

B — Die mündliche Prüfung

B 2.1 Aufgabenformate für Prüfungsteil 1

Seite 14

Lösungsvorschlag:
My name is Peter.
My last name is Schmidt.
S, C, H, M, I, D, T
I am 16 years old.
My favourite colour is blue.
I live in Bremen.
I have one brother and two sisters.
I get to school by bus.
It takes about 25 minutes.

Possible questions:
When is your birthday?
How do you celebrate your birthday?
Tell us about your family?
What is your favourite subject and why?
What do you enjoy doing in your free time?
What did you do yesterday/last weekend?
What are your plans when you leave school?

B 2.2 Aufgabenformate für Prüfungsteil 2

Seite 15

shows, railway station, There are, in the background, centre, summer, are wearing, are going, backpacks, on the left, around, on the right, blond hair, in the middle, hat, are smiling, on a trip, school, holidays, Going on holiday

B 2.3 Aufgabenformate für Prüfungsteil 3

Seite 16

Lösungsvorschlag:
Partner A: I think we should go camping this summer. We could go hiking and rock climbing.
Partner B: I don't want to go camping. You get wet when it rains and I don't like sleeping in a tent. What do you think about the beach?
Partner A: In my opinion the beach is boring. There is nothing to do there. You go swimming and hang out in the sun. It is the same every day. Maybe we could visit a big city.
Partner B: That sounds interesting. There's always something to do in a big city. Where would you like to go?
Partner A: How do you feel about Berlin? I've been there before and I could show you around.
Partner B: But don't you want to see a new city? How about London? I've never been there. Have you?
Partner A: No, but isn't London very expensive?
Partner B: I believe that we can plan ahead and save money by staying in a youth hostel. We could buy our own food and not eat in restaurants. The money we save we can spend on the different sights. What would you like to see?

Partner A: I really want to go on the London Eye. You have a great view of the city from up there. I also want to visit the zoo and the Tower. What about you?

Partner B: I want to go shopping at Harrods, visit some museums and see the changing of the guard at Buckingham Palace.

Partner A: That sounds great. I can't wait to go to London!

B 3.1 Speaking Test 1

Seite 17
Part 1 – Questions
Lösungsvorschlag:

What's your name? My name is Peter Schmidt.
How do you spell your last name? S, c, h, m, i, d, t.
Please tell me where you live! I live in Bremen.
How long have you been living there? I have been living in Bremen for three years.
Do you live in a house or a flat? I live in a house.
Do you have your own room? Yes, I do.
Please describe your room! My room is about 25 square metres in size, with a big window. When you walk through the door, my bed is on the right and my work desk is on the left near the window. The walls are green and white. I also have a comfortable couch and a TV in my room. I have a lot of pictures on the walls and a big shelf full of books and CDs and DVDs. My bed is really big. I have a small shelf next to my pillow with a lamp and some books. My work desk has drawers for my papers and a big shelf for all the books I need for school. I also have some plants on the shelf in front of the window.
Do you have any hobbies?
I love swimming and playing badminton.
Tell us more about your favourite hobby.
I love swimming. That is my favourite hobby. I go to the pool three times a week to practice. I want to get better so I can win some medals at the next competition. I like freestyle and breast-stroke.

Part 2
Lösungsvorschlag:
picture 1
The picture shows a living room with a sofa and a glass coffee table. There are cushions and rugs on the sofa and a plant on the coffee table. On the wall hang two guitars. In the foreground a boy is standing on a thick carpet, holding a vacuum cleaner. He is wearing a check shirt and jeans, and is barefoot. He is looking down at the carpet as if he is proud of his work – it seems he has just been cleaning the carpet. In the background is a window. You can't see it very well, because the photo is taken from floor level, so the boy's body hides it. But you can just see part of a curtain. On the right of the picture is an alcove with window blinds and some things standing on the floor. You can't see them clearly, but they might be a TV and loudspeakers. I think children should also help with the housework. There are lots of jobs they can do. Some of my friends have to go shopping for their parents or help vacuum the living room and the rest of the house. My best friend told me that his whole family cleans their house every Friday for an hour. I think that's a great idea because then you all work together and the house is clean for the weekend.

Seite 18
Lösungsvorschlag:
picture 2
I can see a room. It looks really messy and dirty. There are books and papers on the left. On the right are dirty clothes both on the bed and on the floor. In the front I can see a desk that is covered with papers and rubbish. The boy obviously has problems cleaning up his room. I think that children should clean their own rooms. I don't want my mother to come into my room and go through my stuff, so I have to clean everything myself. Sometimes my mother tells me that she will come in and clean if I don't do it. That usually makes me start right away.
I also have to take the clean dishes out of the dishwasher and put them away, and stack my dirty plates and cups into the dishwasher. And I must help in the garden in summer. I don't get all my pocket money if I don't do those jobs. I think it is important to help in the family and to work for my money. My parents also have to work for the money they earn. Some of my friends don't have to do anything at home, but I think it is a good lesson for kids that nothing in life is free. If you want something, you have to work to get it. I want to get a newspaper round to earn some extra money.

Part 3
Lösungsvorschlag:
A: We want to have a party for the whole class. What do we need to plan?
B: I think we need to decide where and when we want to have the party. I think we should have the party in someone's home. Maybe someone in the class has a nice big garden, so we can have a garden party with a barbecue at night.
A: I think that is a great idea. A barbecue is much better than a picnic. What time do you think will be good for everybody?
B: I think 7pm or 8pm would be good for everyone. We could do it on a Friday or Saturday so we don't have to worry about going to school the next day.
A: Yes, I agree. Do you think we should just invite the class to the party or should we invite other guests, too?
B: I think we should only have all the people from our class there. It is important for us to spend some time together and have some fun. If we have guests or other friends, it won't be a real class party anymore.
A: I agree. Do you want to have music, maybe a DJ? Or should we organize a karaoke machine?
B: I think a DJ would be great. Maybe we can have a group of people to organize everything. They could make a list of things we need and also decide if people want to bring food and drinks, or if the group should buy everything and collect money from everybody.
A: I think that is a great idea. Let's talk to the rest of the class tomorrow and make suggestions. We can find people who want to join the group to organize the party.

B 3.2 Speaking Test 2

Part 1

Lösungsvorschlag:

Hello, how are you today? I am fine. How are you?
What's your name? My name is Timothy MacPherson.
Can you spell your first name for me? My first name is
spelt T, I, M, O, T, H, Y.
Tell me something about your hometown. My hometown
is not very big. It is near the North Sea and has about five
thousand people.
What can you do there in your free time? In the summer
there is a lot to do. You can go swimming in the North Sea
or go walking on the beaches. You can ride your bike and
visit different museums. You can go fishing or meet your
friends. I am in a soccer club and we play against other
teams at the weekend. We have a disco in town and nice
restaurants.
Can you talk about your family? My dad works in a car
company. He is a manager and flies all over the world. He
is not home much. My mother works as a teacher, but she
is home a lot because she only works part-time.
Do you have sisters or brothers? Yes, I have a brother. He
is eight years younger than me, but we get along great.
I can show him things and he looks up to me. We don't
have the same interests, but I can help him with school
or when he has problems with friends.
Tell me about your friends. My best friend is Tim, a boy
who lives next door. I've known him for many years. We
often meet after school. I have other friends from school
and from my hockey team.
Do you have a pet? We have a dog. We got it as a puppy
two years ago. Now he walks with us everywhere and is a
real friend for all of us.

Seite 19
Part 2

Lösungsvorschlag:

I can see a mother and a daughter. The mother is looking
at her watch and is making an angry face. The daughter
looks like she just wants her mother to leave her alone.
Maybe she wants to meet her friends but her mother is
telling her to be home at ten. The daughter wants to be
with her friends and she thinks ten is too early. Maybe
she has come home late before and her mother doesn't
want her to be out so late. She is worried about her.
We have rules at home. During the week I have to be
home by 9 o'clock. I have to sleep so I can concentrate in
school. At the weekend I can stay out longer if I want to.
Most of my friends have the same rules. The girls have to
be home earlier than the boys. I can call my parents and
they will pick me up at night. They want me to be safe. For
my parents, school comes first. I have to finish my homework and study for exams before I can do anything else. I
can only watch an hour of TV a day and they also monitor
my computer access. They think playing computer games
for hours is bad for me. They want to meet my friends
and know who I meet and where. They bought a mobile
phone for me so I can call them and they can call me.
There are a lot of rules at my house and I don't like all of
them but I know that my parents care about me.

Part 3

Lösungsvorschlag:

A: I don't like school uniforms. People all look the same.
B: That's true. But that can be a good thing.
A: What do you mean?
B: Some parents don't have a lot of money and can't buy
their kids nice clothes. In a school uniform nobody
would know if people have more money and can buy
nicer clothes.
A: That's a good argument. But school uniforms are
expensive, too. Sometimes they look awful. The
girls have to wear skirts and blazers. I would feel
uncomfortable in clothes like that.
B: Yes, I can understand that. But we could design a cool
school uniform. The colours could be nice and the
clothes would be comfortable.
A: OK, that could work. How about jeans? We could all
wear jeans and a T-shirt or sweatshirt. Maybe we
could offer different colours for the boys and girls. We
could have blue and green for boys and red and yellow
for girls.
B: I am not sure that our friends would agree. People
really like to choose their own clothes. A lot of people
feel that clothes are part of their personality. They
want to decide what to wear.
A: Do you think we could ever agree on a school uniform?
B: I don't know. People have so many different styles
and opinions.
A: That's true. Why don't we try and compromise. Everybody can wear their own jeans or trousers and socks
and shoes but they all have to wear a school sweatshirt or T-shirt. We can have a competition in school.
Every class can think about a design for a T-shirt or
sweatshirt. The school can choose the nicest ones
that we can buy in different colours. Maybe that would
work.
B: That sounds like a great idea. The clothes would be
comfortable and I can still choose my own colour but
the style would be the same.

B 3.3 Speaking Test 3

Seite 20
Part 1

Lösungsvorschlag:

What's your first name? My name is Laura.
Can you spell your first name, please? L, A, U, R, A
Where do you go to school? I go to school in Hamburg.
What is/are your favourite subject(s)? My favourite subjects are PE, English and Drama.
What other activities do you do in school? I go to drama
class. I really love it because you can be somebody else
in a play. Right now we are doing a detective story and I
am the killer. It is a lot of fun. I am also a member of our
soccer team. We play against other schools all the time.
What is the atmosphere like in your class? The atmosphere is good. I get along with almost everyone, but we
have some outsiders. They don't want to be part of the
class. When we go on a trip they have some excuse not to
come along.
Do you have a lot friends in school? Most of my friends
are at my school. Not all of them are in my class. I know
a lot of people from drama class and soccer. I am also a

member of our local Red Cross group and have friends there who go to a different school.

Part 2
Lösungsvorschlag:
I can see a group of kids smoking. The kid on the right does not have a cigarette but he is, or wants to be, part of the group. One of the other teenagers wants to offer him a cigarette. What will he decide? Will he take the cigarette because he wants to be one of them? Maybe he will walk away because he does not want to start smoking.
I play soccer and basketball. I want to stay fit and eat healthily. I am against smoking so I would never start just to belong to a group. I don't think this is the right way to make friends. You can find friends in sports clubs or at school. Smoking is a bad habit. It costs a lot of money and kills you in the end. I would tell them that I like them but I don't want to start smoking. They have to accept that, or I can't be their friend anymore.

Seite 21
Part 3
Lösungsvorschlag:
Partner A: We need money for our driver's licence. There are some openings for jobs. What sort of job would you like to do?
Partner B: I like working as a waiter. You meet a lot of new people and the tips are good.
Partner A: Yes, that's true, but the pay per hour is not very good. You have to be up on your feet all day and the working hours are bad. What do you think about working in a supermarket? They have regular hours from 8am to 5pm.
Partner B: Yes, that's good but did you look at the pay? And the job is boring. You have to carry boxes all day and stack the products in the shelves. What do you think about delivering newspapers?
Partner A: That is a nice job but it doesn't pay enough money. We need to earn at least 1000 Euros. What do you think about a cleaning job?
Partner B: I really hate cleaning. I have to help my mother at home all the time and I really don't like it. What do you think about gardening?
Partner A: That sounds really good. I like being outside and we would work with flowers and plants. Do you think we could earn enough money doing that job?
Partner B: I think so. I like being outside and if we work together it wouldn't be boring. Let's give them a call and ask about a job.
Partner A: OK, let's do that.

C Arbeitstechniken für die schriftliche Prüfung

C 1.6 Beispielaufgaben (Hörverstehen)

Seite 27
Part 1
1. C
2. B
3. C
4. A
5. A

Seite 29
Part 2: A summer job
6. A
7. A
8. B
9. B
10. C
11. C

Seite 30
Part 3: A new job
12. in March
13. $6 an hour
14. 10 a.m.
15. 1 to 1:30 p.m.
16. 15 tables
17. her feet hurt and she can't sleep

Part 4: The American and German school systems
18. false
19. true
20. false
21. false
22. true
23. true

C 2.6 Textbeispiele mit Aufgaben (Leseverstehen)

Seite 36
Part 1
1. a) false
   b) false
2. a) true
   b) false
3. a) true
   b) false
4. a) true
   b) false
5. a) false
   b) false

Seite 37
Part 2
6. Samir: F
7. Cheryl: C
8. Jonathan: H
9. Emily: D
10. Demelza: B

Für A, E und G gibt es keine passende Person.

Seite 39
Part 3
11. C
12. B
13. A
14. C
15. C

Seite 41
Part 4
Lösungsvorschlag:
16. A lot of people leave school with a diploma that allows them to study at a university. (lines 2–3)
17. The number of students in Schleswig-Holstein right now is 48,000. (lines 13–14)
18. The government in Kiel is trying to offer more living space to students. (lines 6–7)
19. Students are sleeping and living in their cars, in youth hostels and retirement homes. (lines 8–9)
20. Students help older people with shopping, cleaning and getting dressed. (lines 10–11)
21. In October, 5,000 new students will arrive but only 50% of them will have a place to live. (lines 17–18)
22. An idea to help students is "bed surfing" which is an extra bed for a short period of time. (lines 23–25)
23. Rents are high and a lot of students are on a long waiting list for student housing. (lines 28–29)

C 3.1 Aufgabenformate für die Sprachmittlung

Seite 42
Part 1
New York City Bus Tours
Lösungsvorschlag:
Schaut mal, hier kann man eine Bustour durch New York City buchen, die Stadt die niemals schläft. Die Busse haben eine Klimaanlage und ein offenes Dach, so dass man alles gut sehen kann.
Der Bus fährt über zehn Bushaltestellen an. So kann man sich viele der Sehenswürdigkeiten ansehen, zum Beispiel das Empire State Building, das Metropolitan Museum für Kunst, Macys, den Grand Central Bahnhof, den Central Park, Ground Zero und viele mehr.
Der Stadtführer gibt Hinweise in drei Sprachen: Englisch, Spanisch oder Französisch.
Die Rundfahrten beginnen zu jeder vollen Stunde am Busbahnhof und dauern drei Stunden.
Ihr würdet pro Person $35 bezahlen und ich als Kind noch $20. Man kann die Tickets im Voraus online buchen oder bei dieser Telefonnummer anrufen: 475-9843.

Seite 43
Part 2
Lösungsvorschlag:
Lorenzo: So, what do I have to do when I come to school in the morning? I don't understand the first rule. Can I go to the classroom right away?
You: No, you can't go to your classroom. You have to stay in the hall until 7.30. Then you can go to the classrooms.
Lorenzo: During the breaks can I go into town and get something to eat?
You: No, you must stay in the school grounds until school ends.
Lorenzo: Can I stay in the classroom and talk to my friends then?
You: No, you can't do that. During the breaks you can go into the big hall or you can go outside and talk to your friends there.
Lorenzo: Where can I leave my bike?
You: You can leave your bike in the bicycle stand and lock it up.
Lorenzo: When classes are over, can I go home right away?
You: No, you and your classmates must clean the classroom and put your chairs on the tables.
Lorenzo: Are there any other rules that I need to know about?
You: Yes, during the 5-minute break you can only change classrooms or go to the toilet. You cannot go outside.

C 4.1 Aufgabenformate für das Schreiben

Seite 45
An Au Pair Job (Writing a letter)
Lösungsvorschlag:
Jenny Schmidt

Dorfstraße 16
22384 Hamburg
May 10, 2023

Mr John McGuire
19 Currie Street
Edinburgh – GB

Dear Mr McGuire,
I am writing because I read your advertisement in the newspaper. My name is Jenny Schmidt. I am 16 years old and in my last year in high school. My mother works in a bank and my father is a truck driver. I have two brothers and one sister. I am the oldest. I go to school in the morning and in the afternoon I take care of my brothers and sisters while my mother works. I help them with their homework, play with them in the afternoon and prepare their meals. I also babysit regularly for our neighbors who have two small kids (age 2 and 4). I love kids and want to be a nurse in a children's hospital or become a kindergarten teacher. I did an internship for three weeks in a kindergarten last year. I like to read, play games with my friends and play volleyball. It would be a wonderful experience for me to take care of your children and improve my English in a foreign country.
I look forward to hearing from you.

Sincerely,
Jenny Schmidt

Seite 47
Writing a blog entry
Lösungsvorschlag:
Get vaccinated now!
I think that the vaccination is the only protection against the coronavirus. I feel safe with Pfizer or Moderna and got vaccinated as soon as possible. I am a teacher, so I am around teenagers and children all day. In the beginning I was scared but after my vaccination I feel safe to go to work every day. The side effects of the vaccine were mild. I felt sick for a day or two. My family was vaccinated too. My son is ten and there is no vaccine for him yet. I am worried that he might get the infection and have long-term side effects. I hope that scientists will develop a vaccine for him soon. Then we will be first in line for the vaccine. (10th December 2021, Sheila, Virginia)

(135 words)

Seite 49
Writing a report
Lösungsvorschlag:
The exchange visit to England
My friend Karsten went on an exchange visit to England for ten days. He took the Eurostar train through the Channel Tunnel. The trip was very exciting. His guest family met him at the train station. They were very nice. Their daughter Peggy was Karsten's age. The food was good, especially breakfast and the famous English dish fish and chips. Karsten and his family went on a day trip to London, where they shopped for hours and rode on the London Eye. It was a wonderful experience for Karsten. He and Peggy became good friends and he improved his English language skills on the exchange visit.

(106 words)

Seite 50
Writing an e-mail
Lösungsvorschlag:
To: minniemouse@yahoo.com
From: mickeymouse@yahoo.com
Subject: Trip to amusement park

Dear Minnie,   15th May 2023
Last weekend I went on a class trip to an amusement park. First we rode on the bus for an hour. I listened to music on my MP3 player and talked to my friend. We went on all the fun rides in the park. Some of them were scary, especially the roller coaster. We had pizza and coke. At four p.m. we had to go home. We had a really great time.
All the best from Mickey.   (76 words)

Seite 52
Writing a description
Lösungsvorschlag:
This is what my bag looks like:
My sports bag is small. It is square in shape and the color is black. On the outside it says "Star Team" in white letters. It has two handles and a zipper at the top.
These things are in the bag:
In my bag are a pair of blue sneakers, a pair of red shorts, a green T-shirt and a pair of black socks. I also had a bottle of water and tissues in it.

Seite 53
Filling in a form
9. Price category A or B for a single room
10. Date of arrival: 23rd May
11. Date of departure: 26th May

Seite 54
Giving your own opinion
Lösungsvorschlag:
My opinion about school uniforms
First of all I want to say that clothes are not very important to me. I don't buy expensive clothes. They have to be comfortable and nice. I personally think that a school uniform would help us pupils to feel more like a group and identify with our school or class. We would all wear the same clothes and nobody could say anything about clothes being old or "uncool". Most of my friends feel the same way but then there are some girls and boys who spend a lot of money on their clothes and they don't want to wear the same as everybody else. I guess they care more about what is on the outside of a person than what is inside.

(128 words)

C 4.4 Aufgabenformen zur Wortschatzarbeit

Seite 57
words or expressions which mean almost the same
Lösungsvorschlag:
1. (to) better
2. (to) try
3. strange
4. right
5. afraid
6. mean
7. form
8. wonderful
9. big
10. difficult

Seite 58
opposites
Lösungsvorschlag:
1. impolite
2. (to) agree
3. unhappy
4. unhealthy/sick
5. inexpensive/cheap
6. majority
7. illegal
8. divorced
9. high
10. war

name the words
Lösungsvorschlag:
1. (to) improve
2. foreigner
3. (to) trade
4. crowd
5. countryside
6. discussion/argument
7. neighbour
8. author
9. (to) sign
10. headline

definitions
Lösungsvorschlag:
1. the sea between England and France
2. people stand behind one another waiting for something
3. the person who repairs or installs your toilet
4. the job that you learned
5. something to make someone suffer for what they have
   done
6. the noun for high
7. the noun for healthy
8. something that provides electricity
9. someone who is kept as a prisoner
10. unhappy feeling when someone has something you want

Seite 59
chart of word families
Lösungsvorschlag:
improvement, improving/improved
(to) conquer, conquering/conquered
(to) influence, influence
attraction, attractive
(to) interest, interesting
(to) damage, damage
protection, protective

key words
Lösungsvorschlag:
1. furniture
2. colours
3. toys
4. luggage
5. clothes
6. food
7. jobs

Mindmap: Business and Trade
Lösungsvorschlag:

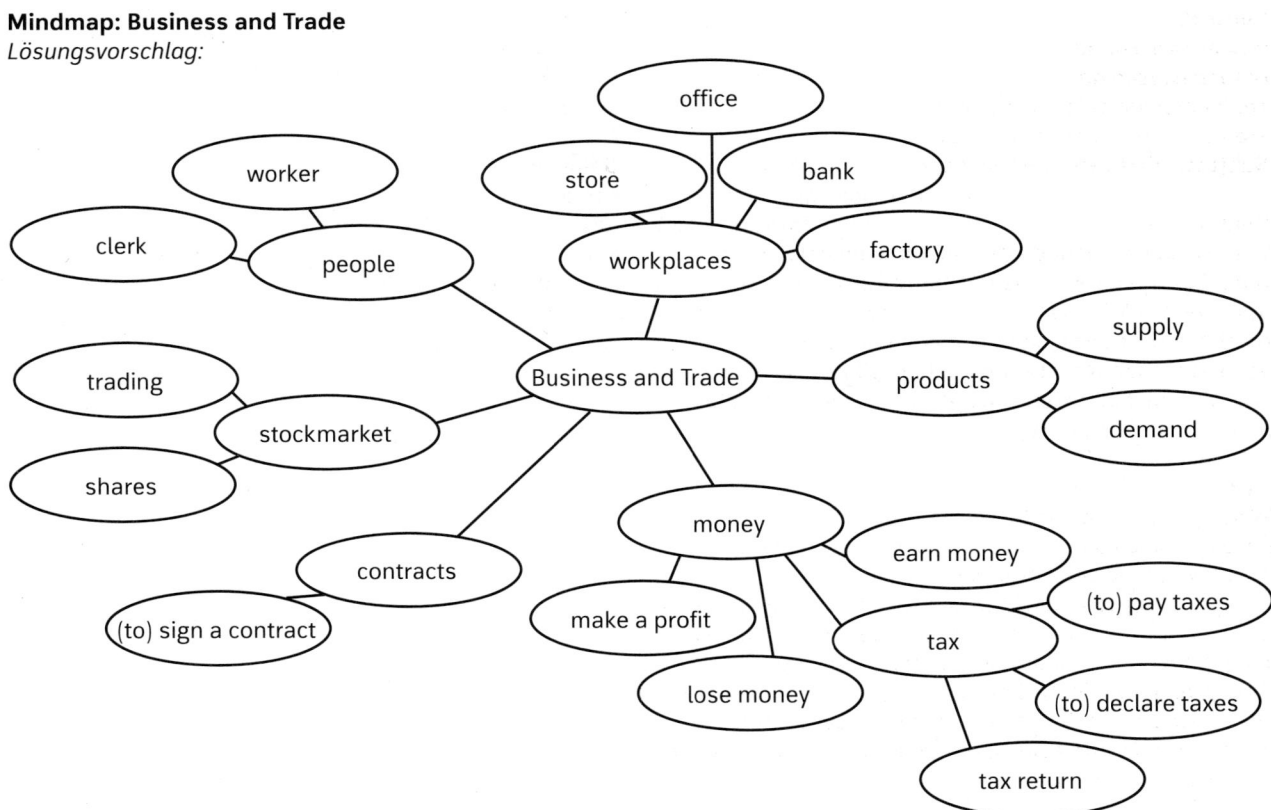

Angeleitete Prüfungsaufgaben

D I. Hörverstehen

Seite 61
Mindmap – Schools in Britain
Lösungsvorschlag:

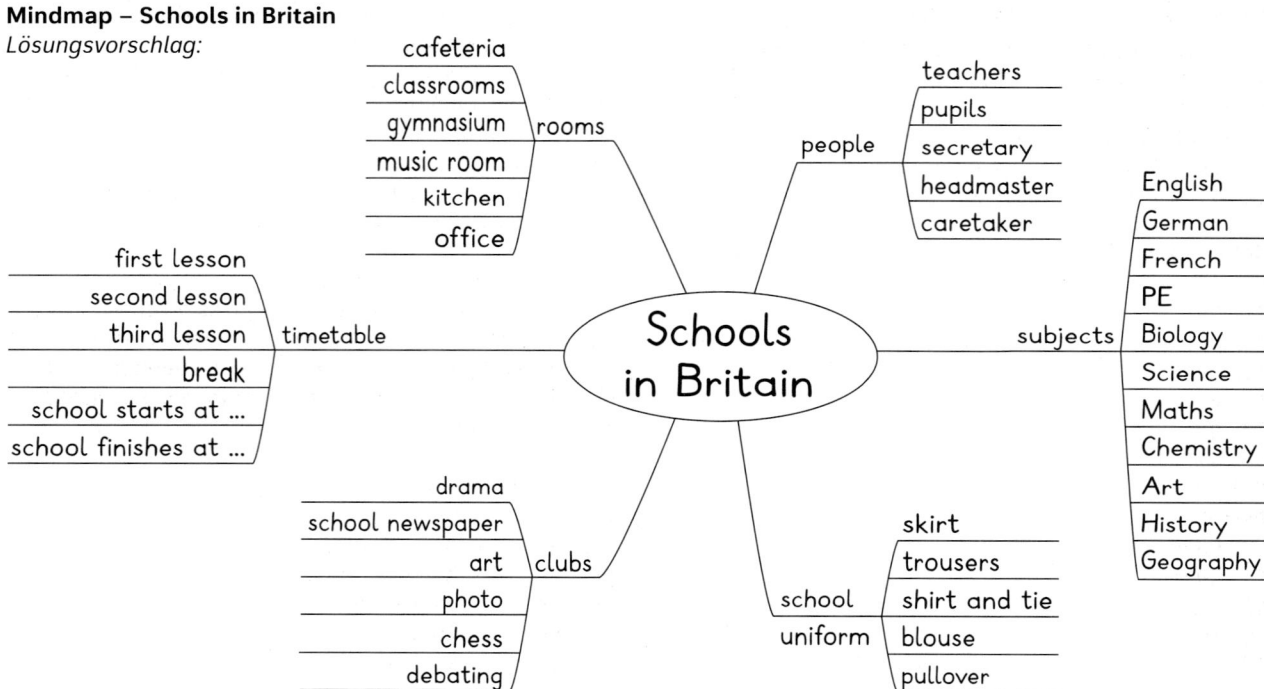

Part 1
Welche Gesprächssituation wird hier präsentiert?
Eine oder mehrere Personen unterhalten sich über einen bestimmten Inhalt.
Worüber wird gesprochen?
Die Personen sprechen über Inhalte von Unterrichtsfächern.
Auf welche Begriffe/Inhalte musst du achten?
Du solltest auf Begriffe achten, die zu den einzelnen Unterrichtsfächern passen (z. B. basketball, cooking, kitchen, colours, countries, numbers, animals).
Informationen bzw. Unterschiede zum britischen Schulsystem:
school uniforms, form, grade, cafeteria, pupils, teachers, subjects, timetable, classroom, homework
Was sollst du aus den Hörtexten heraushören? Was musst du bei dieser Aufgabe beachten?
Du sollst jedem Text ein Unterrichtsfach zuordnen und die richtige Zahl neben das entsprechende Fach schreiben. Du musst auf bestimmte Begriffe achten, die es dir möglich machen, das Unterrichtsfach zu erkennen.

Extract 1:
Shakespeare, famous writer, *Romeo and Juliet* – English
Extract 2:
pizza, water, salt, cheese – Home Economics
Extract 3:
earthquakes, ground shakes, Richter scale – Geography
Extract 4:
100 kilometers per hour, 181 miles – Maths
Extract 5:
painter, picture, artist, colours – Art
Extract 6:
basketball, game, ball – PE
Extract 7:
animals, the ocean, whales, seals – Biology

Seite 64
Part 2
Welche Gesprächssituation wird hier präsentiert?
Es handelt sich bei der Situation um ein Interview.
Worüber wird gesprochen?
Ein Mädchen berichtet über seinen Schulalltag.
Auf welche Begriffe/Inhalte musst du achten?
Achte besonders auf die Vokabeln zum Wortfeld „Schools in Britain".
Was sollst du aus dem Interview heraushören? Was musst du bei dieser Aufgabe beachten?
Du musst gezielt auf die Informationen (z. B. Zahlen) achten, die bei den einzelnen Aufgaben erfragt werden (Alter, Herkunftsland von Naomi).

8. C
9. B
10. C
11. A
12. B

Seite 66
Part 3
13. false
14. false
15. true
16. true
17. true

Lösungshilfen:
vocabulary: lies, rumours, gossip, share, cell phone, video, pictures, humiliating, secrets, threaten,
typische Situationen:
– Jugendliche bedrohen/erpressen andere Mitschüler
– Jugendliche veröffentlichen peinliche Bilder oder Videos von anderen Jugendlichen im Internet (facebook etc.)
– Du sollst Aussagen als richtig oder als falsch erkennen.

Seite 67
Part 4
18. videos.
19. behind your back.
20. entire world.
21. Great Britain.
22. victims.
23. hardly ever get caught.

Lösungshilfen:
a new kind   – eine neue Art von ...
share   – mit anderen teilen
publish   – veröffentlichen
distressing   – unangenehm
humiliating   – peinlich, erniedrigend

Beispiel: They publish humiliating **pictures** and videos.

– Du sollst die Sätze vervollständigen.

D II. Leseverstehen

Seite 69
Part 1
Vorwissen aktivieren:
Anhand der Überschriften kannst du erkennen, dass es sich bei den Texten um Informationen zu vier verschiedenen Städten und Veranstaltungen für Touristen handelt.

englische Begriffe:
sights, museum, opening hours, history, food, drink, activities, season, restaurants, shopping

Aufgabenstellung beachten:
Bei dieser Aufgabe geht es darum, dass du entscheiden musst, ob die Aussagen zu den einzelnen Veranstaltungen richtig oder falsch sind. Lies dir zuerst die Sätze durch und lies dann die Texte und markiere die wichtigsten Textstellen.

Wörter erschließen:
witnessed   – bezeugen
prosperity   – Aufschwung
(to) raise   – hochheben, anheben
(to) host   – eine Party geben
ingredient   – Zutaten
culinary   – kulinarisch
variety   – Vielfalt

1. a) false
   b) true
2. a) true
   b) true
3. a) false
   b) false
4. a) true
   b) false
5. a) true
   b) true

Seite 71
Part 2
Vorwissen aktivieren:
englische Begriffe:
holiday, vacation, attraction, sightseeing, visit, information, opening hours, tourist, parks and gardens, museum, shopping, souvenirs

Aufgabenstellung beachten:
Bei dieser Aufgabe musst du herausfinden, welche Sehenswürdigkeit zu welcher Person passt. Lies die Texte der Personen und der Attraktionen durch und unterstreiche die wichtigsten Angaben.

Wörter erschließen:

estate	–	Landgut
geology	–	Geologie
several	–	mehrere
furnishings	–	Einrichtung
feature	–	Merkmal
stroll	–	Spaziergang
exhibit	–	ausstellen

6. E
7. D
8. A
9. F
10. G

Seite 75
Part 3
Wörter erschließen:

to trade	–	handeln
trade union	–	Gewerkschaft
tax	–	Steuer
migrant	–	(bird) Zugvogel, (Mensch) Zuwanderer, Einwanderer
protection	–	Schutz

Seite 76
Lösungsvorschlag:
11. Migrant workers are people who have to move to the city to find a job. (lines 9–10)
12. Government benefits are tied to the place where you were born. (lines 12–14)
13. In 2016 China produced 34% of the world's clothing exports. (lines 24–25)
14. The average monthly salary of a woman working in the textile industry is about $270 a month. (lines 27–29)
15. The biggest health risk in the textile industry is a technique called sandblasting. (lines 34–35)
16. Humanitarian organisations are trying to defend the workers' rights and raise awareness of the illegal working conditions. (lines 44–45)

Seite 77
Part 4
17. true
18. false
19. not in the text
20. true
21. false
22. true
23. true
24. not in the text

D III. Mediation (Sprachmittlung)

Seite 78
1.
Lösungsvorschlag:
1. Das Postamt befindet sich auf einem schwimmenden Boot im Dal See.
2. Das Postamt wurde im Jahr 2011 eröffnet.
3. Man kann Briefe abschicken, das Internet nutzen und internationale Telefonanrufe tätigen.

4. Das alte Postgebäude ist abgebrannt.
5. Es war ein Lagerhaus (für Bewässerungsrohre) für eine Tomatenplantage.

Seite 80
2.
Thema: Verkaufsgespräch
Situation: Eine englischsprechende Touristin möchte in einem Bekleidungsgeschäft etwas kaufen, spricht aber kein Deutsch und versteht daher den Verkäufer nicht.
Begriffe: bestimmte Marke – brand, Größe – size, im Angebot – on sale, Taille – waist

Lösungsvorschlag:
Can he help you?
Do you want a particular brand?
What size do you need and what colour would you like?
They have jeans by Lovis and Hers in your size and colour for € 75.

D IV. Schreiben

Seite 82
a)
Korrigierter Text:
In 1945 Juneau <u>was</u> the capital of <u>Alaska</u> (sp, wo). In 1953 oil fields <u>were</u> found in Alaska (wo, gr, sp). The population of Alaska is 600,000. In 1959 Alaska <u>was</u> the <u>69th</u> state of the USA (wo, sp). Alaska is the biggest <u>state</u> of the USA (sp). On some days in Alaska <u>there</u> <u>is</u> no daylight and on some days in Alaska <u>there</u> is only daylight and no night (voc, gr). In 1867 the USA <u>bought</u> Alaska from Russia (wo, gr). In 1926 Alaska <u>received</u> a state flag (voc, wo).

b)
Lösungsvorschlag:
Last week I went to the museum of natural history. **In general**, I am not really interested in museums **but** I really liked this one. They had a map in the entry hall **so** the tourists could find information about the different exhibits and continents **that** you could visit. We had a tour guide **but** he was not very good. He always spoke in the same monotonous voice **and** he did not seem excited about the animals in the museum. The different continents and their animals were really interesting **although** some areas of the
museum were boring **because** you had to read a lot of information, **but** you could also rent a pair of headphones. Instead of reading everything by yourself you could also walk **while** listening to the explanations on the tape. I really liked the dinosaurs best **because** there was a lot of action, **which** was exciting. The dinosaurs moved and made noises **so** the whole scene seemed real **and** scary. Some kids were at the controls, **which** were easy to operate **because** you just had to move the lever up and down. **Although** the adults laughed, the smaller kids were really scared **and** started crying.
Afterwards I went to the restaurant **and** enjoyed a cup of coffee. **Although** the souvenir shop was very expensive, I bought a small dinosaur **that** I wanted to take home with me. **Because** visiting this museum was such a good idea **and** I had such a good time, I will go again soon.

Seite 83
Part 1
Schritt 1:
<u>Read the text</u> and write an <u>e-mail to the author</u> of the article. <u>Name arguments for and against the use of digital devices</u> and state <u>your own opinion</u> at the end of the e-mail. Write at least <u>130 words</u>.

Schritt 2:
- Text sorgfältig durchlesen
- eine E-Mail an den Autor schreiben
- Argumente für und gegen das Benutzen von digitalen Geräten nennen
- die eigene Meinung darstellen
- mindestens 130 Wörter schreiben

Schritt 3:
- digitale Geräte
- Gefahrenpotenzial?
- eine Studie (Ergebnisse)

Seite 85
Schritt 4:
influence – beeinflussen, global digitalization – globale Digitalisierung, outcome – Ergebnis, anonymously – anonym, survey – Umfrage, significant – bedeutend, recognize – erkennen

Schritt 5:
Lösungsvorschlag:
Arguments for digital tools:
- vast progress in digital technology
- children learn how to use digital devices
- easy communication with friends etc.
- distance learning is possible
- contact with school, teachers
- classes via video

Arguments against digital tools:
- less exercise
- no more hobbies
- health problems (eyes, weight)
- no "real" contacts with friends
- danger of addiction

Schritt 6:
Lösungsvorschlag:
"Children and teenagers had to stay at home …", "This led to spending more time with and using technological tools", "The study showed more frequent smartphone use …", "This may be related to the social distancing measures …", "The present survey also showed the changing patterns and reasons for the use of smartphones …", "Smartphones were used for social contacts, learning and entertainment. Finally, a significant increase of overuse and addiction was noted", "This led to many health and social problems …"

Schritt 7:
Lösungsvorschlag:
In my opinion we can't live without digital devices any more. I use my smartphone to stay in contact with my friends and family. I can organize my social life and make appointments. I think that we have to talk about the dangers of addiction and make children and teenagers aware of the problems.

Seite 86
Schritt 8:
Lösungsvorschlag:
To: jsmith@yahoo.com
From: marym@yahoo.com
Subject: digital devices

Dear Mrs Smith, I read your article in our local newspaper. I have followed the debate about digital tools for a while now, and I want to add some ideas and my opinion to the discussion. Children and teenagers today can't live without digital tools. They need them for their social life and they need them for school. Teenagers organize their free time and their hobbies with their smartphone. They get in touch with their friends and talk about where to meet and when. In school, they check their schedule, their homework and when they have to take the next exam. They can also look at material for school online or talk to their teacher. Using digital devices makes their life easier. Children also use their devices for entertainment like watching videos or playing computer games. I think we need to talk to children early about the danger of digital addiction, and parents have to monitor their children and the use of their smartphone.
Sincerely   (168 words)

Seite 87
Part 2
Schritt 1:
A <u>new fast-food restaurant</u> is going to open in your hometown. <u>You would love to go</u> and be one of the first people in your class to <u>try the food.</u> You want to <u>invite the exchange student from the USA</u> who is in your class. Her name is <u>Heather</u>. <u>Write an invitation</u> to her.

Schritt 2:
- eine Einladung schreiben
- Name des Restaurants, warum ich gehen möchte
- Ort und Zeit des Treffens
- 60–70 Wörter schreiben

Seite 88
Schritt 3:
Situation: eine Person lädt eine andere in ein Restaurant ein, Verabredung, Uhrzeit, Ort etc.

Schritt 4:
Invite her to come: I would like you…, would you like…?, can you come?, I hope you have time.
Tell her what restaurant you want to go to and why: new restaurant, I like fast food, be one of the first to try it out, tell the rest of the class whether the food is good
Suggest a good place and time to meet: Friday night, meet at 7 p.m. in front of your house

Schritt 5:

Dear Heather,   23th May 2023

A new fast-food restaurant is going to open this Friday
night. I want to invite you to go there with me and try it
out. I really like fast food. I hope you do, too. We could be
the first pupils in our class to eat there.
I could pick you up Friday night at 7 p.m. at your house. I
hope you will come.
Yours, John.   (65 words)

Seite 89
Part 3 (diary entry)
Lösungsvorschlag:
On Saturday the weather was cloudy. We visited the
Museum of Natural History and saw dinosaurs. Later we
went shopping. I bought a new T-shirt. We had coffee at
a music café.
On Sunday we got up late and went for a walk in the park.
We ate at a fast-food restaurant. After that we went to
the cinema and saw an exciting film. We took the train
back home and had a nice dinner with the family. We
talked all evening. I was really tired and went to bed late.
                                                 (91 words)

Lösungshilfen:
Schreibe einen Tagebucheintrag für das Wochenende
(Samstag und Sonntag) und benutze die Wörter aus dem
Kasten. Schreibe einen Text von etwa 80 Wörtern in der
Vergangenheitsform.

Beispiel:
I bought a wonderful new T-shirt. It was cheap and I re-
ally love it. I didn't like the the Museum of Natural History.
It was boring.

Teil E Aufgaben zum selbstständigen Üben – mit Hilfestellung

E I. Hörverstehen

Seite 91
Part 1
1. B
2. B
3. A
4. A
5. B
6. A

Seite 93
Part 2
7. B
8. A
9. C
10. A
11. A
12. B

Seite 94
Part 3
13. Minneapolis
14. spring of 1964
15. summer of 1967
16. Mississippi
17. 1907 feet
18. 115 feet

Seite 95
Part 4
19. false
20. true
21. false
22. true
23. true

E II. Leseverstehen

Part 1
1. a) false
   b) true
2. a) true
   b) true
3. a) true
   b) true
4. a) false
   b) false
5. a) false
   b) false

Seite 97
Part 2
6. Meike: B
7. Max: A
8. Jenny: G
9. Marc: F
10. Peter: C

Seite 98
Part 3
11. true (lines 2–4)
12. false (lines 8–10)
13. false (lines 15–16)
14. true (line 21)
15. true (line 24–25)
16. false (line 35–36)
17. true (lines 40–41)

Seite 100
Part 4
18. B
19. D
20. A
21. C
22. A
23. D
24. B

E III. Mediation (Sprachmittlung)

Seite 101
Part 1
Lösungsvorschläge:
1. Hundekot überträgt Krankheiten!
   Nehmen Sie Ihren Hund an die Leine und entsorgen Sie den Kot.
   Bitte halten Sie diesen Platz sauber.

2. Gras wächst in Zentimetern und stirbt in Quadratmetern.
   Bitte bleiben Sie auf den Wegen.

Seite 102
Part 2
Lösungsvorschlag:
1. You can play this game alone or in a team. You have to throw the frisbee into a basket. You start at the tee (just like in golf) and throw the frisbee. The person with the fewest throws wins. You don't hit a golfball, you throw a frisbee.
2. Men, women and teenagers can play in the club.
3. You need to bring comfortable clothes and sneakers.
4. The club travels to famous golf courses and takes part in friendly tournaments there. Last year they went to Scotland. This year they want to go to Switzerland.
5. You have to contact Horst Meier by phone or via email.
email:
Sehr geehrter Herr Meier,
ich habe einige Fragen zum Discgolf-Verein:
Wie lange dauert der Schnuppertermin? Wie lange dauert das Training? Wo trainiert der Verein? Kann man diesen Ort gut mit öffentlichen Verkehrsmitteln wie U-Bahn oder Bus erreichen?
Vielen Dank für Ihre Antwort.
Mit freundlichen Grüßen

E IV. Schreiben

Seite 104
Part 1

Arguments for "trunk or treat"	Arguments against "trunk or treat"
– easy for parents – don't have to walk around the neighborhood – safe for kids – no traffic – you know the people who give out candy – decorated trunks are really cute – you can trust the people who do it	– not really typical of Halloween – parents don't make an effort – they are lazy – kids miss out on the experience of preparing for adulthood – no "real" memories of Halloween – don't get to know your neighbors

A blog
Lösungsvorschlag:
"Trunk or treat" is a new thing in a lot of rural neighborhoods. The advantages are that it is easier for parents and safer for the kids. They don't have to worry about traffic. You usually know the people who give your kids candy, so you can trust them. A lot of people work hard on decorating their trunks, and when you look at some of the examples the trunks really look cute.
The disadvantages are that "trunk or treat" is not really typical of Halloween. Young kids are supposed to walk around their neighborhood and ask for candy. The parents don't make an effort to make that possible for their kids like meeting and getting to know their neighbors and talking to them. The kids miss this experience for their adulthood and they don't have typical memories of Halloween. That is sad.   (148 words)

Seite 105
Part 2: Writing an e-mail (couch surfing)
Lösungsvorschlag:
To: Sallyp@xxx.com
From: marym@xxx.com
Subject: couch surfing

Dear Sally,   15th May 2023
Thanks for your e-mail. Couch surfing sounds really interesting. Where did you hear about it and how exactly does it work? How do you contact people who offer a place to stay? How long can you stay at their place? Can I offer my apartment to other people, too? I think it would be really exciting to have people visit you from all over the world. Couch surfing makes travelling to foreign countries a lot cheaper and you meet nice people at the same time.
Bye, Mary   (85 words)

Seite 106
Part 3: Interpreting charts
1
Lösungsvorschlag:
This chart shows the vaccination rate for people of different ages in Germany, Bavaria and Berlin. The source of the chart is https://www.zdf.de/nachrichten/politik/corona-impfung-daten-100.html.
The most important numbers are the ones for Germany. 60.8% of the 12- to 17-year-olds have had at least one vaccination, 54.3% have had two and 8.5% have ad a third booster shot.
77.8% of the next age group (18- to 59-year-olds) have had one vaccination, 79.8% have had two and 42.0% three.
In the next age group, the over 60-year-olds, 88.3% have had one shot, 87.4% have had two and 65.3% three.
The numbers in Bavaria and Berlin are similar. Some age groups are a little higher or a little lower than the nation's average.
As a conclusion, we can say that the older population has higher vaccination numbers because they are in more danger from the coronavirus than the younger people.
                                                    (153 words)

2

Lösungsvorschlag:

The source of the chart is https://www.bundesgesund-heitsministerium.de/fileadmin/Dateien/3_Downloads/C/Coronavirus/Befragung_Nichtgeimpfte_-_Forsa-Um-frage_Okt_21.pdf. It shows that the majority of people who do not want to be vaccinated (34%) say, that the vaccines have not been tested enough. 18% are afraid of the side effects of the vaccine. 15% of that group think that the vaccine isn't safe. 12% have doubts about the effective-ness of the vaccine. 8% are hoping for a better vaccine. 5% have recovered from Corona and 2% are too busy to get vaccinated. There are many more opinions but the groups are very small.

As a conclusion, we have to be aware that all the groups against vaccinations have a lot of different opinions. This is not one big group that agrees on one thing. Society needs to take the expressed fear and the scepticism seriously and think about measures how to convince them that the vaccination is the right thing to do for everybody.

(152 words)

Teil F

ORIGINALPRÜFUNG 2022

Lösungen (nicht amtliche Lösungen)

I. Listening

Seite 110
Part 1
1. C
2. A
3. C
4. A
5. B
6. B
7. B

Seite 113
Part 2
8. b
9. c
10. b
11. c
12. a
13. c

Seite 114
Part 3
14. students: second floor / teachers: first floor
15. (on the) keycard
16. 7–10 (am), top floor
17. kitchen staff / people in the kitchen / chef(s)
18. have to leave the hostel / expelled from the hostel
19. make a reservation
20. DHC2022

Seite 115
Part 4
21. false
22. true
23. true
24. false
25. false
26. true

II. Reading

Seite 116
Part 1
1. b
2. c
3. a
4. a
5. b
6. a

Seite 118
Part 2
7. D
8. B
9. H
10. A
11. C
12. F
13. G

Seite 120
Part 3
14. c
15. b
16. c
17. a
18. c
19. a

Seite 122
Part 4
20. true (lines 4–8)
21. false (line 12)
22. false (line 16)
23. true (lines 18–19)
24. false (lines 19–20)
25. false (lines 22–23)
26. true (lines 31–33)

III. Writing – Set I

Seite 124
Part 1 – A complaint: Empty Box

Lösungsvorschlag:
Hello, my name is Max and I ordered Bluetooth ear-phones from your company last week. Today the box came but it was empty. I was really excited about the ear-phones. I saved my money for months, so I could afford them. This weekend I wanted to go running and try them out. But the box is empty and I feel very disappointed. I expect you to send the earphones as fast as possible so that I have them here tomorrow. Thank you.

(82 words)

Seite 125
Part 2 – A Letter of Application: Au Pair Job

Lösungsvorschlag:
To: contact@aupair4u.com

Subject: Applying for an au pair job

Hello,
My name is Sarah, and I am 19 years old. I just got my highschool diploma. My favourite subjects are English and French. I love languages. I am also good at sports. My hobbies are running, swimming, riding my bike and reading books about science fiction. I have two broth-ers and one sister. I babysat them a lot when they were small. I also took care of my aunt's kids, so I have a lot of experience. I think I want to become a teacher. I love working with kids. Activities like playing games and reading books are wonderful. I think I would be the right person for this job because I like kids and get along with everybody. I can spend hours on the playground or read-ing children's books out loud. I have a driving license and my own car and I am very flexible. I would love to take care of your kids.

(156 words)

III. Writing – Set II

Seite 126
Part 1 – A Comment: My parents are forcing me into Apprenticeship

Lösungsvorschlag:
Hi, my name is Gina. Parents always think they know what is right and best for you. Can you blame them? They worry about you all the time. Your parents probably think that you won't be able to support yourself as a musician. If I were you, I would do the apprenticeship in the car dealership. In your free time I would try to advance your career as a musician and maybe in the end it will all work out for you and you can support yourself as a musician.

(89 words)

Seite 127
Part 2 – A Blog Entry: Time Travel into the Past

Lösungsvorschlag:
If I could travel back in time, I would go back to my time in kindergarten. Why would I choose that time? Life as a small child is carefree. You have to do nothing except maybe get dressed and eat. Your parents or the people around you do everything for you. They wake you up, they dress you, they make you food and take you wherever you have to go. When you are in kindergarten, all you have to do is play with your friends all day long. And that's what I would do. I would see all my favourite friends again and play with them and have a wonderful time. When you get older, you have to do a lot of things and take on a lot of responsibility. People expect you to be on time, to be good in school, to have hobbies and to know what you want to do with the rest of your life. So if it was up to me, I would travel back in time and be a small kid again.

(178 words)